❧ Guidance in the Elementary School

Guidance in the Elementary School: A Book of Readings

EDITED BY

HERMAN J. PETERS

ANTHONY C. RICCIO

JOSEPH J. QUARANTA

THE OHIO STATE UNIVERSITY

THE MACMILLAN COMPANY, NEW YORK

COLLIER-MACMILLAN LIMITED, LONDON

Sixth Printing, 1967

Library of Congress catalog card number: 63-13571

The Macmillan Company, New York
Collier-Macmillan Canada, Ltd., Toronto, Ontario

Printed in the United States of America

To the Pioneers in

ELEMENTARY SCHOOL GUIDANCE

Preface

Now that organized guidance services are characteristic of all but a handful of reputable secondary schools, a number of leaders in the guidance movement are turning their attention to the elementary school. The factors responsible for this surge of interest in elementary school guidance are multiple and complex. First, there is the argument that if guidance services are valuable they should be available to elementary school students. Second, there is the theoretical stance that guidance is a process, developmental and continuous in nature, which should assist the individual during his formative years. Third, there is societal pressure to employ guidance workers to identify talented pupils as soon as possible so that these pupils might be encouraged to engage in the pursuit of excellence. These three reasons are not exhaustive, but they appear to be the principal reasons for advocating the establishment of organized guidance services at the elementary school level.

Although there is a great deal of interest in elementary school guidance, materials are relatively scarce in such a new field. This problem is compounded by the fact that few pertinent textbooks share common conceptualization of elementary school guidance services. In effect, then, students enrolled in courses in elementary school guidance see only a part of this broadly expanding field; they see the field through the eyes of their textbook writers, few of whom are in agreement. Hence, there is a need for a well-organized collection of authoritative opinion and research if the student of elementary school guidance is to be exposed to, and stimulated by, the conflicting and complementary ideas that make elementary school guidance such a challenging and exciting area of study. In the educative process, students and in-service personnel should be provided the opportunity of choosing among alternative approaches to real and practical problems. *Guidance in the Elementary School: A Book of Readings* is intended to provide the reader with such an opportunity.

The book is divided into eight parts. The first part is concerned with the conceptualizations which professional educators employ in providing a rationale for the establishment of elementary school guidance programs. The second part treats of the methods which have proven effective in appraising the level of development of elementary school pupils. The third part is focused upon the relationship of the elementary school child to the world of work. Counseling the elementary school child is emphasized in the fourth part. The fifth part deals with the learning situation in the elementary classroom. The status of research in elementary school guidance is discussed in Part Six. Part Seven is concerned with the interpersonal relationships of elementary school guidance personnel. The text is concluded with a discussion of the major issues in the field.

The articles comprising each of these eight parts were selected because, in the judgment of the editors, they represented the best statement of the particular positions taken by leaders in the field.

Representativeness, provocativeness, definitiveness, clarity of expression—these were the criteria employed by the editors. Thus, under one cover, the editors have attempted to present the best thought currently available in the area under study.

Grateful acknowledgment is made to the authors and publishers of the articles which comprise this book for the courteous manner in which they granted permission to reproduce their material. Appropriate citation of the source of each article is given in the text.

H. J. P.
A. C. R.
J. J. Q.

Table of Contents

❧ Guidance in the Elementary School

Part One

CONCEPTUALIZATIONS OF ELEMENTARY SCHOOL GUIDANCE

The Case for Guidance Services in the Elementary School

N. HARRY CAMP, JR.

Despite the fact that leading educators have long contended that the program of guidance services follows the pupil from his first school registration to his graduation from high school, the provision for well-planned guidance programs in the elementary school has lagged considerably. Today there is significant evidence, however, which shows that practice is beginning to catch up with theory. There is a movement to provide a program of guidance services sensitive to the needs of elementary school children.

The rapid growth of guidance services in the elementary school was listed by Jones and Miller as one of the ten most significant trends in pupil personnel and guidance services during the past ten years.[11] This study presented for the first time a nation-wide picture of the extent of guidance counselors who serve in elementary schools. Their report reveals that there are some 711 counselors who serve in elementary schools, 408 of whom devote half time or more to their professional duties. Two additional studies substantiate the Jones and Miller findings. One, covering 611 elementary schools in 19 states, reported that 34.7 per cent of the schools had part or full time services of a counselor.[1] A second, covering 354 elementary schools in 28 states, reported a total of 249 guidance workers, 116 of whom were full time, 31 half-time, and 102 less than half-time.[18]

The recognition of the need for and the growth in the provision for pupil personnel and guidance services in the elementary school shown by these studies reflects the broadening concept of guidance in the United

REPRINTED FROM *EDUCATION,* 75, 7 (MARCH 1955), 419-431, BY PERMISSION OF THE PUBLISHERS AND THE AUTHOR.

States during the past half century. Although this trend is encouraging it should not be taken as a signal for complacency. There are evidences and trends existing in our society today which point to an even greater need for a more general acceptance of guidance services in the elementary school. It is the purpose of this discussion to explore these forces in order to reaffirm the need for expanding the provision for guidance services to young children.

Forces in a Dynamic Modern Society

We live in a world vastly more complicated than that of our forefathers. This is a period of rapid social change and state of national and world uncertainty. We are more than ever aware of the disrupting influences which local, state, national, and world conditions have upon parents and their children. Day by day problems of growing up are intensified by the tension which characterizes our daily environments. It would be impossible to mention here all of these disturbing factors, but for purposes of illustration and emphasis we will discuss four which show poignantly that parents and their children do have more problems to cope with than they had in years gone by. This points up the need for planned guidance services for young children which will recognize their problems sooner and take steps to handle them.

Demands of society. Miraculous discoveries in the physical sciences pour forth so fast that they seem to stumble over each other. With them come new ways of living, working, and communicating among humans. The pace of living is rapid, highly complicated, and extremely competitive, with emphasis upon the achievement of success. Drive and search for it at any cost becomes foremost. Unfortunately, money consciousness and the drive for power become the instruments for achieving success. This warped concept insists upon success in spite of the individual's real endowment. There is a failure to realize that not all people possess the same qualities for achieving success and that only a few can reach the top while others are pushed aside. Many of these individuals refuse to accept their places and try over and over again to better themselves. New frustrations arise and they become resentful and hostile, and may even resort to unlawful ways of behaving.

Mobility of the population. During the past twenty-five years there has been a shift from rural to urban modes of living. Approximately three-fourths of American children live in urban areas. A more recent population trend has been from centers of urban areas to urban suburbs. In addition, there has been a general shift of the population from middle-west to west, from northeastern seaboard to southern middle seaboard, from south to eastern industrial centers, and from the eastern seaboard to Florida and Texas.

Today's families are on the move more than families used to be. During World War II wives with children followed their husbands from one military camp to another while they were stationed in this country. In such instances it was difficult for children to establish a feeling of belongingness to home, friends, neighborhood, and school. The Korean police actions and the threat of World War III have sent fathers into the armed services and their children are being deprived of a father when it is most important. The evils of Momism—the identification of boys with their mothers rather than their fathers—have taken their toll in confusion and adjustment problems. Occupational nomadism is on the increase. Workers migrate with their families from one place to another and settle temporarily whenever they can find employment. Frequent moving deprives children of that feeling of stability which comes when roots can grow in one place.

CHANGES IN FAMILY AND HOME LIFE. Industrialization, world tension, and mobility of the population are in part responsible for disrupting influences in family and home life. Boom town communities are springing up all over the country and cities have grown bigger and bigger. Overcrowding has been the result. This, in turn, creates conditions which invariably add to the child's problems of adapting to his environments. In many areas there is a lack of suitable living quarters, sanitation facilities, police protection, recreation, and educational facilities. Crowdng in industrial neighborhoods tends to destroy a child's sense of individuality and to lessen self-sufficiency. Children become uncomfortable and ill at ease when people are not about. Therefore they seek places where there are crowds—movies, drugstores, pool halls, *et cetera*. These environments often have an unwholesome influence.

Lack of housing leads to overcrowded living conditions. Homes have grown smaller and smaller and the number of children in a family has increased. The inevitable consequence is frustration of children's trust and respect for other people—especially the mother and father. Lazy habits of dress and sexual activities are apt to lead to disillusionment about sex. Because there is no privacy in the home children view openly sexual activities. Without privacy children find it difficult to develop self-concepts and self-respect and their values become warped. All the child does day and night is in full view of everyone in the family. Irritability, touchiness, tension, and adjustment problems inevitably follow.

The rising standard of living and soaring prices have also added to the confusion. Fathers often find it necessary to work considerable distances from home and spend less time with children when they need him most. Mothers work to help support the family or to increase the family income and improve the socio-economic status. While mothers are at work children are often not in competent hands. They are parked with friends and relatives or left to shift for themselves. Working parents become too busy and are too tired to play with their children, to do interesting things with them, or to give them the counseling they desire. The stress and strain of making a living affects the adjustment of parents and creates an unfavorable pattern of family attitude and atmosphere. Parents become emotional and highstrung, and discipline is either erratic or too strict. Overburdened, inadequate, and rejecting mothers often develop strong anxiety feelings. Lack of communication and reduced intimacy between members of the family lead to rejection and punishment of the children. This pattern of inconsistency and show of emotion frightens and confuses the child. As a result, he becomes tense and filled with anxiety, and aggressive, anti-authoritarian, anti-social behavior results. We may have a school learning and behavior problem, and even a budding delinquent on our hands. Emotional tension in the family often leads to broken homes. It is significant that a large share of children with problems come from broken homes or those rendered incomplete by absence of mother or father.

Conflicting social values. The American scene is dominated by different, frequently contradictory cultures, each with its particular customs and mores. One extreme is unethical—the other is puritanical. In the center there is confusion and conflict. Goals and practices are not clear. In this lack of harmony it is difficult to know which path to follow.

Mothers are confused by the wide variety of methods advocated for bringing up children. They become overanxious about their child's growth and development. They worry about whether their child conforms to what is considered the norm in physical-mental-emotional-social growth. Some mothers obsessively count calories, check the number of stools, *et cetera.*

☙ The Rapidly Accelerating Trend Toward Maladjustment

The Extent of Maladjustment.—Most children adapt themselves and learn well in school. For reasons that are self-evident, however, there is a noticeable increase in the number of adjustment problems and serious cases of maladjustment which come to the attention of school personnel. It has been estimated that between ten and twenty per cent of the children enrolled in public elementary schools represent some kind of educational problem.[9] These range from severely disturbed children with emotional and behavior problems, to children with intellectual handicaps and learning difficulties. One in twenty does not adapt or learn successfully in school. These children with adjustment problems need help. The measures taken may vary from the survey of their specific needs, strengths, and limitations and the adjustment of the curriculum and methods of instruction to adjustment of personal relationships in the classroom and, perhaps, supportive therapy by the guidance specialist.

Among the elementary pupils who have adjustment problems, many are so severely disturbed that they need more specialized study and treatment than the school can provide. The Mid-Century White House Conference on Children and Youth (1950) stated that one-fourth of all elementary school children need some kind of special treatment for social-emotional adjustment. Although it is impractical for the guidance personnel to provide complete therapy for these children, they can make the necessary preliminary study.

THE RISE OF JUVENILE DELINQUENCY. Juvenile delinquency is rising sharply. Last year about one million children under 18 in this country were involved with the police because of misbehavior.[6] About one-third of those apprehended came before the juvenile courts. What is even more shocking, however, are the large numbers who are never apprehended. Although most delinquents do not have their first brush with the law until their early teens, there is ample evidence to show that the symptoms of their lack of adjustment were functioning and observable during their attendance in the elementary school. Sheldon and Eleanor Glueck found in their study that nearly half of the delinquents clearly indicated their maladjustment before they were 8 years of age by stealing, playing truant, running away, and destroying property.[8] It is also significant for our discussion that most delinquents are "school misfits." For example, of 187 boys studied at New York State's Randall Island Reformatory, not one could read at his mental ability level, and 90 per cent had failed in school.[14] Cantarow found that two-thirds of the 347 cases at the Delaware County, Pennsylvania, Juvenile Court had misbehaved at school, played truant, or disliked school.[14]

The delinquency problem has to be attacked at its source by the entire community working together. The schools alone cannot change slum neighborhoods or unfavorable home life. They can help to prevent delinquency by identifying boys and girls with predelinquent tendencies and guiding them to use adjustive ways of solving their problems. Through a program of guidance services the elementary school can take steps to help prevent delinquency through: (1) understanding delinquency, (2) identifying early symptoms of anti-social behavior, (3) adjusting the school program to the child, and (4) helping parents to improve family life and attitudes.

Mounting Enrollments in the Elementary Schools

Some 26 million children are presently enrolled in public elementary schools. The schools are faced with the problem of meeting this staggering load because of the tremendous increase in the birth rate during World War II and the continued upward trend since that time. Unfortunately, the situation will become even worse. Reliable estimates indicate that the full extent of the large numbers of births between 1942 and 1953 will not be felt in the elementary schools until 1958. If the present birth rate continues we can expect 30,000,000 pupils in the elementary schools by 1978.[5]

Both the present and future enrollment pose serious problems for the schools. One of these is the basic matter of school housing. This problem has not been met and schools are dangerously overcrowded. Classrooms are bulging and class size has grown too large for effective instruction. Schools have resorted to the use of temporary, ill-equipped facilities and half-day sessions. In September, 1954, it was reported that 600,000 children in the United States were attending half-day sessions.[5]

Another result of increased enrollments is a serious shortage of adequately trained teachers. Forty-six of the forty-eight states report they cannot get enough competent elementary teachers. To meet this shortage it has been necessary to employ inexperienced and partially or completely uncertified teachers. In September, 1954, more substandard or emergency teachers were employed than ever before—72,000 as compared to 70,000 in 1953.[5]

Under these conditions some 4,000,000 children today are not getting the maximum benefit from their days in the elementary school. These children are not being exposed to the kinds of facilities, the quality of instruction, and the individual attention we recognize as being essential to the growth and development of happy adult personalities.

Inadequate Application of Knowledge from Related Disciplines

The implications which the work of specialists in the field of psychology, psychiatry, sociology, and mental hygiene have for elementary guidance are inescapable. Yet, in their actual practice with children, educators across the country neglect to use this valuable source material as effectively as they should.

The knowledge of skills and insights of these disciplines point up the need for providing guidance services for children in the first six grades. We will discuss briefly some of this knowledge.

All children have problems. Every child has major problems as he matures, but fortunately most children are able to solve their problems without the aid of clinical specialists. In meeting their everyday problems, however, children need the help of understanding adults. The problems which loom so enormous to them often never get a hearing from the teacher or parent. The failure to recognize the existence of problems and the failure to provide help in their solution often plants the seeds of maladjustment. Therefore, children need guidance to help them over the mental and emotional hump of growing up. Parents need education in child rearing and teachers need training to become patient and understanding of individual needs and to know that the development of healthy personalities is a slow process.

Developmental guidance is important. In a traditional school it is believed that the pupils bring their minds to school to be trained. The sole purpose is the mastery of subject matter. Pupils have little to say about classroom activities and the teacher's attitude toward her pupils is formal and rigid. The children are expected to be quiet, to respond almost automatically, and to refrain from wiggling or whimpering. The child's need to learn to read, write, master arithmetic, spell, converse, and discuss are clearly recognized, but little attention is given to the development of his normal physical behavior, personality, and social graces.

Specialists give us a clear picture of the functioning of human behavior. A child goes through a process of physical-emotional-mental growth during which he learns to achieve the best possible adjustment for him. The struggle to achieve this aim persists throughout his life and thus is a continuous process highlighted by certain times of crisis when problems are confronted and solved. Such crises can be linked to the child's biological developments and to the stresses and strains he experiences throughout infancy, childhood, and adolescence. We are not positive what age is the most difficult one, but we can say that experiences in childhood are the most important ones for healthy development. These basic truths are often overlooked in planning the elementary school educational program.

Psychologists recognize that children have basic needs in several areas which have to be met for optimal personality growth and development. There are needs to be met in the physical, emotional, and social areas as well as in the intellectual. We know that a great many things take place in the classroom besides intellectual matters. For example, lifetime social attitudes and ways of behaving are learned. It is important to learn the three R's, but we need to spend time stressing learning the fourth R —relationship; that is, emotional relationship.[3] There is need to get away from the idea of the school as a social vacuum where children automatically shed their individual needs, ambitions, and conflicts to assume the stereotyped role of learner. Children bring their insecurities and other emotional problems into the classroom. It is also true that adults cannot automatically shed their particular needs and uncertainties and assume the stereotype of teacher. Consideration of these facts is imperative because of the far-reaching effect they have upon the kind of learning and teaching which results.

The Mid-Century White House Conference on Children and Youth agreed that one of the major objectives of the elementary school should be to further the all-round development of a healthy personality in every child. Specialists agree then that optimal adjustment of the whole child requires consideration of these dynamic factors along with the intellectual. One proof of this is found in the generally accepted fact that vocational maladjustment results because of unsatisfactory personal, emotional, and social factors. This emphasizes the neglect of the dynamic factors of adjustment and points up the need for specialists who can help provide the service necessary to fill this obvious gap in the elementary school program.

A well-planned program of guidance services is needed to facilitate the realization of this aim. Stress in guidance is placed upon all phases of the child's personality growth and development, thus emphasizing a *positive* and *preventive* approach to the adjustment problems of children. The program should be predicated upon the belief that the task of the school is not only to teach subjects but to teach children—to teach children in such a way that they have a feeling of achievement so that their school attendance can be happy. Although this seems self-evident, many elementary school administrators seem more concerned about the school program than about the children.

Developmental guidance implies education based upon the interests, needs, and abilities of the children it serves. First priority is given to the discovery of these patterns in each child. Intelligence testing is essential but more stress than has been given heretofore needs to be placed upon children's aptitudes, interests, and emotions. Children need to be tested periodically with regard to their interests and encouraged in them. Once these interests, capabilities, and needs have been identified, the curriculum can be built around them. Teachers can provide opportunities for developing initiative and creativity and set up the conditions necessary for the discovery and development of all kinds of abilities and talents. This recognition of the individual as a person builds better understanding of each child and enables teachers and parents to get a long range view of the child's growth and development. In this way the child will become a mature, happy adult.

The developmental approach in guidance is in contrast with "crisis" guidance which is predicted in terms of emergencies. When a child fails to progress academically, when a child is truant, when a child is a behavior problem, *et cetera,* guidance personnel are expected to act immediately and come up with sure-fire remedies that will solve the problem or clear up the difficulty. It should be emphasized here that the guidance counselor is concerned with the maturation of the child's learning ability, but does not take over the functions of the teacher. The counselor is also concerned with the child's physical-social-emotional growth, but he does not take over the functions of the medical doctor, psychologist, or psychiatrist. The counselor is needed as a resource person because he is familiar with the work of all these specialists and can integrate into the total educational program the values each of these specialists has to offer.

PREVENTION OF MALADJUSTMENT. It is generally accepted psychological truth that harmful habits of adjustment acquired at an early age are extremely difficult to change and often are the basis for more serious maladjustment. Therefore, early prevention of maladjustment is more important than later efforts at change. This implies early detection of symptoms of non-adjustment and the provision for the appropriate treatment. The first step in helping a child change non-adjustive behavior is to understand his motivations as fully as possible. We therefore have to be constantly on the alert for causes of deviating behavior and then eliminate or alleviate these causative factors. By dealing with the relatively simple problems promptly and constructively, serious maladjustment can be prevented, and the need for clinical services reduced. The need for prevention through early discovery and treatment of adjustment problems was emphasized at the White House Conference on Education for Children and Youth.

The majority of children are born emotionally-physically-mentally normal and healthy. Some few children are relatively handicapped in one or more of these areas. One educational aim should be to strive to protect these normally healthy children from physical or psychological damage by their environments, thereby preventing severe cases of maladjustment from becoming too numerous. Guidance with children can be more effective in the elementary school than at any other educational level. Human behavior specialists are convinced that emotional problems are more amenable to treatment during these years. This is true because the feelings of the child are close to the surface and are readily expressed. We also know that habitual behavior patterns and would-be lifelong attitudes are in the formative stages during the years from 6 to 12. With the proper assistance, positive and preventive steps can be initiated which will do much to forestall the necessity for having to work with serious adjustment problems at the junior and senior high school levels. Counselors at these levels know that learning, emotional, behavior, and personality problems do not wait until junior high school to develop. These specialists believe that elementary school counselors are needed to assist in the recognition of symptoms of adjustment problems and to work with the child, teacher, and his parents in order to prevent future difficulties.

It is evident, then, that the services provided by the elementary school need to be expanded. Besides its educational aim, the school needs to function as an agency for prevention of mental maladjustment. Development of all-round healthy children cannot be the sole responsibility of the classroom teacher. Counselors are needed to help teachers become aware of the emotional difficulties in children because only they can prevent them from developing further. We know that great troubles arise from small ones. We also know that the more promptly mental difficulties or anti-social symptoms can be discovered the better is our possibility of counteracting them. We need, therefore, to give teachers and parents factual knowledge whereby preventive rather than rehabilitative or reformative measures can be taken. With such a preventive program we are able to detect at an early stage the individual who later on becomes a delinquent or criminal. The most effective approach to the needs of children is for the guidance specialist to work with teachers and parents to help them understand the psychological needs and problems of children. Therefore, it should be fully agreed that counselors be given time for this job rather than spend full time giving tests and working with problem children.

CHILDREN VARY IN THEIR ABILITIES. Psychologists have found that children are different and that they mature at their own unique rates of speed. The idea of individual differences precludes that there is a pattern of adjustment that is normal for each child within the framework of the society in which he lives. Traditionally, the aims of education were realized by strict discipline, by excessive homework, and by requiring all children to maintain the same arbitrary standards. This was a mass attempt to mold children into the same formula.

Recognizing individual differences makes the matter of readiness for learning and expectation level extremely important. Although most children are ready to read in the first grade, we may find some who are not ready until second, or even third grade. Many of the expectations we have of children seem unreasonable to them. In some instances levels of expectations are unrealistic. If a child comes to school lacking the experiences which prepare him for reading readiness, the teacher adds to the pressure when she displays impatience with his progress, or when she presents tasks for which he is not ready.

It is inescapable that schools take individual differences into consideration. Because of large classes differentiation is a difficult task, but it can be facilitated by providing guidance specialists on a larger scale than heretofore. These specialists are needed to assist in the identification of slowly maturing children, and to help teachers set up standards of attainment for each child in terms of his needs, aptitudes, interests, and abilities with the primary emphasis upon total personality development. The counselor can aid the teacher by helping her point out to the child that he should try to achieve realistic goals within his reach, simultaneously letting the child know that he will have to postpone the achievement of some of his goals, else he will feel dissatisfied and frustrated. The child should be given to understand that all people have limitations and that accepting them does not mean that they have failed. Only by learning to accept his own limitations and those of his environment will the child be able to adjust adequately. When a child becomes aware of his limitations, he can better adapt himself to his own problems and to the limitations of others. The counselor can also help the teacher understand what kind of pressures each child can stand and from which he can profit most. This is essential because in general a person's ability to adjust depends upon how able he is to endure frustrations. Each person has a certain level of frustration which by and large is determined by his experiences in his home. When an easily frustrated child is put under too much pressure in the classroom, he will react in a negative way—in contrast to the pupil with a high frustration level who will gain by being challenged.

Influence of the home environment. Mental maladjustment and delinquent behavior is the consequence of what an individual feels and sometimes thinks and the way he acts because of his personality make-up. He individuality is molded through his several environments, of which the most important is the home. What basically stimulates us in our life are the experiences we have in our infancy and childhood—in our family and in our community. No one is born bad or maladjusted—he gets that way when put in touch with his environments. It is not enough to respect the child as an individual, but we must know him as a person and understand him in terms of himself and in the ties he knits with his family, community, and society.

Early emotional attachments to mother, father, and siblings provide the basis for later relations with peers, teachers, principals, and other authority figures. When early family attachments have gone smoothly and have provided security for the young child, he has a good start toward making social adjustments outside the home. When he has not been so secure, serious problems may arise. You may have children who become overly dependent upon teachers for love and approval, or cling to the mother, or to another child.

Some parental attitudes have a destructive influence on the child and sometimes tear down what the school tries to do. Although teachers cannot hope to change deep-seated attitudes and the personality structure of the parents, they can aid in the identification of parents who need the help of social workers or psychotherapists. The old idea that the home is where you live and the school is where you learn must give way to the building of a kinship between parents and teachers who are jointly charged with the education and well-being of children.

It takes both the home and the school to insure a well-balanced personality. Guidance personnel are needed as specialists to serve in the capacity of consultants to teachers and parents. Counselors can help teachers help parents change their faulty attitudes and provide a favorable environment of attitudes which will help the child achieve a sense of well-being and happiness.

Inadequacy of Present Services to Pupils

Many elementary schools today fail to meet the needs of their pupils. Recently a panel of six high school students in New York City, discussing the subject "Is Today's Education Meeting the Needs of Youth?" generally agreed that the principal deficiency was the lack of guidance services at crucial points in the lives of boys and girls. The failure of the public schools to provide the necessary services in the form of non-teaching specialists is in part directly responsible for the staggeringly large numbers of seriously maladjusted children. A vast number of the twenty-six million children attending elementary schools receive an educational diet below the subsistence level. Children at both extremes of the normal intelligence distribution go unidentified and therefore are neglected. These are usually referred to as "exceptional children."

GIFTED CHILDREN. Specialists tell us that one-half of our gifted children are not recognized as gifted by parents and teachers.[15] In general, these are children whose IQ's are above 125, and who achieve 18 months beyond grade level placements, and who display exceptional talents in music, art, mechanics, *et cetera*. Even among the gifted whose abilities are recognized, less than three-quarters develop their abilities to the fullest extent. The mental health of the gifted needs to be guarded, especially in the elementary school. It is during the period from 6 to 12 that they face their most difficult problems of personal-social adjustment. Gifted children often suffer at the hands of parental pressure or indifference. Even though gifted children have better than average ability for understanding and solving their own problems, they often need the special help which adults can provide through counseling. The studies made by Terman point out that the exceptionally bright child who is kept with his age group finds little to challenge his intelligence and all too often develops habits of laziness that later wreck his college career. Terman stresses the fact that we need to adopt educational methods which will challenge the gifted, and that this can be done only through early identification, using the appropriate tests and careful observation.[19]

Guidance personnel are needed (1) to aid in the early identification of talented boys and girls, (2) to assist the teacher in providing for their needs, (3) to help parents understand their gifted children and thereby alleviate their problems, should they become emotionally disturbed.

INTELLECTUALLY HANDICAPPED. Another vast group of children at the other extreme of the normal intelligence distribution are tragically neglected in our educational scheme. These are the intellectually handicapped. There are some 700,000 children now enrolled in our schools who are so limited mentally that they are considered mentally retarded.[4] These children have IQ's roughly between 35 and 75 or 80. It is estimated that only fifteen per cent of this group are identified and enrolled in special classes or centers where they can receive the special help they need.[4] These handicapped children should be identified early in the elementary school so that subject matter and teaching methods can be adjusted to their learning abilities. Failure to discover these children at this early age level results in increasing numbers of school failures, truants, emotional and behavior problems, and delinquents in the junior and senior high schools.

Educators are faced with increasingly large numbers of *slow learners*. Roughly, these pupils have IQ's ranging from 75 or 80 to 89, and by the time they enter seventh grade are at least three years retarded in achievement. Although these pupils cannot be expected to make much progress academically, they are still forced in some schools to sit in classes from which they can get little. The slow learner can, however, master the civic, special, and vocational skills he needs for a personally productive life. Counselors should be available to help identify slow learners. It is essential to make sure that the pupil's poor academic progress is due to limited learning ability rather than to an emotional disturbance, poor health, or some other problem which could be overcome by remedial instruction or treatment.

EDUCATIONALLY RETARDED. The educationallv retarded are also neglected. These are children who are 18 months below chronological age level in academic achievement. The vast majority of them have reading difficulties which become seriously handicapping when the child enters junior high school where reading and the language arts skills are indispensable tools for adequate learning. It has been estimated that by the sixth grade only about 70 per cent of school children have learned to read even moderately well. A junior high school counselor stated the problem that worries elementary teachers and counselors most: "Practically every youngster who walks into my office with an educational problem has trouble with reading." [12] Guidance counselors are needed (1) to assist teachers in interpreting survey reading tests, (2) to work with difficult reading cases that involve physical, mental and emotional problems, (3) to help prepare referrals of the more difficult cases to reading specialists, psychologists, physicians, or psychiatric clinics.

DROP-OUTS. The high school drop-out is considered by many to be one of the nation's most serious school problems. It is estimated that 650,000 children dropped out of junior and senior high schools in the 1953 academic year.[10] Although one out of four drop-outs leave school in the 9th grade, it is a continuing problem in the 10th, 11th, and 12th grades. Most drop-outs can be traced back to the elementary school where these pupils did not make the proper adjustment. Their adjustment problems stemmed from many factors, including non-recognition of "problem pupils," overcrowded classrooms, lack of identification of the intellectually handicapped, failure to adjust the curriculum to "slow learners," *et cetera*.[13] As these pupils progress through school without their basic needs being met, their deficiencies become more pronounced. The end result is usually their being unable to adjust educationally-emotionally-socially to the junior high school. Their deficiencies cause feelings of inadequacy which lead them to drop out of school, and in some cases even to become delinquent. Attack upon this problem calls for early identification of potential drop-outs and broadening of the offerings of the school.

FAILURE TO IDENTIFY SYMPTOMS. Many classroom teachers today fail to do an efficient job of identifying behavior which is symptomatic of adjustment problems. Kaplan found that teachers are more apt to react to behavior that is annoying than to behavior that might be symptomatic of serious adjustment problems.[17] One of the services which the personnel worker can render is to impart to teachers the principles of mental hygiene and indicate their application to children in their classes. Counselors can help teachers ferret out the root causes of emotional, learning, and undesirable behavior problems. They can use tools which aid them in bringing to light the obscure factors that are responsible and help them in detecting the contributing causes that aggravate behavior problems.

These facts point up the crying need for more guidance facilities in the elementary school where the emphasis can be placed on the prevention of mental-emotional maladjustment. Not only their number, but their diversity, make it impossible for one teacher or single group of teachers to meet all the pupil needs we have been discussing. To effectively offer services aimed at alleviation of these needs, many nonteaching school and community resources must be called upon. Unquestionably good teaching is the heart of elementary guidance, but it takes more than individual good teaching to do a complete job of assisting children to make an adequate transition from home to school, and to society in general.

Teachers Desire Specialized Help

Our ideas of what a classroom teacher can accomplish in the modern school are not based upon reality. In the past the teacher within her classroom was expected to assume the entire responsibility for the growth and development of the child's personality in all its phases. It is true that our best teachers fulfill their major function which is to teach and act as the integrating force that brings into play factors necessary for the child's physical-social-emotional-moral growth. It is self-evident, however, that the very immensity of the assignment makes it impossible to complete. Although the ability of the teacher to perform her duty is not questioned, the classroom teacher cannot do her job without assistance.

In our increasingly complicated world teachers have neither the time, the training, the resources, nor the experience to incorporate into their teaching the entire body of truths we know about mental hygiene and child development. It is not possible for the teacher to provide the kind of individual help the guidance counselor can give the child who so urgently needs it. The teacher needs and almost daily seeks the assistance of the guidance specialist. Thus the guidance counselor is essential to function as the medium through which the guidance and mental hygiene points of view are kept constantly a part of the atmosphere of the school. In addition, the trained guidance counselor should be available as a consultant and as a worker who can perform the intensive and more specialized guidance tasks. It is imperative that we note here that another group of persons is essential if education is to meet its objective of fostering the optimal adjustment of each child. These specialists are the nurse doctor, social worker, psychologist, and psychiatrist who make their specialities available when they are needed. In a well-rounded guidance program, then, teachers, guidance specialists, and clinical specialists have a specific part to play in the growth and development of every child.

Summary

This presentation has spelled out the need for the provision of guidance services for elementary school children. The specific needs discussed grew out of the following general trends in our society today: (1) forces in a dynamic, modern society, such as the rapid pace of living, mobility of the population, changes in family and home life, and conflicting social values; (2) the rapidly accelerating trend toward maladjustment noted in the greater extent of emotional maladjustment and the rise of juvenile delinquency; (3) mounting enrollments in the elementary school; (4) inadequate application of the knowledge of psychological and medical specialists; (5) inadequacy of present services to pupils; and (6) teachers' desire for specialized help.

The feeling reflected here is the fact that the entire elementary educational program will benefit immeasurably by the provision for specialists to coordinate and carry out a program of guidance services.

REFERENCES

1. The National Association of Guidance Supervisors and Counselor Trainers, *A National Study of Existing and Recommended Practices for Assisting Youth Adjustment in Selected Elementary Schools of the United States* (Ann Arbor, Mich.: Ann Arbor Publishers, 1933).

2. David Abrahamsen, *Who Are the Guilty?: A Study of Education and Crime* (New York: Holt, Rinehart & Winston, 1952).

3. "Are the Schools Meeting the Child's Needs?" *The University of Chicago Round Table,* No. 766 (November 30, 1959).

4. "Education in Review," *New York Times* (February 28, 1954).

5. "Education in Review," *New York Times* (September 1954).

6. Martha M. Eliot, "There Are Also Juvenile Non-Delinquents," *New York Times Magazine* (November 7, 1954).

7. K.G. Garrison and B.W. Cunningham, "Personal Problems in Ninth Grade Pupils," *School Review,* 60 (January 1952), 80.

8. Sheldon and Eleanor Glueck, *Unravelling Juvenile Delinquency* (The Commonwealth Fund, 1950).

9. *Guidance for Today's Children,* 33rd Yearbook of *The National Elementary School Principal,* **24**, 1 (September 1954).

10. *Guidance Newsletter* (Chicago: Science Research Associates, October 1953).

11. Arthur J. Jones and Leonard M. Miller, "The National Picture of Pupil Personnel and Guidance Services," *The Bulletin,* **38**, 200 (The National Association of Secondary School Principals of the N.E.A., February 1954).

12. *Junior Guidance Newsletter* (Chicago: Science Research Associates, November 1951).

13. *Junior Guidance Newsletter* (Science Research Associates, February 1952).

14. *Junior Guidance Newsletter* (Science Research Associates, February 1953).

15. *Junior Guidance Newsletter* (Science Research Associates, May 1952).

16. Leo Kanner, *Child Psychiatry,* 2nd ed. (Springfield, Ill.: Charles C. Thomas, 1948).

17. Lois Kaplan, "The Annoyances of Elementary School Teachers," *Journal of Educational Research* (May 1952), p. 649.

18. Frank Sievers, *Principles and Practices in Elementary School Guidance* (unpublished doctorate thesis, Teachers College, University of Nebraska, 1954).

19. Lewis M. Terman, *Genetic Studies of Genius IV—The Gifted Child Grows Up* (Palo Alto, Calif.: Stanford University Press, 1947).

Guidance

HAROLD F. COTTINGHAM

Anyone active in educational work at the elementary-school level can hardly read a journal, textbook or professional publication without being aware of the current emphasis on guidance functions in the elementary school. This trend is indeed of recent origin: much of the material has appeared within the past five years, and even older references do not carry a dateline much prior to 1948.

Let us look at the reasons for the relatively recent emergence of guidance activities at the elementary level. Then let us classify some of the early literature, especially as to the approach recommended for elementary guidance. Finally, we will outline several areas of emphasis or agreement now characterizing guidance for elementary pupils.

In considering the recent emphasis on guidance in the elementary school, we need first to look at the history of the development. Guidance services were first provided for out-of-school youth (in Boston in 1908). Later, such services were extended to secondary-school pupils, and now we are developing a guidance program for elementary-school children.

One factor which has spurred the extension of guidance for grade-schoolers has been the developing awareness that guidance activities need not be reserved exclusively for specialists but may be shared by teachers as well. (This development has come as a direct result of the increased support of the view that classroom teachers play a key role in studying and in changing child behavior.)

Finally, even further extension has taken place because of acceptance of the view that guidance services should be available to *all* pupils, not just to those with reading problems or other difficulties. Obviously, if all students are to be helped, we need to have many professional people in-

REPRINTED FROM *GRADE TEACHER*, 76, 5 (JANUARY 1959), 56-57, BY PERMISSION OF THE PUBLISHERS AND THE AUTHOR.

volved, and at various training levels. Thus it becomes not only advisable, but also necessary, for teachers to assume some of these guidance responsibilities.

Society and Guidance

Over the past twenty years, greater concern has been shown for meeting the emotional, as well as the intellectual, needs of children. Such evidence as failures, drop-outs, increasing numbers of maladjustments and referrals to psychological clinics has shown the validity of these allegations. Within the past few years much interest has also been aroused in the general question of manpower utilization, with particular reference to pupils who could succeed in scientific careers. These attitudes have been accentuated by an interest in the early location of general and specialized talent, as well as the identification of children who may become problems at upper-grade levels. With greater expenditures devoted to pupil personnel services, the public is demanding greater emphasis on the preventive aspects of guidance.

When we examine the different approaches by various authors to guidance in the elementary school, we find at least six somewhat distinct conceptualizations. Some of the earlier texts in the field (Hatch [1] and Bernard, Zeran and Evan[2]) proposed that guidance functions in the elementary school be patterned after the services commonly accepted for the secondary school. A second conceptual position, now somewhat passé, is that elementary guidance is almost synonymous with "good teaching" (Willey[3]). A modification of this idea is stressed in a recent book by Barr [4] who sees the teacher, aided by parents, specialists and administrators, as carrying "the largest share of guidance services." Still another basis is the mental health or problem-centered one, as expounded by Detjen and Detjen.[5]

Another attack on the problem (Driscoll[6] and Cutts[7]) might be called the school psychologist and specialist approach, implying that much of the guidance in the elementary school should be provided by school or child psychologists, supplemented by specialists such as visiting teachers or social welfare personnel. The application of human development principles through child study methods constitutes yet another concept of elementary-school guidance. The writings of Gordon[8], Prescott[9], and Los Angeles County[10] reflect this position.

One feature inherent in several of the views listed above is their stress upon roles of personnel or assumed services, rather than on *locally designed* functions to help the child become effective in his school and home environment. Some people consider as more practical this approach of coordinated effort, where guidance consists of organizing various resources within and beyond instruction (emphasized by Martinson and Smallenburg[11], ASCD Yearbook[12], Cottingham[13] and Strang[14]). Naturally, even these sources have differences in viewpoint, in spite of the common element mentioned above.

Guidance Principles

A casual overview of the leading publications which offer a description of the nature of guidance in the elementary school indicates several characteristics upon which a number of these writers agree. The presence of certain common concepts possibly indicates a trend toward accepting a basic set of beliefs which set forth the unique features of elementary-school guidance functions. A few of the more obvious principles which describe guidance work at this level are:

1. Guidance functions consist of a total, coordinated plan of services to pupils, parents and teachers.
2. Guidance is provided by teachers as well as special personnel, both within and beyond the curriculum.
3. While the classroom teacher is the center of guidance activity, additional personnel workers are often necessary to meet all needs.
4. The problem areas presented by children at the elementary-school level emphasize an understanding and acceptance of the self, a satisfactory relation with social groups, and successful experiences in the academic phase of the school program.
5. The activities underlying the teacher's and specialist's guidance role involve procedures to know and understand children, as well as ways of assisting them with personal and social problems.
6. The needs of children in general, and the local school enrollment in particular, should determine the types of services comprising an adequate pattern of guidance in an elementary school. Because of the diversity of pupil needs within a school, many approaches involving both individual and group contacts are necessary.
7. The teacher has a dual role, not only in providing methods and ma-

terials of instruction in basic skills demanded by society, but in providing appropriate procedures to help children with personal and social difficulties which stem from psychological needs.

8. Effective elementary-school guidance is contingent upon the knowledge, skill and professional attitude of mentally healthy teachers, specialists and administrators. An indispensable characteristic of a well-qualified guidance person (teacher or counselor) is a recognizable respect for the integrity of each individual child.

REFERENCES

1. Raymond N. Hatch, *Guidance Services in the Elementary School* (Dubuque, Iowa: William C. Brown Co.).

2. Harold Bernard, Franklin Zeran, and James E. Evan, *Guidance Services in Elementary Schools* (New York: Chartwell House, Inc., 1954).

3. Roy D. Willey, *Guidance in Elementary Education* (New York: Harper and Brothers, 1952).

4. John A. Barr, *The Elementary Teacher and Guidance* (New York: Holt, Rinehart & Winston, 1958).

5. Mary F. and Ervin W. Detjen, *Elementary School Guidance* (New York: McGraw-Hill, 1952).

6. Gertrude P. Driscoll, *Child Guidance in the Classroom* (New York: Bureau of Publications, Teachers College, Columbia University, 1955).

7. Norman E. Cutts (ed.), *School Psychologists at Mid-Century* (Washington, D.C.: American Psychological Association, 1955).

8. Ira Gordon, *The Teacher as Guidance Worker* (New York: Harper and Brothers, 1956).

9. Daniel A. Prescott, *The Child in the Educative Process* (New York: McGraw-Hill, 1957).

10. *Guidance Handbook for Elementary Schools* (Los Angeles: California Test Bureau, Division of Research and Guidance, Los Angeles County Schools, 1948).

11. Ruth Martinson and Harry W. Smallenburg, *Guidance in Elementary Schools* (Englewood Cliffs, N.J.: Prentice-Hall, 1958).

12. *Guidance in the Curriculum,* 1955 Yearbook, Association for Supervision and Curriculum Development (Washington, D.C.: NEA).

13. Harold F. Cottingham, *Guidance in Elementary Schools* (Bloomington, Ill.: McKnight and McKnight, 1956).

14. Ruth Strang, "Guidance in the Elementary School," *Guidance for Today's Children,* Thirty-third Yearbook, Bulletin of Department of Elementary School Principals (Washington, D.C.: NEA, 1954).

15. Dugald Arbuckle, *Guidance and Counseling in the Classroom* (Boston: Allyn & Bacon, 1957).

Developing an Understanding of Human Behavior at the Elementary School Level *

FRANCES SMYTHE STILES

Human behavior may be approached in two ways. On the one hand, it may be viewed in its overt form and the form described as it appears. On the other hand, the behavior may be discussed in terms of the factors that produced it—the motives and other factors that were its immediate and remote antecedents.

For example, let us consider an aggressive child. His behavior can be described in terms of what he does, when he does it and what society's attitude is toward this behavior, or it can be discussed in terms of the factors or conditions that led up to behavior. For convenience, the first approach may be called non-analytical and the second, analytical.

The two approaches may lead to significant differences in the ways in which others would react to the behavior and the methods they would use in attempting to change it. In the non-analytical approach a label may be attached to the behavior and some arbitrary method of dealing with it may be adopted. The child may be censured, expelled from school, deprived of several recesses, or perhaps ostracized by the other children. The analytical approach, on the other hand, takes into consideration possible motivational forces that are operative.

* We need to know more about why children behave as they do. The author of this [article] presents data on the results achieved from a program designed to modify social behavior. [The] article is based on a doctoral dissertation which was completed in August 1947, under the direction of Dr. Ralph Ojemann. The dissertation is on file at the State University of Iowa under the title of *A Study of Materials and Programs for Developing an Understanding of Behavior at the Elementary School Level.*

REPRINTED FROM *JOURNAL OF EDUCATIONAL RESEARCH,* 43, 7 (MARCH 1950), 516-524, BY PERMISSION OF THE PUBLISHERS AND THE AUTHOR.

The application of an analytical approach may be illustrated by amplifying the example of the aggressive child. Suppose this child bullies others, picks on children younger and weaker than himself, takes things away from them or threatens them. Suppose, in addition, he continually brags about himself. What may have produced this behavior? One possible cause may be that he may have been frequently frustrated in his attempts to build up status. Perhaps there is an older sibling in the family whose attainments are impossible for this child, yet these attainments are accepted as rigid standards by his parents and he experiences frequent failure in his endeavor to live up to them. One's reactions to this behavior would take into account the frustrations the child is experiencing.

It should be emphasized here that there are many possible causes for any given form of behavior. If behavior is to be understood the characteristics of the situation as well as the characteristics of the child who reacts in this situation must be considered. Also, behavior patterns may vary widely in complexity. It is well known that some patterns are far too complex to be understood and reorganized by the lay individual by means of methods within his ability to learn. However, some everyday behavior patterns do lend themselves to analysis by an individual who has acquired such techniques as will enable him better to understand himself and others. It is with these patterns that this study is concerned.

The question now arises: How is one to acquire an understanding of some of the basic principles underlying behavior and its development so that he can begin to look at the behavior he meets in everyday situations in terms of the causes and what would be the effects of such an extension of insight?

There are numerous sources from which an individual may acquire some degree of understanding of the analytical approach to behavior if appropriate experiences were provided. Such sources may be the home, the church, the school, neighborhood play groups, and such media as the radio, motion pictures, lectures, books and periodicals.

Since the school is an important source of experiences, it provides an excellent situation for studying the effects of a carefully designed learning program in developing an understanding of the analytical approach to behavior.

There is some evidence that insight into human behavior and its development can be extended through planned programs at the youth level and that such experiences change the behavior of the young person toward others.[1, 2, 3]

The questions which now arise are these: Can similar experiences be designed for the elementary school level and, if so, how effective would such experiences be? If an understanding and appreciation of behavior are valuable to an individual, it seems reasonable to suppose that the earlier these concepts are acquired, the better. The present study was planned to observe the changes in the social behavior of elementary school children as a result of a learning program especially designed for them. In conducting the study the following procedures were followed: (1) designing a learning program for the intermediate grades, (2) presenting it to the pupils, (3) measuring for its effectiveness.

Procedure

DESIGN OF THE LEARNING PROGRAM

Five patterns of behavior which were common to the experiences of the children, which were of interest to them and which were of a nature that lent themselves to a rather simple analysis of possible causes were selected. These behavior patterns were chosen on the basis of observations of elementary school children, conferences with experienced elementary school teachers and principals and selected readings in the field of mental hygiene.

A pupil's manual and a teacher's manual were prepared by the investigator. The pupil's manual contained an introduction to the pupil, three stories and a summary. The teacher's manual contained, in addition to the materials of the pupil's manual, an introduction to the teacher, discussion guides for the stories and additional discussion guides giving rather detailed analyses of related behavior patterns.

The five behavior patterns introduced by three stories and discussion guides were as follows: (1) behavior toward school playground rules; (2) teasing or bullying (one or the other presented for discussion), (3) trespassing; (4) behavior toward property; and (5) audience behavior.

In the preparation of these materials the investigator kept in mind two main understandings which were to be stressed: the same behavior may have many causes; and it is helpful to discover the causes in order to understand or to change behavior. The term "cause" as used in this discussion means a factor or a condition which led up to the behavior described.

Selected readings in the field of mental hygiene suggested factors or conditions which were utilized in developing the stories and discussions guides contained in the manuals. Some of the factors and conditions which recurred throughout the learning program were: (1) the operation of such motives as the desire for physical activity following a period of "sitting still," the desire for new experiences, the desire to belong to a group, the desire to do something worth-while, and the desire to avoid situations which may lead to feelings of insecurity; (2) the attempt to overcome a feeling of frustration when such motives as the above are blocked; and (3) the lack of sufficient understanding, knowledge or skill.

PRESENTATION OF THE LEARNING PROGRAM

The learning program was presented to 172 children in the fourth, fifth and sixth grades of a consolidated school in a small town and farming community in Iowa. For these children the mean chronological age was ten years, seven months; the mean IQ (Otis) was 103.8. The program was administered through one-hour discussion periods on six consecutive school days. During the first five discussion periods the teacher and the children analyzed behavior patterns which were introduced through stories and discussion guides contained in the manuals. The last or sixth day of class discussion in each grade was taken over by the investigator. At this meeting a sample problem drawn from the group was analyzed and the ideas developed in the preceding discussions were applied.

METHOD OF MEASUREMENT

The effects of the learning program were measured by the degree to which the child demonstrated an analytical approach to the behavior problems which confronted him for solution in the room council situation. In the room council meetings held in this school, problems affecting the children were introduced for discussion. They were discussed by the children with a child as leader and the teacher as just another participant, and procedures were selected by vote. The vote was more than something theoretical to the child. It was something that actually was carried out, and the child knew that similar decisions might be applied to himself as well as to others.

When a motion concerning a plan for dealing with behavior was brought to a vote the investigator would request a written ballot. Each child was asked to write his ballot number to assure a secret vote. The investigator felt that a child would express himself more freely if his ballot could not be identified by the other children. Along with his ballot number the child wrote his vote which usually was expressed either in terms of "yes" or "no" or by a letter ("A," "B," "C," etc.) which designated his preference for one of the possible methods that had evolved in the discussion for changing behavior. The child then was asked to turn the ballot over and write why he thought the way he voted was a good way.

The statements written on the ballot were scored on a seven-point scale as to the extent to which consideration had been given in the child's vote to the underlying factors producing the behavior in question. These statements were interpreted in light of the way in which the child voted and the manner in which the problem was brought up and discussed in the council meetings.

Ballots were scored for the four weekly council meetings before the learning program and for the four weekly council meetings after the learning program. Three points on the scale used in scoring the ballots are described below.

SCORE	CLASSIFICATION
1	This score was assigned when the decision made showed no consideration of the factors producing the behavior. For example, if the subjects voted for some form of deprivation of fun, hostile criticism, appeal to precedent, or some arbitrary form of punishment without any recognition of the factors underlying behavior, a score of "1" was given. *Examples:* "Vote for staying in three recesses because they will miss the fun"; "vote for staying after school because it serves them right."
4	If the subject recognized some relation, explicitly stated, between the causes of the behavior but made only a very partial analysis he was given a score of "4." *Examples:* "Vote for giving him another chance this week because it will help him improve more"; "vote for having the teacher talk to him because that may help him to remember."
7	The ballot statement received a score of "7" if it demonstrated that the subject recognized the probable cause or causes of the behavior which was brought up for discussion in the council meeting and if the subject by his vote and statement showed an attempt to change behavior by changing the underlying factor or factors producing it. *Example:* "Vote for having the best ball players teach those boys (who lack skill) how to play so they will help us have a better team instead of annoying us to get attention."

The above illustrations show the extremes and mid-point of the scale. A score of "2" or "3" was given if there was an implication of a beginning recognition of the relation of the method of changing behavior to the causes but only an implication. A score of "5" or "6" was given if there was a rather clear recognition of the relation of the method of changing behavior to the causes but the causes named were not extensive.

Reliability of the scale was determined by per cent agreement between two observers who scored independently two hundred ballots. There was 85 per cent complete agreement.

Results and Conclusions

An analysis of changes in behavior as evidenced by the ballot scores was made.

Table 1 gives the results and significance of differences on the mean ballot scores for the experimental subjects. In all cases these differences are statistically significant beyond the 1 per cent level of confidence. The mean ballot score for each subject was obtained by averaging the ballot scores from four council meetings prior to and the scores from the four meetings following the learning program. The data show significant gains for all groups.

Results of Test of Significance of Differences on Ballot Scores for Experimental Subjects

Grade	*N**	*Mean Initial Score*	*Mean Final Score*	*Mean Gain*	*"t"*	*Level of Significance*
IV[1]	23	1.41	2.98	1.57	8.81	Beyond 1%
IV[2]	19	1.56	2.72	1.16	6.61	Beyond 1%
V[1]	34	1.68	3.26	1.58	17.07	Beyond 1%
V[2]	33	1.41	2.25	.84	7.90	Beyond 1%
VI[1]	29	2.22	2.87	.65	4.22	Beyond 1%
VI[2]	30	1.61	2.32	.71	9.11	Beyond 1%

* Complete scores available for only 168 subjects.

Some evidence that gains are not the result of sheer practice in council sessions is furnished by ballot scores obtained from fifth grade subjects in the University Elementary School. The mean ballot scores for nineteen fifth grade pupils for each of six consecutive meetings without an intervening learning program are as follows:

Council Meetings

Grade	N	1	2	3	4	5	6
V	19	1.21	1.63	1.55	1.42	1.37	1.32

Practice effects alone, therefore, do not seem to account for the gains given in Table 1.

Although the gains are not large, they are significant and indicate that a learning program such as the one introduced in this study has made a small beginning in helping the children to develop a more analytical approach to problems of human behavior which confront them.

Before accepting this finding, however, and to aid us in interpreting the data more adequately we may ask a number of questions:

1. Are the changes due to the ability of the children to express themselves on paper?

Since such a possibility was recognized by the investigator she took precautions to keep this factor at a minimum. During the balloting procedure the children were assured that no premium was to be placed on spelling or writing but rather that the investigator was interested solely in why they thought what they voted for was a good choice.

As a further answer to this question semester grades in language were selected as the best available measure of the child's ability to express himself, and correlations were obtained between language grades and ballot score changes. Since teacher grades are not considered very satisfactory the unreliability of such measures must be taken into account in interpreting the correlations. The actual calculation of the correlations was done from raw scores; however, scatter diagrams were made of each distribution and in each case the spread of scores seemed reasonably satisfactory. The correlations between ballot score changes and the semester language grades range from —.25 to +.33 which indicate little or no relationship.

2. Are the changes due to the reading ability of the children?

When the reading materials were being prepared the investigator attempted to simplify them so that they would be within the reading comprehension of the children. As a first measure, the investigator asked each of three children to read orally two pages picked at random from the pupil's manual. These children who scored at the average third grade level on the Iowa Every Pupil Reading Test encountered little difficulty in reading and in understanding the sections of the stories which the investigator asked them to read.

As a second measure, the investigator subjected the materials to two formulæ which have been used to ascertain the reading level of elementary school reading materials. The two methods do not agree, but with one exception the readings tend to show a difficulty at or below the fourth grade level.

In addition to these tests, the investigator throughout the writing of the stories kept in mind elements which studies have shown tend to affect comprehension difficulty of children's reading materials.

Correlations were obtained between ballot score changes and the reading scores of the subjects. The reading scores are the total reading scores received on the Iowa Every Pupil Reading Test which was given to the experimental subjects. These scores indicate a measure of both vocabulary and reading comprehension. Here again the correlations are near zero with one exception. The correlation for Grade IV^2 is +.47 (N=17). For the group as a whole, however, the correlations are not significant.

3. How are the changes related to sex differences?

The mean gain on ballot scores for each sex shows very little difference:

Sex	*N*	*Mean Gain*
M	72	.97
F	99	1.12

4. Are the changes related to differences in the intelligence of the children?

There is very little relationship between ballot score changes and intelligence (Otis). One exception appears in Grade IV^2 where the figure is +.64. There is perhaps a slight tendency for a positive correlation but the figures are not too consistent from grade to grade. Apparently the learning program did not unduly favor the high or low in intelligence.

The above findings tend to indicate that the changes in ballot scores cannot be accounted for on the basis of practice in using ballots as employed in this study, nor does it seem that the changes are related to verbal facility or intelligence as measured by the tests used. The evidence points consistently in the direction of a significant change in the actual approach to the behavior of others.

This finding has a two-fold significance. Changes in the child's approach to the behavior and in his understanding of that behavior can be made on the elementary school level provided appropriate influences are brought to bear. If it is desirable to develop in children an understanding of the behavior of others and the ability to approach behavior in an analytical way, a contribution can be made through elementary school experiences.

The second implication relates to the study of the child's development in his behavior toward others. Whenever one tries to explain the child's growth in behavior toward others it is necessary to take into account the fact that this growth depends in part upon whether the child has had an opportunity to extend his insight through experiences designed along the lines indicated in this study.

It cannot be concluded from this study that the particular experiences incorporated in the learning program are the most efficient experiences we can devise. One can think of numerous changes and extensions that could be made in the program. Only a limited number of patterns of behavior were included. Many more and different types could be tested.

Also, the subject's behavior when he considers the problem in council sessions is only one test of change in behavior. Many more tests could be made. For example, in one of the grades in which the trial program was carried out there appeared some weeks later the problem of pupil behavior during classroom discussion of a natural science topic. The teacher stopped the class discussion and asked whether the pupils who were creating the disturbance should be put out in the hall. One of the pupils suggested that from the discussions about behavior they had had several weeks ago it seemed they should first ask the question as to why the children were creating the disturbance—whether it was because the discussions did not have any meaning or value to them. More investigation is needed to determine how extensive such reactions following the learning program are and under what conditions they appear.

Finally, studies can be made of the types of pupils who show gains and those who do not. What causes the differences? Such studies could throw much light on the dynamics of changing behavior.

This study has taken only the first step to show that some changes can be made in this area of the child's development.

REFERENCES

1. Bessie McNiel, "Development at the Youth Level of a Conception of the Cause of Behavior and the Effectiveness of a Learning Program in This Area," *Journal of Experimental Education,* 13 (December 1944), 81-85.

2. Ralph Ojemann, Anne Nugent, and Mildred Morgan, "Study of Human Behavior in the Social Science Program," *Social Education,* 11 (January 1947), 25-28.

3. Ralph Ojemann and Mildred Morgan, "The Effect of a Learning Program Designed to Assist Youth in an Understanding of Behavior and Its Development," *Child Development,* 13 (September 1942), 181-194.

Guidance: A Longitudinal and a Differential View

GAIL F. FARWELL
HERMAN J. PETERS

A comprehensive guidance program starts with the child's entry into the school setting. The guidance program is for *all* boys and girls at *all* school levels. If the basic concept emphasizes a sensitivity to prevention rather than a resort to correction and cure, then our guidance point of view, which has as its basic tenet the assisting of boys and girls toward optimum psychological, sociological, and physical maturity, must be put into operation early in the school life of boys and girls.

What kind of a person do we want to entrust with the responsibilities implied above? What is this guidance worker to be like?

First a person of character who can sustain the demands of intimate inter-personal relationships and who by virtue of his own maturity can enrich these relationships. Guidance is no mechanical process. Inadequate people can go through the motions but the young person gains little, if indeed he is not harmed. Behind the various procedures and techniques useful in guidance programs must be a substantial person, warm, open, knowing of the feelings of others, deeply respectful of the rights of others. It is very likely that the young person (and all of us) can work out significant changes in personality only in a close and meaningful relationship with another person.

Second a person of broad experience seriously reflected upon. The person should have had enough experience to know that his own experiences, rich as they are, cannot provide adequate patterns for another

REPRINTED FROM *THE ELEMENTARY SCHOOL JOURNAL*, 57, 8 (MAY 1957), 26-31, BY PERMISSION OF THE PUBLISHERS AND THE AUTHORS.

person. We need guidance workers who know people well and know the world in which they live.

Third a person who is bright, intelligent. A person of average intellectual ability will simply not be able to help those youngsters of great creative potential who will be our leaders of tomorrow.

Finally a person who is technically competent. This is the relatively simple side of the matter. Given a person with the qualities noted above, it is easy to train him to be a good counselor, a good diagnostician, a good planner of programs, a good guidance worker.

We should recognize that the guidance process is somewhat different at the elementary-school level than it is at the junior and senior high school levels. The point of view expressed above emphasizes "helping boys and girls toward maturity," and we must recognize at what maturity level each pupil has arrived if our guidance procedures are to function effectively. In moving toward maturity, we need to provide bases for making decisions and to provide yardsticks against which the individual can appraise his own development. The classroom teacher, sensitized to the guidance point of view and capable of empathic relationships with boys and girls, has a most important role in the elementary-school phase of the guidance program. The school counselor or a guidance committee, headed by a person at least semi-skilled in guidance procedures, should co-ordinate the activities at this level.

The extent of the capacity for insightful introspection is questionable in the case of young children, but we need to keep this process in mind and, as the boys and girls move along in our school system, encourage this activity as soon as the maturity level will justify the action.

Guidance Throughout School Years

If one considers a guidance program on a longitudinal basis, a firm foundation for understanding the uniqueness of each boy and girl in our schools must begin at the kindergarten level. It is folly to permit our children and youth to proceed toward maturity without a record of their ongoing psychological, sociological, mental, and physical development. To this end a program of guidance services is dedicated.

The services approach to the guidance program—inventory service, information service, counseling service, placement service, and follow-up service—can be viewed as having implications across the entire school system, but certain phases of these services are much more applicable at some levels than at others. In the elementary school the guidance program is most concerned with pupil inventory; with the provision of appropriately graded information about schooling, social-personal relationships, and the world of work; and with orientation and with grade and subject-area placement of the pupil. It is imperative that the service aspect of the guidance program be co-ordinated. Otherwise, incidentalism prevails, and the major crime of incidental guidance is not what it does but what it leaves undone. Also, incidentalism breeds much overlap in function and accomplishment.

As we move into the later stages of the elementary school and the junior high school, the need for counseling service and placement service becomes greater. Also in the junior high school some follow-up studies of the effectiveness of the guidance program of the elementary school are in order. At this stage of maturity the pupils evidence much greater sensitivity to peer and adult relationships, and the guidance workers should begin placing emphasis on boys' and girls' understanding of "the self" and also the implications for interrelationships with "other selves." In the junior and senior high school, extensive emphasis should be placed on the role of educational, occupational, and social-personal information in providing boys and girls with a background for making intelligent choices about future schooling and careers and for establishing satisfactory human relations.

In the junior and senior high school, the group approach to ascertaining, providing, and interpreting information about "self" and about the impinging environmental influences should be supplemented and complemented by individual counseling service. The right of each pupil to expect recognition of his unique individuality implies that time, staff, and budget must be provided for individual counseling service.

The senior high school youth become concerned about external placement—placement in part-time or full-time jobs and in institutions of advanced education (apprenticeship programs, non-degree programs, and college programs). Adolescents need adequate assistance in selection of, accomplishment in, and interpretation of, their career and educational programs. In the over-all placement service we include internal placement (which is concerned with grade and subject-area placement) and external placement (which is concerned with making a student's "next steps" realistic and meaningful).

The follow-up or research aspect of the guidance program has implications at all levels, for it is through research that evaluation of our methods and the effectiveness of the program can be ascertained. This evidence should be the basis for making changes in the guidance program as well as for deciding on the worthiness of those operations we wish to maintain.

Differential Factors in Elementary-School Guidance

Guidance in the elementary school has a number of distinguishing hallmarks. Numerous articles on guidance in the elementary school have focused discussion on how guidance at this level is similar to guidance services at the secondary-school level. It may be worthwhile to consider how guidance in the elementary school differs from guidance in the secondary school. Emphasis on the factors unique to elementary-school guidance may assist elementary-school staff members to do a better job in their respective guidance roles.

One of the basic factors affecting guidance in the elementary school is related to child development. It is in the period of six to twelve years of age that the child brings together in integrated fashion the forces of the home, the school, the church, and peer relationships, which structure the foundation for his adolescent years. All these forces begin to blend into a harmonious whole. Adolescence seems to be more concerned with the differentiating aspects of the above-mentioned diverse factors rather than the integrative aspects, as during childhood.

The expressiveness of children reveals the harmony between their overt and covert motivation. Beginning with adolescence there may be more differentiation between outer behavior and inner feelings and thinking. Thus, through childhood there is a learning of controlled expressiveness—in a sense, a learned inhibitiveness within the demands of the cultural framework.

A third factor differentiating elementary-school guidance is that children cannot verbalize their feelings to the extent that the maturing adolescent is capable of doing. Because the reasoning process in children is not developed to its fullest, it, too, is a differential factor in an elementary-school pupil's being insightful into the cause and effect of his behavior. Two cautions in interpretation of the last statement are in order here: (1) The mere fact that the elementary-school boy or girl may not have reached the highest level in his reasoning powers does not mean that his feelings are not as sensitive or impressionable as are the adolescent's. (2) The mere fact that the pupil is in the adolescent stage does not necessarily mean that his reasoning powers insure insightful self-understanding.

A fourth differential factor in the guidance of elementary-school children is related to the fact that children do not have a sense of immediacy in deciding on advanced education, making career decisions, and dealing with familial factors that affect their progress toward adulthood. Elementary-school children do have the immediate problems of learning basic skills, of socialization, and of relating to a reality world as contrasted to the fantasy world of early childhood. The elementary-school child is in need of guidance which will help him build a firm personality core from which he can develop the variations in living required in adolescence and adulthood.

The limits of choices of behavior by elementary-school boys and girls is a fifth differentiating factor in their guidance. The choices which children may make are more often than not within an adult framework of limitations, and in most cases the adult involved is the one in their current situation. The adolescent, on the other hand, may more often make decisions within societal limitations rather than within the limits set by the adults in his life space situation.

A sixth differential factor concerns the use of guidance services. Whereas the adolescent may use guidance services directly, the elementary-school child receives the benefits of guidance services through the school staff. The guidance services are more teacher-centered than pupil-centered in the elementary school. One example will illustrate. A tenth-grade student may discuss his aptitude-test results with a school counselor. In the elementary school the guidance-minded teacher will use the test results in developing a meaningful program of learning for the pupil; there probably will be no direct communication with the child concerning his record on a test.

A seventh differential factor is the difference in the organization of the elementary school from that of the secondary school. The elementary-school teacher has full guidance responsibility for his pupils. The high-school teacher has a definite guidance role to play, but it is usually so delineated as to include only one or two phases of the high-school student's total life situation. The high-school counselor becomes the unifying agent, as well as specialist, in assisting the adolescent to know, accept, and direct himself. In the elementary school the classroom teacher functions as the school counselor.

Concluding Comment

Guidance in the elementary school should assist the pupil to develop a harmonious and integrated personality core through carefully planned school experiences which reflect the integration of all the forces impinging on the individual. This is in contrast to guidance services in the secondary school, which assist adolescents to extend themselves to the optimum in all the various aspects of adolescent and adult living, such as educational planning, career choice, personal relationships, and living with one's self. In the elementary school the classroom teacher is *the* guidance worker. In the secondary school each classroom teacher must play a role in the guidance program, but it is the officially appointed, time-released, school counselor who correlates the guidance program for the teachers and unifies the assistance given boys and girls who need his help in greater or lesser amounts.

At both elementary- and secondary-school levels, the school, particularly the co-ordinating head of the guidance program (preferably a school counselor), needs to have a perspective of the over-all guidance program. The program needs to be placed on a longitudinal basis that avoids duplication; makes optimum use of the potentialities of all school staff members at their operational level in the system; and is designed, altered, and reinforced in its procedural approach to meet the needs of all boys and girls. The guidance point of view is a philosophy that must pervade the school system if the maximum potentiality of boys and girls is to be realized.

Guidance Services Recommended by Public- and Parochial-School Teachers

ANTHONY C. RICCIO
DONALD J. WEHMEYER

In a recent report, Leona E. Tyler indicates that there is a definite need to improve guidance services in private schools. Further, she notes the effort "to get private school counselors into the [National Defense Education Act] program has been almost completely unsuccessful."[1] Many persons believe that private-school personnel do not enroll in guidance and counseling training institutes because they do not receive the handsome stipends afforded public-school participants. Others think that the problem is more basic. They hold that guidance services are not as well received in private as in public schools, primarily because of the emphasis on traditional approaches to education in private schools. They see the issue as directly related to conflicting philosophies of education.

This paper reports a study designed to ascertain whether there are noticeable or significant differences in the guidance services recommended by public and private (parochial) elementary-school teachers for particular problem situations. By law neither public nor private elementary-school teachers are allowed to enroll in NDEA counseling and guidance training institutes and thus are ineligible to profit professionally or financially from external pressures to improve the quality of counseling and guidance services; it seemed desirable, therefore, to use elementary-school teachers to measure genuine attitudinal differences toward guidance services. The study incidentally yielded data pertinent to the future of guidance services at the elementary-school level.

REPRINTED FROM *EDUCATIONAL RESEARCH BULLETIN*, 40, 1 (JANUARY 1961), 12-18, BY PERMISSION OF THE PUBLISHERS AND THE AUTHORS.

Several attempts have been made to study the reactions of educational groups to the kind of guidance services that should be employed in particular problem situations. Lawrence H. Stewart administered Robinson's "What Should Be Done?" questionnaire to 94 counselors and 169 classroom teachers in the San Francisco Bay area to learn whether these groups had different conceptions of the guidance services most appropriate for particular problem situations. He found few outstanding differences in the recommendations of the two groups and noted that large numbers in both groups recommended actions which were "inadequate and often inappropriate." He suggested that his findings conceivably were related to the current practice of assigning teachers to counseling positions rather than persons qualified in the field.[2]

Mangan conducted a similar study using a sample of elementary- and secondary-school teachers in Ohio.[3] He administered the same questionnaire to 111 secondary-school teachers and an adaptation of it to an equal number of elementary-school teachers. Observing few differences between the guidance services recommended by the groups under study, he discerned a tendency for secondary-school teachers to suggest intensive guidance procedures for students with various kinds of academic difficulties.[3] The writers used this adaptation in the present study.[1] The questionnaire follows:

WHAT SHOULD BE DONE?

Following are brief descriptions of pupils in the sixth grade of an elementary school. The members of the staff are discussing the relationship which their guidance program should have to each pupil. As a preliminary step they are placing each pupil in one of the following five categories. If you were there, what rating would you give each pupil? (Place a category number before each pupil.)

0 Probably no need for guidance program to work with this pupil.

1 Routine use made of conferences and activities with pupil and/or parents; nothing especially planned for pupil at this time.

2 Special plans made to fit this pupil's needs with particular emphasis placed or non-conference personnel methods, e.g., activities, change of grade, enrichment, etc.

3 Special plans made to fit this pupil's needs with particular emphasis placed on the school providing intensive counseling help or play therapy.

4 Refer the pupil to some agency outside of school for help.

[1] The writers make grateful acknowledgment for permission to use the questionnaire and other data appearing in Mr. Mangan's thesis.

........*Athlete*	A natural athlete. Is the star in all physical education held in class. Has average intellectual ability and achievement to match; has a pleasing personality.
........*Bright*	Very bright pupil; I.Q. 170. Particularly likes arithmetic but gets outstanding grades in all class work with little or no effort (his success with poor study methods makes it difficult to convince other pupils that they might benefit from learning better study methods). Accepted by others; often a leader.
........*Cqueer*	He's so odd we spell it "Cqueer." Tense, withdrawn, and often smiles or talks to himself. Erratic in behavior. Doing very poor school work; rejected by other pupils.
........*Dumb and Deficient*	Doubly troubled, I.Q. 75. Three grades below level in school; has difficulty in doing class work. He is older and bigger than other pupils and is accepted by them in such activities as physical education.
........*Engineer*	Has his heart set on becoming an engineer. He has high ability and grades. Has many mechanical and electrical hobbies. Not too socially inclined, but is well liked by pupils.
........*Failing*	Pupil has average ability and is doing satisfactory work in everything but arithmetic which he is failing. Much upset by failing grade. Has always had trouble with arithmetic, just as his mother did. Liked by fellow pupils.
........*Gauche*	Not particularly liked by other pupils. Dresses in poor taste. Not always clean, poor manners, seems awkward for age, does good work in school however.
........*Homely*	She just isn't good looking at all. She has a pleasant personality, good social skills, and is accepted by other pupils in class work. Outside of school, however, she is not in a group and other girls tend less often now to be seen with her. Has been pubescent for one year. Does good work in school.
........*Ill*	Constantly has colds or other respiratory ailments. Lately has had a bad cough and has lost weight. Says she doesn't feel well. When she does attend school, she does good work and is liked by the pupils.
........*Jerk*	A "teacher's pet." Does well in school; goes out of his way to please his teacher. Rushes home after school "to be with Mother." Immature, even "babyish" in his relations with other pupils, disliked by other pupils.
........*Kiddish*	Girl's behavior is immature; baby talk, over-dependency on mother, fails to make own decision, etc. Her "cute" manner

makes her popular with many of the boys. To get average grades in school her parents force her to study and help her with school work.

........*Loafer*	Very high ability; average grades. Liked by pupils; active in school affairs. Plans to go to a private high school which has very high standards.
........*Medicine*	Wants to become a doctor; but has low ability and low grades. Will probably have difficulty in high school; parents want him to be a doctor.
........*Not Known*	Not mentioned by anyone on a Guess Who test. Does average work in school but doesn't discuss in class; teacher says nothing about her stands out. Comes from a farm nearby; not active in group work. Not rejected; just sort of "mousy."

This questionnaire was administered to 103 parochial elementary-school teachers in attendance at the 1960 Summer Session of the University of Notre Dame. Their responses were compared to Mangan's data (1959) on 111 public elementary-school teachers in Ohio in two ways. First, a comparison was made of the percentage distribution of choice of guidance services by both groups for each of the fourteen problem situations. Second, in accordance with Mangan's treatment of his data, the five categories listed in the directions accompanying the questionnaire were reduced to two. Categories 0, 1, and 2 were termed "routine"; categories 3 and 4 "intensive." The chi-square test was used to determine whether there were significant differences in the extent to which the study groups recommended routine or intensive guidance services. The .05 level of confidence was selected as the criterion of significance.

Table 1 presents a percentage breakdown by category of the responses of the study groups. The table should be read as follows: for the case called Athlete, 58 per cent of the parochial and 52 per cent of the public elementary-school teachers thought that no guidance was needed; 37 per cent of the parochial and 43 per cent of the public-school teachers suggested a routine conference; and so on. An analysis of Table 1 indicates a remarkable similarity in the categories selected for each problem situation. In only four of the fourteen categories (Cqueer, Engineer, Homely, and Kiddish) were there different modal responses, and in only one case (Cqueer) was there a difference larger than 20 per cent. In addition, there was a decided tendency for both groups to suggest intensive counseling or referral for students characterized by social or academic deficiencies. This observation was also reported by Robinson[4] and by Stewart.[2]

On the other hand, less than 10 per cent of the members of either group suggested intensive guidance services for the superior or well-adjusted students (Athlete, Bright, and Engineer). This finding runs counter to one of the purposes of the National Defense Education Act: to use guidance services as a means of helping talented students to make optimal contributions in the interests of national defense. It also suggests that Mr. Conant's recent interest in using guidance services to identify, encourage, and develop talented students[5] has yet to be accepted or practiced at the grass-roots level, for guidance services were viewed by study-group members as remedial and preventive rather than developmental.

TABLE 1 Percentage of Parochial and Public Elementary-School Teachers' Responses for Guidance Action, by Category

Student	*No Guidance Needed* 0		*Routine Conference* 1		*Special Non-Conference* 2		*Intensive Counseling* 3		*Referral to Outside Agency* 4	
	Par.	Pub.	Par.	Pub.	Par.	Pub.	Par.	Pub.	Par.	Pub.
(1)	(2)	(3)	(4)	(5)	(6)	(7)	(8)	(9)	(10)	(11)
Athlete	58	52	37	43	4	5	1	0	0	0
Bright	7	7	15	15	69	70	6	8	3	0
Cqueer	0	0	0	4	3	3	25	53	72	40
Dumb and Deficient	1	0	2	10	20	25	43	40	34	25
Engineer	15	26	43	33	33	35	8	4	1	2
Failing	0	2	30	28	38	49	29	20	3	1
Gauche	2	2	32	29	6	21	52	43	8	5
Homely	7	3	28	25	16	36	42	32	7	4
Ill	4	3	10	24	3	5	8	10	75	58
Jerk	0	1	17	18	14	14	63	61	6	6
Kiddish	0	2	38	29	20	22	37	41	5	6
Loafer	2	3	20	24	62	52	15	21	1	0
Medicine	0	0	46	47	18	18	32	33	4	2
Not Known	3	6	29	27	26	32	40	35	2	0

The data contained in Table 1 do not augur well for the future. Since there are relatively few elementary-school counselors at present, elementary-school teachers will have to bear the brunt of guidance activities. If the study-group members are representative of their co-workers, they will devote much time to working with the deficient and maladjusted at the expense of the superior and the well-adjusted student. Since the elementary-school counselors of the future in all probability will come from the present crop of elementary-school teachers, there is reason to believe that to a large extent they will continue to view guidance services as remedial and preventive. The talented and potentially superior students in our society will suffer—as will the entire nation—if this negative view of guidance services is not radically altered. Undoubtedly one of the major tasks of both teacher- and counselor-education programs in this decade will be to communicate to future teachers and counselors the belief that guidance services have just as much, if not more, to offer to the development of the superior student as to the rehabilitation of the deficient or unmotivated student.

TABLE 2 Analysis of Observed Differences Between Public and Parochial Elementary-School Teachers' Recommendations of Routine and Intensive Guidance Service *

Student (1)	*Chi Square* (2)	*Level of Significance* (3)
Athlete	.0071	.95
Bright	.0275	.90
Cqueer	2.0208	.20
Dumb and Deficient	3.6019	.10
Engineer	1.7099	.20
Failing	3.5422	.10
Gauche	3.3291	.10
Homely	3.4297	.10
Ill	6.3347	.02
Jerk	.1254	.80
Kiddish	.5625	.50
Loafer	.9644	.50
Medicine	.0144	.95
Not Known	.9883	.50

* Degree of freedom = 1

Table 2 presents the results of a chi-square analysis of the significance of the differences between public and parochial elementary-school teachers' recommendations of routine and intensive guidance services. The table shows that in one case only (Ill) was there a significant difference in the recommendations of the study groups. In view of the data contained in Table 1, this finding is not surprising. It should be noted, however, that there were greater differences in the guidance recommendations of the Ohio elementary- and secondary-school groups studied by Mangan[3, p. 34] than in the responses of the parochial and public elementary-school teachers. It is conceivable that the elementary-secondary dimension may be more important than the public-private school one. This possibility bears further investigation.

To the extent that the study groups are representative of public- and private- (parochial) school teachers, it is possible to conclude that there are no distinguishing general attitudes toward guidance services between these two groups. It seems, therefore, that if administrators in parochial schools were to place guidance services at the disposal of teachers, they would be used at least as often by parochial-school teachers as by public-school teachers. What is most noticeable, however, is that both private and public elementary-school teachers perceive guidance services as means of rehabilitating the deficient rather than as avenues of developing the talented. Here, perhaps, is a major challenge to elementary-school administrators. Through in-service education or other means, they must make their teachers aware of the advantages of the developmental approach to guidance services. A successful developmental guidance program may obviate much of the work required by remedial or preventive guidance programs.

Unfortunately, students also have a tendency to view guidance services from other than a developmental point of view.[6] They share with their teachers the notion that guidance is for those who are performing at a less than satisfactory level on some behavioral dimension. They do not view it as a means of assisting the mediocre to perform at a superior level or as a vehicle for helping the superior student to perform at an exceptional level. They must come to realize that the counseling interview is basically a learning situation and that the well-motivated, intelligent student stands to profit far more from counseling than does the unmotivated, less intelligent student.[7] Perhaps it is in this area that Mr. Conant's report will make its greatest contribution to the modern school; for as students who are known to be excellent are seen in fairly frequent contact with guidance personnel, the stigma currently attached to taking part in a counseling interview will gradually disappear. In sum, until there is a radical departure from a negative, problem-oriented conception of guidance services on the part of teachers and students, the concept of guidance for all youth will be but a counselor-educator's dream.

REFERENCES

1. *The National Defense Counseling and Guidance Training Institutes Program: a Report of the First 50 Institutes,* Bulletin 31 (Washington, D.C.: Office of Education, U. S. Department of Health, Education and Welfare, 1960), p. 73.

2. Lawrence H. Stewart, "Teachers and Counselors Look at Students: Some Implications for Guidance Practice," *Personnel and Guidance Journal,* **35** (May 1957), 565-568.

3. John C. Mangan, "Teachers' Recommendation for Guidance Services" (Master's thesis, Ohio State University, 1959).

4. Francis P. Robinson, "Guidance for All: in Principle and in Practice," *Personnel and Guidance Journal,* **31** (May 1953), 500-504.

5. James B. Conant, *The American High School Today: a First Report to Interested Citizens* (New York: McGraw-Hill, 1959), 44-46.

6. Marilyn Heilfron, "The Function of Counseling as Perceived by High School Students," *Personnel and Guidance Journal,* **39** (October 1960), 133-136.

7. Herman J. Peters, "Counseling Services for Talented Students," *Working with Superior Students: Theories and Practices,* ed. Bruce Shertzer (Chicago: Science Research Associates, 1960), 203.

The Guidance-Oriented Elementary Teacher

FRANCES R. HARPER

Unlike guidance at the secondary-school level with its growing use of specialists, elementary-school guidance remains primarily the ongoing responsibility of the classroom teacher.

The National Defense Education Act of 1958 authorizes the use of federal funds to improve guidance, testing, and counseling services at the secondary level. The legislators had nothing to say about guidance in the elementary school. For the time being, the shortage of trained personnel and the emphasis on search for talent at the secondary level will probably prevent any major new developments in guidance practices in the elementary school.

The practical concept of guidance for the grade-school child may be considered just about forty years old. The Commonwealth Fund in the 1920's sponsored a dual program which provided for the establishment of experimental child-guidance clinics and visiting-teacher services.

While the child-guidance movement has grown steadily, the visiting-teacher movement developed very slowly. Since 1945, however, many state departments of education, in their efforts to improve school attendance, have sponsored the employment of visiting teachers (also called school, social workers, elementary counsellors, and pupil personnel workers).

Activities of the visiting teacher, like those of other special consultants to the elementary school, are designed to assist the teacher in his efforts to bring out children's talents and strengths as well as to correct or offset their shortcomings and weaknesses. For the most part, elementary-school

REPRINTED FROM THE *NEA JOURNAL*, 49, (MARCH 1960), BY PERMISSION OF THE PUBLISHERS AND THE AUTHOR.

teachers and administrators have been readily able to blend the concepts of guidance with their interest in teaching "the whole child."

Fortunately, elementary educators seldom visualize guidance in their schools either as a watered-down version of secondary-school guidance or as designed only for those children whose behavior is disturbing or deficient.

Certain administrative requirements lie back of the assumption that the classroom teacher is primarily responsible for the day-to-day guidance of all his students. One of these is that teachers who are assigned to a particular grade will understand not only the subject matter but also the physical, social, and emotional characteristics of children of that age. Another assumption is that pupils with marked physical, mental, or emotional difficulties will not be placed in the regular classroom.

Guidance at the elementary level is most significantly a point of view to be adopted and developed by the classroom teacher. This point of view, first of all, rejects an authoritarian approach and accepts mutual respect as a basis for all relationships.

Using this approach, teachers avoid such labels as good and bad, right and wrong, superior and inferior. Rather than comparing one child with another, they look for talents, assets, and strong points within the individual child. Giftedness may be social, psychological, scholastic, artistic, or mechanical.

Jerry, for example, bothers his neighbors, leaves his seat to look at exhibits, and interrupts with questions. The teacher does not jump to the conclusion that he is an emotionally disturbed child who has been overindulged at home and who needs to be disciplined into realizing that his excessive demands for attention cannot always be met.

Observation of Jerry in a number of situations may reveal him to be a bright, alert, and curious child. Here, indeed, may be, not the neurotic who needs to be subdued, but the potential scientist for whom we are searching so assiduously at the secondary level. The guidance Jerry needs may well be the constructive opening of broader and deeper vistas than those now offered to him.

Linda, on the other hand, is very quiet and conforming. Her presence is so unobtrusive that one scarcely notices her frequent absences.

With a child like Linda, the guidance-oriented teacher does not unconcernedly accept written excuses from home regarding colds and other minor illnesses. Realizing that here may be a seriously disturbed child who is having difficulty separating herself from her mother, the teacher may seek the help of the visiting teacher, the nurse, or other professional consultants.

Guidance, like other aspects of modern education, needs to be increasingly rooted in the scientific method, which calls for a conscious and systematic collection and examination of pertinent data before a tentative conclusion is reached. New information may change not only some details but the whole trend of evaluation of a child or a class of children.

One primary teacher, by way of illustration, had a rather negative impression of the guidance concept. She began by studying (superficially) the three or four children most difficult for her to discipline. After reaching a tentative diagnosis of "emotionally disturbed," she considered her study completed and turned her attention to the next most obstreperous group. As she proceeded from group to group with this negative point of view, she in effect created a whole class of "exceedingly difficult" children.

Toward the end of the first term, this teacher had to resign to care for her ill mother. The teacher who replaced her thought of guidance as a positive continuing process for all children. Most of the acute problems subsided. This class of "exceedingly difficult" children was transformed, mainly by a change in teacher attitude, into an effective social unit of children who wanted to learn.

This group of children has been followed closely for six years. With but two exceptions, they have made satisfactory to excellent progress. Special services have been required for two of the children because of unusually disordered home situations. Significantly, however, these two children were not among those on whom the original teacher focused her early negative diagnoses.

While teachers need to be careful not to jump to negative conclusions, they should not, on the other hand, continue to gloss over potentially serious disturbances. As in the case of Linda, co-operative as well as unco-operative children need to be carefully studied.

The earlier a child's emotional difficulties are perceived and treated, of course, the better. Clinical practitioners assure us that faulty emotional behavior is at least as difficult to modify as faulty study or learning habits and that early treatment should be the rule.

There has been a tendency in many elementary schools to wait to see if a child will outgrow emotional problems. Although such a judgment is sometimes justified, it is certainly a hazardous general rule. Far too often, behavioral difficulties reappear in somewhat different forms, but with increased intensity, under the stress of adolescence. It is generally advisable to have a plan for direct and active guidance of children with problems rather than to count on nature to effect a magical growth cure.

Two guidance functions which are usually carried out according to standardized procedures are testing and record keeping. The uniform and objective appearance of record sheets, however, should not so intimidate the classroom teacher that he will never question the reliability or validity of the data reported. The perfect test has not yet been conceived, and automation will probably never fully remove human errors from record keeping.

The alert teacher, for example, may quite accurately see Kenneth as a bright child instead of the dull child reported by the mental-abilities test. It may be that the difference between his observations and the record derives from a reading disability, and Kenneth may need the help of a specialist.

Tests and records are by no means, however, proper objects for a teacher's scorn and ridicule. Imperfect though they are, they provide the best source of information about the developing child—his early and present state of health, his family and social history, and his school achievement and adjustment.

The guidance-oriented teacher not only draws from, but also adds to, the development record of the child. His synopsis of a year's observations of a child will provide the most important beginning for the next teacher's understanding.

In conclusion, then, the concept of guidance is nothing new or threatening to the well-trained elementary-school educator. At its best, it is the clarifying, integrating, and implementing of what the teacher and administrator have been trying to do all along (and, all handicaps considered, doing quite well). Elementary-school guidance is an organized effort to help the teacher more effectively understand and meet the most important needs of the individual child.

Guidance in the Elementary School

ANNA R. MEEKS

One of the most important current trends in guidance is the growth of organized programs at the elementary level.

The urgency of the demand for guidance in the elementary school has become greater as the greater complexity of modern living has increased the pressures which can be factors in a child's maladjustment and which hinder learning. Teachers have seen, for example, that emotional pressures upon the child by the school, his parents, or his peers may create an emotional block which will prevent his learning to read until, through counseling or other help, the block is removed.

More significant than the recognition of the usefulness of guidance in the correction of maladjustment has been the acceptance of guidance as an integral part of the whole educational program. Guidance is now regarded as much more than a privilege accorded the maladjusted; it is also needed by other children and requires programs that have as their major objective helping all children to be at ease with themselves and with others.

Such an approach calls for a carefully organized program of services within the individual school, supplemented by services provided through a central office staff. Helping children meet their personal, social, educational, and vocational needs is facilitated by participation of administrators, teachers, parents, guidance specialists (counselors), school nurses, school psychologists, and community agencies.

The principal is responsible for policies, organization, and leadership. Through effective and democratic leadership, he promotes an over-all school climate in which guidance can be effective. The teacher is a participant in and not merely a recipient of guidance services for his pupils.

REPRINTED FROM THE *NEA JOURNAL*, 51, (MARCH 1962), BY PERMISSION OF THE PUBLISHERS AND THE AUTHOR.

He shares with the counselor many responsibilities including the identification of children with special needs. In identifying these children and in fulfilling his key role in guidance services, the teacher makes use of his own observations, anecdotal records, sociograms, informal interviews, and the insight gained from study of his pupils' autobiographies and other creative forms of expression.

The counseling process in the elementary school differs from counseling at other levels only in its use of some specialized techniques which are particularly suited to the developmental level of the younger child. The counselor's office with its toys, pictures, and books offers a relaxing situation in which the child can handle his tensions, face his concept of himself and others, and learn to live with himself and his fellow classmates.

The uncommunicative child may be able to talk to the counselor on a toy telephone, or may express his hostile feelings by abusing a toy. No attempt is made to diagnose emotional problems or to structure therapy sessions through toys, but their use has a legitimate place in the counseling of elementary children, as the following example shows.

One day fourth-grader Mary came into the counselor's office and stood looking at the toy shelves. Apparently she was not ready to talk about whatever was troubling her but soon she began manipulating two hand puppets, one representing a baby; the other, a little girl. "That's Buddy and this is me," she explained and proceeded to let Buddy beat her badly in a vigorous fight.

On subsequent visits to the counselor, Mary repeated the puppet act several times. When Mary's mother visited the school, the counselor told her about the fights and got this startled reply, "Come to think of it, that baby is licking the whole family! It's time we took him in hand."

Armed with new insight, the mother and the counselor were able to help Mary see herself as a valued person. The teacher, in turn, was able to help her find more satisfaction in her school work.

Of course, had Mary's emotional troubles been more deep-seated, the counselor would have referred her to other specialists. Or, if Mary's problems had been common to those of several other children in her school, she might have been counseled with them in a group, rather than individually.

Small groups of intermediate children often benefit from talking together in the counselor's office. They discuss their school experiences, help each other recognize strengths and weaknesses, and decide how they can improve their strengths and remove their weaknesses. In working with these groups, the counselor will supplement unstructured conversation with effective methods of group work, such as sociodramas and role playing.

In some cases, group counseling is especially effective with underachievers.

A fifth-grade teacher, for instance, was troubled by the fact that two of his boys, Ted and Billy, were not working up to their ability. When he mentioned this to the counselor, he found that she had just scheduled some weekly sessions for five other boys from intermediate grades who were also underachievers. Ted and Billy would be welcome to join.

From these sessions, the boys emerged with a greater sense of responsibility and new confidence in their ability to learn.

Effective though group counseling may be in correcting some results of underachievement, it is far better to prevent underachievement from ever becoming a problem by early and continuous identification of children with superior mental ability.

As pointed out at greater length in the chapter I wrote last year for the study, *Guidance for the Underachiever with Superior Ability* (published by the U. S. Department of Health, Education, and Welfare), bright children share with all children the many needs that are met by guidance services. In addition, they have unique needs arising from their superior ability. They may need help in their relationships with less mature children; routines and drills may become irksome and cause them to lose their motivations for learning; adult expectations for the academically able child may exert pressures which adversely affect the pupil.

The guidance process can also have important bearing on another aspect of underachievement. While there has been a wide acceptance of a readiness level for reading instruction, many schools have failed to recognize that there are readiness levels for all types of learning and that an individual child may have wide differences in readiness levels, as Johnny's story illustrates.

Johnny's reading-readiness score indicated he was ready for formal reading and should make good progress in school. After a few weeks, however, he was having difficulty in both reading and arithmetic. Constantly urged by his parents to do better, he had become an unhappy, confused child.

Miss Brown, his teacher, consulted the counselor and after studying all the factors in his case, they concluded that his reading-readiness score reflected his rich home background more than his mental maturity and that it did not indicate readiness for all learning. When the parents had the situation explained to them, they stopped pressuring Johnny to make rapid progress, with the result that he was able to lead a more comfortable and realistic school life.

The concept of readiness for learning in this broader application needs the greater clarification that can come through child study and through extension and intensification of elementary-school guidance.

Certainly, the problem of the underachiever with superior ability will be greater at the secondary and college levels if guidance has been lacking or ineffective in early school experience.

To sum up, the elementary-school counselor is a professionally trained person with depth of understanding and knowledge in child development, theories of counseling, group dynamics, classroom teaching, curriculum trends, school administration, public relations, and the organization of guidance services.

These requirements explain in part why well-trained counselors are in woefully short supply. The main reason, however, is that few school budgets have adequately allowed for counseling services, particularly at the elementary level. Even the provisions of the National Defense Education Act of 1958 were specifically written for secondary schools.

These facts notwithstanding, I believe that in the next ten years, elementary-school guidance will grow rapidly. It is essential, however, that such guidance not be a pale replica of secondary-school guidance. Rather, the two programs must complement each other and provide continuous coverage for each child from the school's first contact with him until he goes from high school to the right college or the right job.

Part Two

INDIVIDUAL APPRAISAL OF THE ELEMENTARY SCHOOL CHILD

Techniques of Studying Children

SYBIL RICHARDSON

School systems have been studying children for years and have devised a variety of interesting approaches for use in their studies. We might begin our discussion by reviewing some of our assumptions about the principal's role in studying children. Obviously, principals cannot initiate a program of child study by order or by fiat, for to get teachers to look with sensitivity at children, consideration must be given to whatever questions or problems that are of concern to the teachers. We are interested in long-term planning for the study of children, not just a study of a child here and there. Therefore, we must have a plan for maintaining a comprehensive program of child study.

We have long recognized that the principal's behavior plays an important part in creating the child study atmosphere of the school. Certainly his day-by-day behavior has a powerful influence upon the teachers' interest in studying children. For instance, the principal visits classrooms to help teachers with the problems of curriculum, of securing and using materials, and of room arrangement, he does not at first comment on the teacher's methods of handling children. Later, however, he raises questions about the boy in the back of the room who does not seem to be interested, or the girl who apparently requires so much attention. In these ways he stimulates the teacher's interest in each child in the class. Many principals regularly observe during the medical examinations of children to gather important information about certain children which they convey to the children's teachers so that they can better understand the children's classroom behavior. Many principals spend a great deal of time dealing patiently and thoughtfully with each child who continues to be sent to their offices by teachers. The provisions which princi-

REPRINTED FROM *CALIFORNIA JOURNAL OF ELEMENTARY EDUCATION,* 26, 10 (MAY 1958), 227-236, BY PERMISSION OF THE PUBLISHERS AND THE AUTHOR.

pals make for cumulative records, for collection of data, and for the transfer of records also contribute to teachers' understanding of children. Our California professional organizations of principals and supervisors have made an unusual contribution to a system of cumulative records which can be used and transferred from one school to another. These are a few of the ways in which principals play essential roles in helping teachers to understand children. They interpret children to teachers and teachers and children to parents. In a sense, principals play a three-way intermediary role as they listen to each one and try to help each understand the other.

We might briefly review three methods of child study with which many are familiar. One of these, the case study conference method, which was first used by child guidance clinics, has been used extensively in California. Another, the three-year child study program originally sponsored by the Institute of Child Study at the University of Maryland is now being sponsored by certain of the institutions of higher learning in our state. This program provides for continuity in teachers' study of children. Then we have some typical studies of children's responses. Many teachers use this type of study consistently and continuously as a means of determining what curriculum experiences the children need.

The Child Guidance Conference, a Means of Studying Children

Use of the case study conference in California began many years ago. The State Department of Institutions (now the State Department of Mental Hygiene) maintained a traveling clinic which provided services to many school districts. In most communities the school district or the county superintendent of schools subsequently took over these services because both principals and teachers recognized their values.

In a child guidance conference the principal has a key role in helping teachers to select children who need to be studied by a psychologist, social worker, or physician. Certain observations are required to secure information needed about each child and the principal must give the teacher help in recording this information. Teachers were at first so overwhelmed by the job of collecting the material which was required in making case studies that the principal's help and encouragement was essential. Usually, in making a case study the psychologist or the counselor takes major responsibility for completing a synthesis of the results of observations made by teachers and specialists, and for reporting recommendations for the child's improvement. These conferences are open to all teachers not only those concerned with a particular child.

The guidance conference method has been consistently used as an in-service activity to help teachers understand children. Many principals report that even where the services of specialists, such as psychologists and social workers, are not available the activity proves to be fruitful. At certain faculty meetings, attention is centered upon one or two children by the principal asking questions about the children. For the next month or two each member of the staff makes it his business to observe the children while they are on the playground, in the cafeteria, or in the hall and to use the results of his observation to understand each child better. Then in another faculty meeting the teachers and principal discuss what they learned through their observations. Many staffs report that such concerted study produced most worth-while results.

The Three-year Program of Child Study

The child study program originally sponsored by the University of Maryland is extending throughout many parts of the state. This program is voluntary. However, teachers who wish to participate must enroll for three years. During the first year, the emphasis is upon improving observation records of behavior. The activities of the second year are designed to help teachers understand the child within the context of a six area framework. During the third year, study is focused upon the child's self-concept and adjustment. The University of California, Los Angeles, has recently offered graduate credit to teachers enrolling in this child study program. In this program a teacher selects one child each year for intensive study. The child so selected for study is not disturbed or maladjusted, but a child in whom the teacher is especially interested. Teachers usually report that they find that through participation in this study they get a great deal of help in teaching the children studied and that their understanding of all children improves. Probably another strength of the program is that the teachers work in a group and find some personal security from doing so. Many of the leaders for the program are teachers who have had special training for assuming the responsibility.

Observing and Listening to Children, a Part of Curriculum Development

A third type of child study involves the use of questions by principals and their staffs as guides for observing children and as means of encouraging children to talk. Information thus collected helps them to make wise decisions regarding how each child can best be given the help he needs. We are making decisions about youngsters every day all day long, but too often thoughtlessly, routinely, and traditionally.

Studying Children's Intellectual Development

Standardized tests have been used extensively in studying children's intellectual growth. When the results secured by using these tests are discussed, teachers often comment that somehow they think the children have learned more and that they (the teachers) have taught more than is revealed in the tests.

In the beginning of a social studies unit the principal who raises a simple question such as "What do you suppose the children already know about this topic?" may lead teachers to an interesting study. One group of teachers, for instance, who were planning a study of California for children who had recently come from many parts of the country, wondered what the children knew about California. The children were, therefore, asked to write or talk about California. The results showed wide diversity in the children's concepts and understanding. One little girl who lived in a trailer court wrote, "People like to come to California because it is beautiful. I wish I were there right now this very minute." This child apparently did not realize she was actually living in California. Her drab surroundings did not resemble the glamorous California she had heard and read about.

Another group interested in children's understanding of geography had the children answer questions such as "What makes a river?" "Why is a river important?" "What makes rain?" In looking over the children's responses the teachers sensed the full impact of the enormous differences in understanding among the children. Almost for the first time they recognized the extent to which each child's life experience influences what he knows and what he can learn. Children who had spent a good deal of time in California, for instance, gave answers that described a river as a stone ditch that they could not play in or a ditch with wire around it. Certain children who had seen the Mississippi or those who had more verbal fluency gave long and complete answers. One child wrote, "In the early millions of years ago, when the mountains were forming, water washing through the valley made rivers, and today, water melting from the mountains goes down these washes." Through analyzing the responses the teachers began to find ways of utilizing the children's abilities so that all might learn from one another's experiences.

One of the principal's tasks is to help teachers classify and analyze the answers collected. This may result in grouping the children according to those who are unable to respond, those who made confused or erroneous responses, those who made very simple and matter-of-fact reponses, and those who made quite complex responses. In making the analysis the teachers may become especially interested in such points as the creative expressions, unusual responses, and the way in which words are used.

Whether the children should sign their written responses depends upon how the responses are to be used. Generally, the children are not at first required to sign their names and are told that they do not have to worry especially about their spelling or grammar. This leaves them free to respond to the questions as they wish. Later the children may voluntarily sign their papers or identify the papers they wrote.

In one school the eighth grade teachers were especially interested in children's ideas about democracy. They, therefore, asked their pupils to write responses to questions such as: "What does democracy mean to you?" "Can you think of anything that happened to you recently which was undemocratic?" While they were studying the responses, the teachers began to ask, "What would younger children say?" "When was this learned?" "Was this learned at home or at school?" They then decided to ask the sixth grade boys and girls to answer questions like those the pupils in the eighth grade had answered. A comparison of the two sets of responses revealed the growth children make from year to year. For instance, in one typical sixth grade class, 24 children gave some indication of understanding the concept of democracy. They said such things as "it means being fair and square," "having equal rights," "having freedom," or "the right to protest." However, the answers of ten children indicated that they were confused. For instance, one child said, "Democracy is what Hitler told the people and it's all lies." Another child said, "It's when you do something wrong." Four children said, "It's some kind of punishment." This answer raised several questions in the teachers' minds about the words they had used in trying to improve children's behavior. Five children were unable to answer any of the questions.

All the children in the eighth grade were able to give a rather complex statement on the concept of democracy. Many of them not only used such phrases as "it is a way of government in which people are concerned" or "in which we have freedom," but added the more subtle statement that "it is a way of living and working together or helping one another." In the eighth grade, too, all the pupils gave some evidence that they were able to evaluate their experiences in terms of the concept of democracy. One impression obtained from the responses was the amount of injustice which children face and of which adults are unaware. For instance, the children told stories of not being waited on in the store, or of not receiving correct change and being told to leave when they asked for it. The lack of sensitivity of others to the problems which children face was clearly revealed. On the other hand, many children reported evidences of democratic practices at home, at school, and in their neighborhood.

One eighth grade pupil wrote, "I think democracy means to have a free country and a right to go to the church of your choice, to have plenty to eat, and to be safe in your own house. It also means that you can pick your own friends." As an example of a democratic incident that happened to her, she adds, "My next door neighbor gave me some papers for our paper drive and she also gave me some cactus for my small garden." Another child wrote, "Democracy means more than just a form of government, it is a government and a life for the people, and with people and by the people, it is being fair, honest, and helpful." Another pupil wrote, "Democracy is to help everyone by living fair and honest, and you have freedom of speech, religion, and thought." This child went on to say, "In our home we have a democratic form of government. We have a court, our meeting place is the dining room table, our judge is my father. We decide as a whole what to do on some days, but we mostly decide things like what time to have bed time and how to punish, and we are all convinced that the majority is almost always right."

Many questions occur as we look at these ways of trying to assess children's intellectual growth. Our standardized testing programs need to be studied. Some staffs have become interested in trying to assess how the children themselves feel about taking frequent standardized tests. They want answers to questions such as: How do the children feel about the fairness or unfairness of such tests? How do they feel about how well they did? What parts were hardest for the children? What parts were easiest for the children? Do the children who consistently score low recognize this? Do the children meet routine standardized tests with a defensive sense of defeat? The suspicion is growing that repeated testing does not improve diagnosis and that it lessens the motivation of the very children who already have the poorest motivation.

Studying Children's Social Behaviors and Adjustment

In studying children's social behavior, Foshay's *Children's Social Values*[1] is a helpful reference. Teachers describe the many ways in which they tried to study children's social values and social behavior. For instance, several teachers raised questions about children's sense of follow-through and responsibility. They asked, "Why is it that some children who promise to bring apple boxes for the store, money for milk, or books from home consistently fail to do so? How can we help these children to develop the responsibility and follow-through that is part of character?" Their first hypothesis was that the children who verbally committed themselves and said "I will bring this Tuesday" were the ones who brought the material. Many of us who had worked on adult committees might have predicted that the teachers would find this hypothesis to be faulty. We know that people may glibly promise to do something and then forget to do the required job. The teachers found, however, that the children whose security in the group was revealed by sociometric ratings, who had friends, were liked, and who felt this was a good school and a fine class were the children who generally carried out their promises. The teachers concluded that if they wanted to develop character in youngsters, they should not talk *at* them about character, or scold, or moralize, but should instead work hard at making the children feel comfortable and secure in their group."

One group of teachers studied children's aggression. The observations the teachers had made of incidents of hitting, pushing, and shoving on the playground had made them wonder whether the undesirable incidents were caused by a few children or were produced by all. To secure the information needed for their study the teachers recorded information about the acts of aggression which they observed. They also gathered information by having the children answer questions such as "How do people make you feel bad? How do people hurt your feelings? What do people do to you when they want to be mean?"

The children's answers included references to many of the same kinds of undesirable behavior, such as hitting and pushing, that the teachers had observed. The children also reported many behaviors which they thought to be unfair and undesirable but which adults seldom give much if any attention. Apparently, the children thought that not being invited to a birthday party, being turned away from a group they wished to join, and having a face made at them were as undesirable as any of the behaviors adults classify as bad. The teachers began to wonder how children interpret hitting and pushing. They secured the desired answers by composing little stories of the incidents observed and asking the children questions about them such as "Why do you think Jimmie hit Joe?" and "Why did Sally push Mary?" In most incidents the children interpreted aggression as "getting back," saying, "Well, it must have been last week Sally did something to Mary. Something happened before this." The teachers concluded that too often adults attempt to settle incidents of aggression without fully understanding the history of the acts.

Teachers can deepen their understanding of children's social behavior by having the children express themselves regarding the following questions and then analyzing the children's responses. "Who are the big shots among the pupils?" "What do you have to do to get to be a wheel in a group of pupils?" "Who are the pupils that teachers favor or that are most popular with the teachers?" By encouraging teachers to use techniques, principals have frequently helped teachers to discover the children who are overlooked and to help all to build a feeling of group belonging.

In using the sociometric techniques one group of teachers asked the children questions like "Do you like to work alone?" "Do you like to work with others better than to work alone?" Most of the children stated they preferred to work with others. Some of them gave the following reasons for their preferences. "Two heads are better than one." "People have different kinds of knowledge they can pool." The teachers became interested in the children who didn't want to work in groups because, as the children said, "Then you wouldn't get all the credit" or "Somebody else would be lazy and make you do all the work." One child asked, "How would the teacher know who did it if we worked together?" The information gathered served as a springboard for a study of the children who were developing individualistic and competitive attitudes. The teachers concluded that all the children needed help in determining when it is best to work alone and when is it best to work with others.

Many questions for study are related to discipline. For example, the children in one group were asked to list rules that adults follow, rules that children follow, and why we have rules. The children's responses made it apparent that the school had done an effective job of teaching important rules, especially those of safety. Two-thirds of the children indicated in their responses that they thought rules were necessary because of man's "evil" nature, giving such reasons as "Everybody would be killing one another," or "Everybody would be stealing from one another." The teachers agreed that perhaps the children had too often thought of the need for rules in relation to horrible examples. They agreed that for their own happiness and security, children need to view other human beings as honest, friendly, and helpful, rather than with suspicion and distrust.

Studying Children's Questions, Interests, and Anxieties

In his interest survey, Jersild found that only one subject, social studies, was mentioned by children in almost all grades as being disliked, more than liked. Many principals and teachers thought that this would not be true in California and, therefore, surveyed their pupils. The teachers were right. They found that social studies was not disliked as much as it was liked, but that English was mentioned most frequently as more disliked than liked.

In the report card study described in the *California Journal of Elementary Education*[2] several teachers made tape recordings of children's discussions of their report cards. In one group the children were guessing at the meaning of items on their report cards. One child said, "I wonder what it means 'to put away materials'." "What do they mean by that?" and another one would say, "Well, maybe it's art," and another one would say, "No, it couldn't be art because there is another place for that." Apparently children are not clear about the behaviors that are evaluated. The children were confused regarding such terms as self-control. One child, for instance, said, "I got a need to improve in self-control," and another quickly said, "Well, you are new to school and had to get acquainted, didn't you? That's okay." Another child said, "I got a need to improve in self-control because the kids at my table all tell such good jokes."

Principals and teachers have planned parent-teacher association meetings around children's own responses. One interesting study was based on the children's unsigned reactions to questions. These included, "When my mother sees my report card she usually ———," "When my father sees my report card he usually ———." The parent committee was impressed with the different family attitudes which were revealed. Some families apparently give immediate support to the children when he brings his report card home, others apparently exert continuous pressure on children to get better marks. Such study is important in helping parents, teachers, and children to understand one another.

Another meeting was centered upon the responses children made in completing the statement: "I'd like to do my best work at school, and usually I try. When I don't, it's because ———." The reasons that the children gave were used as a basis for class discussions and conferences. The kinds of problems and solutions which the young people formulate are impressive. In a recent teen-age conference, seventh and eighth grade pupils made a long list of problems and then had certain pupils suggest solutions to the problems of each type. The suggestions made give us a basis for having confidence in children's insights and in the soundness of their judgments. The follow through on suggestions and recommendations is, of course, important.

Perhaps the many specifics can be brought together in several principles regarding our own ways of working as principals. To help teachers look at children and listen to children, we ourselves must have an attitude of inquiry. We have to be sensitive to any question, however trivial, which may serve as a springboard for continued study. Secondly, we have to have an attitude of acceptance, and this again means not sitting in judgment of others as we are often quick to do. As adults study the responses of children they often seem to discount them with responses such as: "Well, they are just being silly. That's just to show-off. They just said that to please you." We cannot afford to make such judgments but must consider expression and feelings as facts, true at least for the moment. Principals must be sensitive to their role of helping teachers, parents, and children to perceive and communicate clearly with one another. This is hard, for these three groups have a strong impact upon the principal who must absorb complaints, anger, and hostility sometimes from parents, sometimes from teachers, sometimes from children. It is difficult not to pass these feelings on to others. It is often hard to avoid reaction and to stress mutual understanding. We can support others when we understand them. This does not imply full endorsement of their actions. The principal's leadership role involves continuously helping teachers to study children so that a school environment will be created in which co-operative and productive teamwork flourishes.

REFERENCES

1. Arthur W. Foshay *et al., Children's Social Values: An Action Research Study* (New York: Bureau of Publications, Teachers College, Columbia University, 1954).

2. Sybil Richardson, "How Do Children Feel About Reports to Parents?" *California Journal of Elementary Education,* **24** (November 1955), 106-107.

Teacher Knowledge of Pupil Data and Marking Practices at the Elementary School Level

ROBERT L. BAKER
ROY P. DOYLE

In January of 1954, a committee of representatives from the school community began the study of several problems relating to guidance practices in Madison Elementary School District, Phoenix, Arizona. Special subcommittees were created to work intensively on each problem being studied. The Subcommittee on Pupil Data undertook the study of problems involved in the collection and utilization of information about pupils.

Members of this subcommittee set for themselves three objectives: (1) the development of an adequate testing program; (2) the promotion of other techniques for obtaining information about pupils; and (3) the encouragement of teachers to make optimum use of all available pupil data in pupil guidance.

Careful study of the principal tests of intelligence and achievement led to the adoption of a district-wide testing program. The subcommittee also planned and conducted a series of faculty meetings designed to promote effective use of sociograms, student autobiographies, and anecdotal records in accumulating information about pupils. In addition, emphasis was placed on interpretation of test results to pupils and parents.

The Subcommittee on Pupil Data held that the value of guidance activities at the elementary school level depends, in large part, on the

REPRINTED FROM *THE PERSONNEL AND GUIDANCE JOURNAL*, 37, 9 (MAY 1959), 644-647, BY PERMISSION OF THE PUBLISHERS AND THE AUTHORS.

ability of the teacher to make effective use of pupil information in helping the learner achieve optimum adjustment.

Evaluating Results

In the spring of 1957, the Subcommittee on Pupil Data turned its primary attention to the evaluation of the effects of its work to date. It was recognized that knowledge of facts about individual pupils is not enough, and that until these facts result in desirable modifications of teacher behavior they have served no useful purpose. For this reason the committee felt that the success of the program should not be judged by the volume of pupil data available but by evidence that this condition fostered improved teacher understanding of individual pupils and resulted in more effective services to these children.

A Criterion of Success

It was agreed that one desired result of the recent increased emphasis on pupil data was improved student evaluation which should be reflected in changes in teachers' marking practices.

As an individualized system of marking was employed in the Madison schools, the marks assigned purportedly indicated the extent to which each individual pupil's progress was commensurate with his potential. The committee reasoned that if teachers were cognizant of the capabilities and limitations of each child, and if they used this knowledge to adapt the curriculum to him, children of less ability would work as near their capacity as those who were more capable. Under these conditions, in which the teacher's expectations vary with the ability of each child, it was assumed that the relationship between assigned marks and intelligence test scores would approach zero.

If, on the other hand, teachers are not sensitive to appraisal techniques or are unable to identify certain pupil characteristics, it was assumed that they will tend more frequently to expect some standard performance from a child instead of individualizing their evaluations. In these circumstances, a disproportionately large number of unsatisfactory marks would be assigned to the less intelligent pupils while the same would be true of the satisfactory marks assigned to those with more than an average degree of intelligence. This would result in a moderate to moderately high correlation coefficient between marks and intelligence test scores.

The basic assumption, that a reduction in the correlation coefficient between intelligence test scores and school marks should be considered evidence of increased effectiveness on the part of teachers in implementing the schools' philosophy of evaluating pupil progress and assigning marks, was accepted by the committee as a criterion for evaluating the effects of its emphasis on pupil data.

The Study

One part of evaluating the effectiveness of the in-service program in this regard, then, is to determine the extent to which intelligence and grades are related under the conditions which prevailed before the in-service program went into operation, and to compare these *r*-values with those derived from the correlation of grades and intelligence test scores after the pupil data program had been functioning for a period of time. If the latter *r*-values are significantly lower than the former, there is evidence to indicate that the grading philosophy, in part at least, is being implemented effectively by the teachers.

The hypothesis to be tested with respect to each of the subject matter achievement areas being studied is: there is no difference between the predictive effectiveness of intelligence test scores under the two conditions, 1953 and 1956.

Procedure

Data were gathered for the year 1953 by determining first those pupils currently in each 6th, 7th, and 8th grade classroom who had received first semester grades as 3rd, 4th, and 5th grade pupils in 1953 and for whom intelligence test scores were available. A random sample of five of these pupils was selected from each classroom. The score from the intelligence test, as well as the first semester marks received in reading, spelling, language, and arithmetic, were recorded for each pupil in the sample. Marks received in the column headed Satisfactory Progress were recorded as satisfactory. Those received in the columns headed Improving—More Progress Desired and Little Progress Shown were recorded as unsatisfactory.

For each school subject, a point biserial correlation coefficient was computed to determine the relationship between school marks and intelligence test scores received by this group of pupils.

To study grading practices in 1956, five pupils were selected randomly from each current 3rd, 4th, and 5th grade classroom. The same procedure was used which was employed in studying 1953 marking practices.

Twenty-eight teachers were involved in the 1953 portion of the study. With the exception of teacher personnel changes in five classes and the fact that one class was dropped between 1953 and 1956, the teacher personnel involved in the study remained the same. This meant that 22 teachers in the 1956 portion of the study were members of the original group of 1953 teachers.

Results

TABLE 1 shows the point biserial *r* data between intelligence test scores and grades for 1953 and 1956. Inspection of this table indicates that a larger percentage of unsatisfactory grades was assigned for all subjects in 1956. This may mean that in general teachers had achieved greater confidence as a result of increased knowledge of pupil data. In 1953, they felt unable to appraise accurately pupil ability and under an individualized marking program felt reluctant to assign unsatisfactory marks to some

TABLE 1 Point Biserial Correlation Coefficient Data Between Intelligence Test Scores and School Marks Received in 1953 and 1956

Subject	*Date*	*Mark*	*No.*	*%*	*Mean IQ*	r_p
Reading	1953	Satisfactory	122	87.14	113.22	0.450
		Unsatisfactory	18	12.86	93.28	
	1956	Satisfactory	107	79.26	114.92	0.250
		Unsatisfactory	28	20.74	106.75	
Spelling	1953	Satisfactory	120	85.71	112.98	0.379
		Unsatisfactory	20	14.29	96.70	
	1956	Satisfactory	104	77.04	114.62	0.192
		Unsatisfactory	31	22.96	108.55	
Language	1953	Satisfactory	129	92.17	111.39	0.169
		Unsatisfactory	11	7.83	102.09	
	1956	Satisfactory	112	82.96	114.48	0.209
		Unsatisfactory	23	17.04	107.09	
Arithmetic	1953	Satisfactory	118	84.29	112.81	0.337
		Unsatisfactory	22	15.71	99.14	
	1956	Satisfactory	106	78.51	115.37	0.306
		Unsatisfactory	29	21.48	105.38	

pupils who actually were not performing up to expectancy, whereas in 1956, the increased knowledge of existing pupil characteristics gave them the necessary basis for more sensitive mark assignment.

For reading and spelling, the r-values computed in 1956 were considerably lower than those derived from 1953 data. In the case of reading, the r-value in 1953 indicated a moderate relationship ($r = 0.45$) between intelligence and marks; the r-value in 1956 was a moderately low positive value ($r = 0.25$).

In the case of language and arithmetic, there was no significant difference between the r-values computed for 1953 and 1956. They were moderate to moderately low positive values.

Conclusions

The results of this study indicate that in 1953, when teachers had few objective measures of pupil ability to guide them, a moderate positive correlation existed between intelligence and school marks in reading, $r = 0.45$, and spelling, $r = 0.38$. Since the school marks were purported to measure the degree to which each child's achievement was commensurate with his ability, these correlations indicated that a larger proportion of the more capable pupils were judged by their teachers to be working up to their level of ability than were the less capable.

In 1956, after the adoption of a district-wide testing program and increased emphasis on the importance of collecting and utilizing pupil data, the correlations between intelligence and marks in reading, $r = 0.25$, and spelling, $r = 0.19$, were considerably lower than they were in 1953.

It appeared also that as teachers gained more information about their pupils, they increased the number of unsatisfactory marks which they assigned to the more capable students, indicating greater confidence in their ability to assign grades on an individualized basis.

It is difficult to establish with any degree of certainty that the reductions in these correlations were brought about primarily as a result of emphasis on the collection and use of pupil data and not some other factor also operating in the school system during this period. However, it should be pointed out that in previous years extensive study of the marking philosophy and procedure was carried on and reports and recommendations were made available to teachers. Inspection of the records indicates that teachers' marking practices changed very little during periods when this was the object of direct study. On the other hand, marked changes occurred during the period when primary emphasis was placed upon the utilization of test results and other pupil data.

The Subcommittee on Pupil Data felt that this study produced the most encouraging evidence to date that the increased interest which this group had stimulated in the utilization of pupil data was having a desirable influence on educational practices in the Madison schools. Although the evidence is of a rather limited nature, it is noteworthy that it indicates a change in teacher behavior and not merely an increase in the inventory of the tools available to them.

Identifying Children Through Measurements[1]

HERBERT J. KLAUSMEIER

Increasingly school systems are attempting to improve educational opportunities for all children. In the process of improvement, more careful attention is being given to identifying pupils of markedly inferior and markedly superior learning abilities. Whether heterogeneous classes or special classes for part or all of the instructional program are operated, it is essential to ascertain pupils' learning abilities if best provisions for all children are to be made. Reliable identification of pupils' learning abilities is crucial if special classes are arranged for educable mentally retarded children or for pupils of superior learning abilities, or if pupils are placed in ungraded or primary or intermediate schools. Some first results of a longitudinal study started in 1956-1957 are subsequently reported in this article. This study was undertaken in part to ascertain the relationships among various physical, intellectual, social, and emotional measures among children of low, average, and high learning ability but of the same chronological age.

Measures and Children

The measures secured on each child, starting in 1956-1957 and continued annually through 1958-1959 are as follows:

1. Height to the nearest 1/4 inch, obtained with a standard rule
2. Weight to the nearest 1/8 pound, obtained with a standard beam scale

[1] The research reported herein was performed pursuant to a contract with the United States Office of Education, Department of Health, Education, and Welfare.

REPRINTED FROM *EDUCATION*, 80, 3 (NOVEMBER 1959), 167-171, BY PERMISSION OF THE PUBLISHERS AND THE AUTHOR.

3. Strength of grip to the nearest 1/10 kilogram, obtained with a Stoelting dynamo meter
4. Number of permanent teeth, counted by a practicing dentist
5. Bone development of the hand and wrist to the nearest month, obtained by X-ray and read by two radiologists
6. I.Q. score, using the Wechsler Intelligence Scale for Children
7. Reading achievement, California Test, Form AA, 1950, to the nearest month
8. Arithmetic achievement, California Test, Form AA, 1950, to the nearest month
9. Language achievement, California Test, Form AA, 1950, to the nearest month
10. Chronological age to the nearest month
11. Emotional adjustment, rated from 0, poor, to 10, excellent, by clinical or school psychologists using the Rorschach, three cards from the Thematic Apperception Test, one Figure Drawing, and a clinical interview
12. Achievement in relation to capacity, rated by the psychologists from 0, considerable underachievement, to 10, considerable overachievement, with WISC I.Q. used as the primary criterion of capacity
13. Integration of self-concept, rated by the psychologists from 0, poorly integrated, to 10, well integrated
14. Expression of emotion, rated by the psychologists from 0, highly introverted, to 10, highly extroverted
15. Behavior pattern, rated by the psychologists from 0, highly withdrawing, to 10, highly aggressive
16. The child's estimate of his own learning abilities, rated by the psychologists from 0, greatly underestimated, to 10, greatly overestimated
17. Sociability as ascertained by administering sociometric tests

The first ten measures except the I.Q. were secured on each child within a four-week period during the month of October of each school year; the last seven and the I.Q. were secured during the next five months of the school year.

The children included twenty boys and twenty girls of low intelligence (WISC I.Q.'s 56-81), twenty boys and twenty girls of average intelligence (WISC I.Q.'s 90-110), and twenty boys and twenty girls of high intelligence (WISC I.Q.'s 120-146). The children of average and high intelligence were enrolled in regular heterogeneous classes in Madison, Wisconsin. The children with low I.Q.'s were enrolled in special classes for educable mentally retarded children in Madison and Milwaukee. Excluded from the study were children with low I.Q.'s who exhibited a second severe handicap, as of vision, or definite organic symptoms of retardation, such as mongolism.

All children had birthdates between September 15, 1947, and December 15, 1948. Thus, chronological age was held constant for the three I.Q. levels, and no average- or high-I.Q. child was included who had spent more or less than five calendar years in completing the first five grades of the elementary school. The mean age of the children was 101 months as of October 15, 1956; 113 months as of October 15, 1957; and 125 months as of October 15, 1958. October 15 was the midpoint in time for securing the annual physical and achievement measures.

Results

Space does not permit the inclusion of the lengthy tables,[2] showing raw scores, correlations, analyses of variance and covariance, and factor analysis. Also, only the results through the 1957-1958 year are given. These main results are now presented.

1. The weight, number of permanent teeth, and carpal age of the three I.Q. groups is the same. That is, the high-I.Q. group is neither heavier nor lighter; has neither more nor less permanent teeth; is neither more advanced nor more retarded in total anatomical development (carpal age) than is either of the other two groups. One could have inferred nothing about the learning abilities of the particular children being studied on the basis of weight, number of permanent teeth, and carpal age.

2. The high-I.Q. children are slightly taller than those of average and low intelligence; however, the overlap in height among the three I.Q. groups is far greater than the small but statistically significant difference between the high and the other two groups. The school should probably not consider height when attempting to identify children of low and high learning ability.

3. A marked difference is found in strength of grip among the three I.Q. groups. The high-I.Q. children are stronger than either the average or low, and the average are considerably stronger than the low. Strength of grip is the only measure of vitality in the present study. It appears that the high-I.Q. children have far greater vitality than do the low-I.Q. children. In addition, it appears that both on a physical task and probably also on a mental task, the high-I.Q. child has not only more energy to bring to bear on the task but also is able to concentrate his total energy

[2] The tables presenting all the data of this research are included in the official report to the U. S. Office of Education, Department of Health, Education, and Welfare.

more efficiently on a particular task. While there is some overlap in strength among the three I.Q. groups, the difference in strength among the three groups is almost as great as is the difference among the three groups in arithmetic achievement. It is possible that other measures of vitality along with strength of grip would prove useful in identifying children of inferior and superior learning abilities.

4. In tested reading, arithmetic, and language achievements, the high-I.Q. group is distinctly superior and the low-I.Q. group is distinctly inferior. There is no overlap in tested reading achievement between the low- and average-I.Q. children. There is considerable overlap of scores between the average and the high in both reading and arithmetic, and most overlap occurs in arithmetic. The high-I.Q. children are not so far advanced above the average in arithmetic as they are in reading.

5. As based upon the psychologists' ratings (variables 11 to 16 reported previously), no difference among the three I.Q. groups is significant at the .01 level for the following traits: emotional adjustment, achievement in relation to capacity, integration of self-concept, expression of emotion, behavior pattern, and the child's estimate of his own ability. At the .02 level, however, the sixty girls have better integration of self-concept and give a higher estimate of their own abilities than do boys.

The incidence of emotional maladjustment, however, is quite high in all three I.Q. groups, with some quite severely disturbed individuals being found in all three I.Q. groups. This result must be interpreted in light of the low-I.Q. children being enrolled in special classes for the educable mentally retarded and their having no second severe handicap. Were these low-I.Q. children to be enrolled in regular heterogeneous classes, it is entirely possible that their emotional adjustment would be much poorer in relation to that of the children of average and high intelligence. Further, though there is no difference in integration of self-concept as based on the psychologists' ratings, informal observation leads to the conclusion that the self-concepts of the low-I.Q. are less well differentiated than those of the average- and high-I.Q. children.

In another investigation of children in regular heterogeneous third- and fifth-grade classes, it was found that the low-achievers with a mean I.Q. around 100 were not so well adjusted emotionally as were the high-achievers, based on teacher estimates. In addition, the low-achievers had a higher incidence of boys and a higher incidence of children from lower socio-economic status. In the present study also, though not significantly different from other groups, boys of average intelligence in regular heterogeneous classrooms are found to have poorer emotional adjustment and lower achievement than the average I.Q. girls in the same classrooms.

6. There is no difference in sociability among the three groups as measured by sociometric tests. Differences in preference for friends of the same sex are far greater among fourth-grade children than are differences based upon I.Q. For example, girls choose other girls, regardless of I.Q., to a much greater extent than they choose boys, and the same holds for boys. Based upon many informal observations of the children in the classrooms in which they were enrolled, it appears that the special classes for the educable mentally retarded have an environment which encourages friendly and helpful relationships among children to a higher extent than do the regular classes for the average- and high-I.Q. children.

7. For the combined group of sixty boys and sixty girls, there is a tendency for variability in physical growth within the child (split growth) to be accompanied by low achievement. Boys and girls who are growing quite consistently in height, weight, strength of grip, and bone development achieve slightly higher than do those who are not growing consistently in all areas.

8. For the combined group of sixty boys and sixty girls, there is a tendency for variability in physical growth within the child (split growth) to be accompanied by emotional disturbance. No cause of the tendency towards split growth has been ascertained. It is possible that with further analysis it may be found that split growth in the readily observed characteristics—height, weight, or strength—may be associated with the lower achievement and poorer emotional adjustment, or there possibly may be some sort of physiological or chemical imbalance leading to the variable pattern of physical growth, the lower achievement, and the tendency toward emotional disturbance.

9. There is no difference among the three I.Q. groups in the within-child variability in reading, arithmetic, and language. The children in the low-I.Q. group tend to be high in one achievement area and low in another to the same extent as do the average- and high-I.Q. children. If three different teachers had these three groups of forty children, each teacher would have an equally difficult or equally easy time in providing reading, arithmetic, or language materials to suit the needs of each child within the groups of forty.

10. There is no difference in the variability of the three I.Q. groups in any area of achievement. The forty low-I.Q. children as a group are just as variable in reading achievements as are the forty average- and the forty

high-I.Q. children. Again, if three teachers had the three I.Q. groups of forty pupils, the teacher of the low-I.Q. children would need to have as wide a range of reading materials to meet the needs of her group as would the teacher of the high-I.Q. children.

11. The following clusters of measures correlate positively and significantly with each other: (a) height, weight, strength of grip, and carpal age; (b) strength of grip, I.Q., reading achievement, arithmetic achievement, and language achievement; (c) emotional adjustment, achievement in relation to capacity, and integration of self-concept; (d) expression of emotion, pattern of emotional behavior, and the child's estimate of his own abilities. Number of permanent teeth was found not to correlate significantly with any other variable. In addition, there are few positive and significant correlations between variables in any of the two groups above. For example, carpal age and weight do not correlate significantly with any measures other than the physical measures. Factor analyses of the correlation matrices from 1957-1958 and from 1958-1959 will be made to ascertain the extent to which growth in the physical, intellectual, and emotional areas may be a general factor or specific factors. At the present time the researcher doubts that there is a general growth factor with children of this age. The correlations thus far suggest that there are quite specific physical, intellectual, and emotional growth factors.

The researcher believes that the findings concerning the average- and high-I.Q. children will hold for other samples of children drawn by the same criteria in many cities of the United States. There is no basis for assuming that the regular heterogeneous classes from which the average- and high-I.Q. children were drawn differ greatly from other classes in similar cities where the mean I.Q. of the child population in the elementary school is around 108. The findings pertaining to the low-I.Q. children might not hold for institutionalized low-I.Q. children, for low-I.Q. children with a second severe handicap, or for low-I.Q. children remaining with average- and high-I.Q. children in regular heterogeneous classrooms. In addition, the results reported for these children at a mean age of 101 months in October, 1956, and 113 months in October, 1957, might not hold for these same children four years from now. Finally, the personality ratings were made by experienced clinical and school psychologists, using projective methods. These techniques and instruments are tools of their professional work, and their independent ratings of children were found reliable through correlation techniques. It is possible that, had group tests of personality been used, the results would have been different. The researcher, however, assumes that other well-prepared, experienced school and clinical psychologists would have secured approximately the same ratings on these children.

Summary

Height, weight, number of permanent teeth, carpal age, sociability or friendliness, emotional adjustment, achievement in relation to capacity, integration of self-concept, manner of expressing emotion, behavior pattern, and the child's estimate of own learning abilities as defined in this study are of little if any value in helping the teacher identify pupils of superior learning ability at a mean age of 113 months or of normally fourth-grade age. Individual I.Q. test results, achievement test results, and strength of grip or vitality are exceedingly useful.

Identifying the Insecure Child: III. The Use of Children's Drawings

WILLIAM E. MARTIN

This study attempted to answer three questions: (a) Do children express their feelings of security or insecurity in their drawings? (b) Can such graphic expression be described and measured? (c) Can the drawings of secure children thus be distinguished from those of insecure children?

In answering these questions, we used the following procedure: We first identified the most secure and most insecure children in three different groups, using methods which did not involve a consideration of their drawings. Then we obtained a sample drawing from each child so identified. Next we procured ratings of pertinent characteristics in each drawing. Finally, we compared the ratings of drawings of secure with those of drawings of insecure children.

Identifying Secure and Insecure Children

We began with a total of 75 children: 24 kindergarten, 25 Grade 1 and 26 Grade 2 children in a University laboratory school. The number of boys and girls in each group was approximately the same. The mean chronological age and intelligence quotient, as derived from the 1937 Revision of the Stanford-Binet, for each group respectively, were as follows: 5.9, 123; 6.7, 132; 7.9, 125. The socio-economic status may be considered high in view of the fact that most of the fathers were employed in professional or managerial activities or were graduate students in the University.

REPRINTED FROM *THE JOURNAL OF GENETIC PSYCHOLOGY*, 86, (JUNE 1955), 327-338, BY PERMISSION OF THE PUBLISHERS AND THE AUTHOR. THIS RESEARCH WAS SUPPORTED BY A GRANT FROM THE BUREAU OF EDUCATIONAL RESEARCH OF THE UNIVERSITY OF ILLINOIS.

We first administered to each child a revised form of the Wolff Security Test.[2] This instrument consists of nine pairs of drawings of situations involving children. For each pair the child is asked which one he would rather be. The child who, by reason of his choices, seems to be apprehensive, timid, inactive, and socially retiring is identified as being relatively insecure. On the other hand, the child whose preferences indicate that he is bold, outgoing, active, and socially participant, is considered relatively secure. We expressed the results of this test as the number of "insecure" responses. The range of possible scores was from 0 to 9.

We then asked each member of the teaching staff to rate each child with whom they were acquainted on the Prichard-Ojemann Behavior Rating Scale.[4] This scale describes six kinds of behavior: (a) voluntary withdrawal from group; (b) non-acceptance by group; (c) bidding for attention of adults; (d) crying; (e) apprehensiveness; and (f) hyperactivity. Prichard and Ojemann reported that the frequency of each of these behaviors as rated on a five-point scale differentiated between children nominated as secure and those nominated as insecure by their teachers. We obtained at least nine independent ratings on this scale for each of the children in our sample. We expressed the results in the form of an average score for each child for the total scale. The range of possible scores was from 6, the most insecure score, to 30, the most secure score.

On a later occasion, we asked our raters to nominate from each group the three children they considered most secure and the three children they considered most insecure. The result for each child was simply the number of nominations of each kind he received.

Originally, our hope was that the results obtained from these three methods of identifying secure and insecure children would agree to such an extent that we could pool them and thus have one group of secure and one group of insecure children at each age level. Unfortunately, as indicated in an earlier report[2], there was no such agreement in the results. We arrived, therefore, at this point in the study with six, rather than two, groups at each age level: a group of secure children and a group of insecure children as identified by each of the three methods.

In order to define these groups exactly, it was of course necessary to establish arbitrarily cutting points for each distribution of scores. On the Wolff Security Test, we placed a child with a score of 5 or more in the insecure group and one with a score of 0 or 1 in the secure group. On the Prichard-Ojemann Behavior Rating Scale, we defined a child who had a score of 20 or less as insecure and one who had a score of 26 or more as secure. Finally, we chose for consideration any child with three or more nominations as most insecure or three or more nominations as most secure.

After applying these cutting points, 54 of the original 75 children remained, all of them appearing in at least one of the criterion groups, many of them appearing in more than one. For example, one child was in the "secure" groups as identified by behavior ratings and by teachers'

TABLE 1

Sex, Chronological Age (CA), Mental Age (MA), Intelligence Quotient (IQ), Wolff Security Test Score (W), Prichard-Ojemann Behavior Rating Scale Score (P) and Number of Teachers' Nominations as Most Secure (TS) and Most Insecure (TI)

Group	Child No.	Sex	CA	MA[a]	IQ	W[b]	R[c]	TS	TI
Kindergarten									
	1	F	5.6	6.8	120	2	26.7	2	0
	2	M	5.7	6.8	120	1	22.5	0	0
	3	F	5.4	7.4	136	1	26.2	4	0
	4	F	5.6	7.8	140	2	25.0	5	0
	5	M	5.5	7.2	130	1	22.8	3	0
	6	F	5.8	6.9	118	2	17.6	0	5
	7	M	6.1	6.2	101	1	20.7	0	4
	8	M	6.2	6.0	96	5	19.2	0	4
	9	F	6.3	7.0	110	2	26.5	2	0
	10	M	5.8	7.2	122	4	15.9	0	7
	11	M	5.8	8.2	140	5	21.1	0	0
First Grade									
	21	F	6.4	8.0	125	1	19.1	0	6
	22	M	6.9	9.9	143	3	26.8	5	0
	23	M	7.1	11.7	165	1	22.8	1	0
	24	M	6.9	9.6	139	1	25.0	1	0
	25	F	7.0	8.2	116	6	25.6	1	1
	26	F	7.1	9.2	129	1	26.6	6	0
	27	M	6.8	10.9	160	1	27.3	1	0
	28	F	6.8	7.8	115	2	19.7	0	5
	29	F	6.9	9.9	143	3	27.1	2	0
	30	M	6.7	7.8	117	7	20.0	0	4
	31	M	6.6	7.3	111	3	19.3	0	5
Second Grade									
	41	M	7.6	8.1	107	1	27.9	6	0
	42	F	8.7	10.8	125	6	22.9	0	0
	43	F	8.3	11.2	135	6	26.0	1	0
	44	M	7.7	9.7	126	2	27.2	1	0
	45	M	7.7	9.7	126	2	13.9	0	6
	46	M	7.6	10.0	132	0	17.0	0	2
	47	F	7.9	9.8	123	7	18.3	0	1
	48	F	7.3	12.5	170	3	26.8	3	0
	49	M	7.9	9.6	121	1	26.9	3	0

[a] 1937 Revision of the Stanford-Binet.
[b] The number of "insecure" responses.
[c] The most "secure" score is 30; the least "secure" score is 6.

nominations but in the "insecure" group as identified by the Wolff Security Test.

Circumstances were such that we were able to obtain drawings from only 31 of these children, selected at random from the total possible number of 54. Table 1 contains the pertinent data for each of these subjects, 11 kindergarten children, 11 first graders, and 9 second graders. Table 2 shows how these subjects were distributed in the various criterion groups.

TABLE 2 Insecure and Secure Subjects According to Each of Three Criterion Measures

CRITERION	WOLFF SECURITY TEST		PRICHARD-OJEMANN BEHAVIOR RATING SCALE		TEACHERS' NOMINATIONS	
Sub-group	Insecure No.	Secure No.	Insecure No.	Secure No.	Insecure No.	Secure No.
Kindergarten	8	2	6	1	6	3
	11	3	8	3	7	4
		5	10	9	8	5
		7			10	
First Grade	25	21	21	22	21	22
	30	23	28	26	28	26
		24	30	27	30	
		26	31	29	31	
		27				
Second Grade	42	41	45	41	45	41
	43	46	46	43		48
	47	49	47	44		49
				48		
				49		
N	7	12	10	12	9	8

Obtaining the Drawings

In order to obtain the sample drawings, we invited each child to our office, seated him at a small table, provided him with a black crayon and a piece of manila drawing paper, 12 × 9 inches in size, and suggested that he draw us a picture of his family. He received no further instructions and was left to his own devices until he finished the drawing. We carefully avoided watching the artist at work, giving our attention to other activities during the period of production. Our procedure failed only in the case of one second-grade girl who felt that "It" was all very silly.

Rating the Drawings

Wolff [5] has suggested certain graphic characteristics as expressive of a child's feelings of security and insecurity. We selected 11 of these for consideration in our sample of drawings and described them in such a way that their presence would be evidence of security and their absence evidence of insecurity, assuming, for the moment, the validity of the Wolff suggestions. The terms below will indicate briefly the nature of these graphic characteristics:

In the drawing as a whole:

1. Symmetry
2. Determination of strokes
3. Continuity of strokes
4. Pressure of strokes
5. Expansiveness
6. Degree to which graphic elements are centered

Individual figures in the drawing:

7. Symmetry
8. Sharpness and distinctness of features
9. Clarity of position of natural features
10. Expansiveness
11. Activity

For each drawing, a rater judged the amount of each characteristic he found to exist on a five-point scale: very much, much, some, little, very little. He could indicate his rating at any point on a given line corresponding to a given characteristic. Afterwards we further subdivided the line into 10 equal parts and assigned values ranging from 1 (at the "very little" end of the scale) to 11 (at the "very much" end of the scale).

The raters were 13 university juniors and seniors, 8 males and 5 females, all majoring in art. They accepted the drawings as art products and nothing else; they did not know of our concern with the graphic expression of personality.

Our board of judges rated the art products in groups: all five-year-old drawings or all first-grade drawings or all second-grade drawings. In order to eliminate the effects of practice and fatigue, we adopted this procedure: (a) The judges were divided into two approximately equal groups, Group *A* and Group *B*; (b) Group *A* first rated the kindergarten drawings, then the first-grade and finally the second-grade drawings, while Group *B* undertook their ratings in the reverse order; (c) No judge rated the characteristics in the same order as any other judge; (d) No judge rated the characteristics in the same order from one group of drawings to another.

TABLE 3 Means and Standard Deviations of Ratings of Thirteen Judges of Thirty-One Drawings on Each of Eleven Scales

Scale	Mean	Standard Deviation
1. Symmetry of drawing as a whole	6.8	1.3
2. Determination of strokes	7.0	1.3
3. Continuity of strokes	6.9	1.0
4. Pressure of strokes	6.8	1.6
5. Expansiveness of drawing as a whole	6.9	1.7
6. Dregree to which graphic elements are centered in the drawing as a whole	6.7	1.1
7. Symmetry of individual figures in the drawing	7.0	1.1
8. Sharpness and distinctiveness of features of individual figures in the drawing	6.3	1.5
9. Clarity of position of natural features of individual figures in the drawing	6.3	1.6
10. Expansiveness of individual figures in the drawing	6.5	1.3
11. Activity of individual figures in the drawing	5.6	1.6

Martin and Damrin[3] have already presented a detailed analysis of these ratings on the basis of which they concluded that they were "highly reliable." Since they also found no significant differences among the means of the ratings on any scale for the three age groups, it is possible to ignore the factor of age in the present report. Table 3 gives the means and standard deviations of the ratings of these 13 judges on the total collection of drawings.

Comparing the Drawings of Secure and Insecure Children

In Table 4 are the means and the standard errors of the means of the ratings on each scale for the groups of insecure and secure children as identified by three different methods. The use of the "*t*" test discloses but one significant difference between means, that between secure and insecure children as identified by behavior ratings on Scale 10, Expansiveness of Individual Figures. In this case, the value of "*t*" is 2.18, which is

TABLE 4 Means and Standard Errors of Means of Ratings of Thirteen Judges on Each of Eleven Scales of Drawings of Children Classified as Secure or Insecure

CRITERION		WOLFF SECURITY TEST				PRICHARD-OJEMANN BEHAVIOR RATING SCALE				TEACHERS' NOMINATIONS			
Sub-group		Insecure		Secure		Insecure		Secure		Insecure		Secure	
N		7		12		10		12		9		8	
		Mean	SE	Mean	SE	Mean	SE	Mean	SE	Mean	SE	Mean	SE
Scale	1	7.04	.62	6.28	.30	6.74	.48	6.35	.36	6.75	.46	7.09	.48
	2	7.03	.31	6.41	.37	6.59	.47	7.54	.32	6.63	.45	7.19	.36
	3	6.87	.28	6.68	.32	6.21	.38	7.12	.27	6.40	.34	7.10	.23
	4	6.69	.66	6.30	.42	6.52	.58	7.35	.45	6.29	.52	7.05	.42
	5	7.51	.90	6.72	.48	7.18	.53	6.10	.53	6.91	.54	6.69	.59
	6	7.03	.52	6.42	.31	6.40	.38	6.56	.33	6.34	.37	7.16	.36
	7	6.60	.41	6.67	.33	7.00	.28	7.33	.27	6.95	.26	7.35	.35
	8	6.50	.71	5.40	.31	6.06	.51	6.70	.32	5.82	.48	6.26	.58
	9	6.59	.77	5.74	.39	5.74	.46	6.88	.39	5.62	.37	6.53	.57
	10	6.71	.73	6.10	.30	6.91	.40	5.82	.30	6.69	.34	6.41	.34
	11	5.47	.84	6.18	.49	5.16	.39	5.14	.50	4.81	.39	5.83	.45

significant at the five per cent level. Unfortunately, even this one difference is contrary to expectation, since it is the insecure rather than the secure group which showed the greater expansiveness.

Discussion of Some Individual Drawings

Despite these negative findings, an examination of some of the drawings may be of interest. Table 5 contains the mean ratings expressed as *T*-scores on the drawings of five of the children in our sample.

TABLE 5 Mean Ratings Expressed as Standard Scores of Thirteen Judges on Each of Eleven Scales of Drawings of Selected Children

CHILD NO.	3		30		5		47		7	
Scale	Mean rating	T	Mean rating	T	Mean rating	T	Mean rating	T	Mean rating	T
1	6.2	45	7.2	53	7.8	58	8.2	61	6.6	48
2	7.9	57	7.0	50	5.5	38	7.9	57	6.5	46
3	7.1	52	6.6	47	6.5	46	6.9	50	6.6	47
4	8.5	61	7.9	57	5.5	42	9.5	67	6.1	46
5	5.2	40	9.2	64	6.5	48	9.3	64	5.9	44
6	5.4	38	6.9	52	7.2	55	7.8	60	6.1	45
7	7.6	55	6.1	42	5.7	38	8.1	60	6.8	48
8	6.0	48	6.6	52	3.2	29	8.5	65	4.8	40
9	6.9	54	6.2	49	3.8	34	8.2	62	5.2	43
10	5.3	41	7.8	60	6.4	49	9.1	70	5.4	42
11	6.1	53	5.6	50	5.8	51	7.2	60	3.7	38
Mean		50		52		44		62		44

The three criterion measures agreed in identifying Child No. 3 as a secure child. Yet the judges' ratings of her drawing (Figure 1) did not confirm this identification. Only in Pressure and Determination of Strokes (Scales 2 and 4) were the ratings conspicuously above the mean. In Expansiveness and Centering of Graphic Elements (Scales 5, 6, and 10), the ratings were definitely below the mean. For all scales, the average *T*-score was 50. Whatever feelings of security characterized this child, she did not seem to express them in the drawing of her family.

In Child No. 30, we have a boy who was placed in the insecure category according to all three criteria. Yet, when we look at his drawing (Figure 2) and the ratings of it, we again find no confirmation of this placement. He obtained a relatively low rating on Symmetry of Individual Figures (Scale 7) but relatively high ratings on Pressure of Strokes and Expan-

FIGURE 1 Drawing of Child No. 3

FIGURE 2 Drawing of Child No. 30

siveness (Scales 4, 5, and 10). On the remaining scales, the ratings were more often above than below the average. His mean *T*-score was 52.

The drawing of Child No. 5 (Figure 3) received an average rating of 44. In general, the judges found an absence of those characteristics which presumably denote feelings of security, the only exceptions being Symmetry of the Drawing as a Whole (Scale 1) and possibly Centering of Graphic Elements (Scale 6). Yet, according to the Wolff Security Test *and* teachers' nominations, this boy was identified as a secure child.

In the case of Child No. 47 (Figure 4) we have a drawing which received uniformly high ratings, as indicated by a mean *T*-score of 62. In fact, not a single rating fell below the mean for the total group. We would conclude, from the drawing alone, that we were dealing with a secure child. But, in terms of scores on the Wolff Security Test and on the Prichard-Ojemann Behavior Rating Scale, this girl was a member of our insecure group.

As a final example, there is the drawing of Child No. 7 (Figure 5). All ratings given this drawing were below the average for the group, implying an insecure child. It is true that four different teachers nominated him as one of the three most insecure children in his group. But,

FIGURE 3 Drawing of Child No. 5

FIGURE 4 Drawing of Child No. 47

FIGURE 5 Drawing of Child No. 7

on the Wolff Security Test, he gave but one insecure response out of a possible nine. Perhaps, this was a case in which the secure responses were reactions to or compensations for feelings of insecurity.

The results reported in detail for these five drawings are representative of those for the total sample. They furnish no basis for concluding that drawings of insecure children differ from those of secure children.

Limitations in the Present Study

It is only fair to point out certain recognized limitations in the present study. The sample of children was inadequate on at least two counts. For one thing, it was too small. However, since Wolff [5] does not give the number of children which he studied, we cannot say which of the two studies should be given the greater weight on this factor. Our sample was also too homogeneous with respect to intelligence and socio-economic status, being highly selected with respect to both factors.

In previous papers [1,2] we have expressed dissatisfaction with our means of identifying secure and insecure children. Perhaps, clinical methods would improve the selection and definition of our groups.

Moreover, we consider the sample of drawings far from adequate, since we obtained only one drawing from each child. Evidence concerning the amount of intra-individual variation in expressive content of drawings is lacking, but it is reasonable to assume the existence of some.

Finally, we recognize that the ratings of the drawings might be considered inadequate in some respects. In the attempt to make the judgments as objective and reliable as possible, we may have lost something in the drawings. Wolff implies that such judgments are an art rather than a science[5, pp. 222-223] and then demonstrates his own artistry in the "blind" analyses of children from their drawings. Whether or not judgments as art can be investigated by acceptable scientific methods is a moot point. Perhaps, we could have supplemented our procedures by asking clinical psychologists to determine from an inspection of a drawing whether the artist was secure or insecure and thus obtained more reassuring results. Only further study can settle this matter.

Summary

This study investigated the possibility of identifying the insecure child through an analysis of the expressive content in his drawings. Within the limitations of the study as stated, we must conclude that characteristics which Wolff has suggested to be expressive of feelings of security do not differentiate between the drawings of secure and insecure children. This conclusion holds, ironically, even when the subjects are identified as secure or insecure by means of a screening device originated by Wolff himself.

REFERENCES

1. William E. Martin, "Identifying the Insecure Child: I. The Wolff Security Test," *Journal of Genetic Psychology,* **78** (1951), 217-232.

2. ———, "Identifying the Insecure Child: II. The Validity of Some Suggested Methods," *Journal of Genetic Psychology,* **80** (1952), 25-33.

3. ——— and D.E. Damrin, "An Analysis of the Reliability and Factorial Composition of Ratings of Children's Drawings," *Child Development,* **22** (1951), 133-144.

4. E. Prichard and R.H. Ojemann, "An Approach to the Measurement of Insecurity," *Journal of Experimental Education,* **10** (1941), 114-118.

5. W. Wolff, *The Personality of the Preschool Child* (New York: Grune & Stratton, 1946).

Situational Play Therapy with Normal Children

CLARK E. MOUSTAKAS

In the past two decades much clinical insight has been derived from studying the inner world of the disturbed child. Various theories and techniques of play therapy have been presented and evaluated by psychotherapists, and analytical and neoanalytical case studies, with complete interpretations, have appeared regularly and increasingly.

Client-centered recordings of nondirective play therapy sessions have dramatically portrayed the process of attitudinal reorganization in young children. Almost all the children described in these reports have had some degree of personal and social maladjustment, fixated psychosexual paths, or inadequate self-concepts.

The present study was concerned with normal children who were faced with a disturbing new family experience which they perceived as threatening to themselves, and who were given an opportunity to resolve their feelings in situational play therapy sessions. In the two cases here described in some detail both children were faced with one of the commonest crises of childhood, the arrival of a new baby in the family. Of a number of instances in which play therapy sessions were equally effective, these two were selected as providing interesting and clear-cut illustrations of the method.

The New Baby Crisis

Normal children who experience such catastrophes as fires and floods, or who have accidents or illnesses, or are subjected to such family crises

REPRINTED FROM *JOURNAL OF CONSULTING PSYCHOLOGY,* 15 (1951), 225-230, BY PERMISSION OF THE PUBLISHERS AND THE AUTHOR.

as divorce and death, often show confusion, hostility, uncontrollable aggression, hate, and anxiety. The arrival of a new baby in the family is one of the commonest sources of such a disturbance in the child's behavior. To all children such an event brings a period of stress, for however stable, well organized, and rooted in positive emotions the family relationships may be, the arrival of a new family member requires some modification of role in each person in the family. Some family disorganization may result, at least temporarily, and the older child or children are often faced with a difficult adjustment to the new situation.

For neither of the two children, Tommy and Susan, whose play therapy sessions are reported was the arrival of a new baby a surprise. Both had been informed of the coming event two or three months in advance, and both had expressed pleasure in the prospect.

The Case of Tommy

Tommy, four years old, had been rated as fairly well adjusted both personally and socially by his nursery school teacher, the nursery school director, and the psychologist. His relations with other nursery school children were satisfactory, he came to school happily, and he talked with pride of his home and parents. His parents, in turn, talked of him with pleasure and pride and regarded him as a happy, secure, confident child who easily accepted limits and responsibilities.

When Tommy was four and one-half, an adopted girl of thirteen was suddenly brought into the home, and three months later his mother gave birth to a daughter. During this period Tommy's behavior showed a radical change, both at school and at home. At school he became sulky, refused to accept even simple, clear, and reasonable limits, showed a tendency to retreat from child groups whenever things did not go his way, and often withdrew into long sessions of solitary play. At home he became fidgety at mealtimes, refused to eat foods that he had accepted before, cried, attempted to destroy the family record player, and often appeared ill-tempered and irritable. His mother, after attempting to deal with the situation by explanations and supports of many kinds, requested that he be given play therapy.

Three play sessions were conducted with Tommy. During the first he played with airplanes and trucks the entire time and was relatively quiet. In the second session Tommy appeared to focus on his attitudes about himself and what the two new members of the family would mean in terms of his role. He perceived them as potential threats, but once he had recognized these feelings and they had been accepted and clarified, he could accept his siblings and share with them his emotional and material possessions, and see his altered role as one that did not threaten his real self. A transcript of this session from the tape recording follows.

Second Play Session with Tommy

***T*. You can use these things in any way that you want, Tommy.

†*C*. You know what? I could make a little castle out of that. [Indicates sand in sandbox.]

T. You could make a castle.

C. These are two boats. Look.

T. Mm-hm.

C. You know what kind? This one is a ship and this one is a ferry.

T. One's a ship and one's a ferry.

C. This is the ocean. [Points to sand.] This is the way that they use them in New Mexico.

T. In New Mexico, they use them like that.

C. Now do you know what we have to do? We have to get some water and smooth it. [Refers to sand.] You know what I can do? I can make an ocean liner and put it in the sand.

T. You can do that.

C. Then this can be the dock. [Points to hill of sand.] Then the ocean liner can go on it. It can go right on the hill.

T. Mm-hm.

C. There is just room for two boats to be on it. There. Now I'll make another boat. This can be the parking space. [Points to spot in the sand.] See? This is a great big parking lot for it.

T. A great big one.

C. See? This is where the little boat goes. He goes way up there. There's a parking lot for the big boat and one for the little boat. We have to do this over at the dock. Toot, toot, toot go the boats. Look where this boat has to go. He goes to get the sand. I'm putting it right in.

T. You're putting it right inside.

C. I'm pretending this is a ship. This is where they really go. Right over here. [Points to spot in sand.]

T. That's really the place for them to go.

C. This is the stuff that they carry into the dock. [Sand.] Look what he has to do. He's going to bury this whole big boat.

T. He'll bury the whole big boat.

C. See? I can bury him.

T. You're really burying him.

C. So no one will ever find him again.

* *T*, Therapist. † *C*, Child.

T. He will be lost for good.

C. He'll be lost for good. It can't get out now. You see, this is the little boat's dock and no one ever goes in this dock. Because that's his dock.

T. Just his.

C. You know what he's going to do? He's going to put sand and water on this boat. [Points to big boat which he has taken out of sand.] Then he'll clean it up.

T. He'll make it clean.

C. Hi, Joe. Howdy. You see, this big one that comes along is his brother. You see, these two boats are brother boats.

T. One is the brother of the other one.

C. Yeah. One is the brother of the other one. Hey! Who messed my dock up? "Well, I did," says the big boat. See? He has some sand in him. He carries people in his boat, and this one has sand in his, too.

T. They both have sand.

C. You know what? They dump out the sand there. He [little boat] scrubs his boat off. Then he [big boat] scrubs his boat off. Both of them go. You know where they're going now? In the . . . in the brink the ship goes first [big boat]. Say, what do you know, Joe? I have to make another dock for this boat [a tiny boat].

T. Another dock for another boat.

C. Yeah. Oh, I know a nice dock. What do you know, Joe? He'll be lost forever. What do you suppose I'll have to do? Hey! What's the matter with my garage? That's what it will be. What do you know, Joe?

T. What do you know?

C. This is the littlest boat. I have to build so many docks around here.

T. So many docks you have to build.

C. Yes, and all these are brothers. This is the best one [picks up middle boat], because, look. He can carry more sand than the other ones.

T. He's the best one of all.

C. You know what? You know what I have to do? See this boat here? That's the littlest one, and this one is the biggest one, and see, those are brothers. These two are brothers and these two are brothers.

T. They're all brothers.

C. Yes. And they all have some docks, but he [middle boat] has the coziest one.

T. He has the nicest, coziest one.

C. And this [big boat] and this [little boat] each have one, but he [middle boat] can carry nice soft dirt for people to the lake. We better not use this boat [tiny boat]. You know, this is the guy who stands and has to watch all of these things. [Picks up policeman figure and gestures toward boats.] And this one. You know what? I'm pretending that this is an oil place and that's where the boats get their power. You know, they don't have any power when they start off. They come around and after awhile they put their boats in this space where they can get power.

T. That's what they do.

C. I know what I'm doing. You know what I'm pretending? This is all the family, the whole family, the whole family. This is the family.

T. You're pretending it's the whole family.

C. Yeah. I have to. Well, what do you know? What do you know, Joe? What do you know, Joe? Linga, linga, linga, linga, linga, linga. Hey! I'm pretending. You see these cowboys? They're the guards.

T. They are the guards, huh?

C. All of them. They're the guards of these garages.

T. They guard them.

C. They guard them. There's the guard. You see, if anyone comes around to steal the boats . . . well, they'll shoot them.

T. They shoot anyone who tries to steal the boats.

C. There's another guard. He's a husky one. Look, there's sand in this boat [middle one]. He carries it well. Golly, he's stuck in a ditch, but he's cozy. Cozy, but him and him . . . no, really every three of them are the coziest.

T. Every three of them.

C. This is the best cowboy and he guards this boat [the middle boat]. Linga, linga, linga. You know what? They watch to see that no one steals anything. They watch the garages, too. One guard's in front of each garage.

T. One in front of each garage.

C. See, these are very lucky because they have guards. They're very lucky.

T. Very, very lucky because they have guards.

C. No one else has guards but them.

T. No one but them.

C. This guard watches this [big boat]. This guard watches this [middle boat]. And this guards this one [tiny boat]. This guy [middle boat] is lucky. He's lucky because he has the nicest house, the nicest house of all. He has the best house of all. He can just fit in right well. These [the other two boats] are lucky, too. They have power. They squeeze right in. He has power, too. He goes over and gets his power.

T. You have just a short while longer to play.

C. There he goes. See? He goes to his brother's place.

T. He's going right to his brother's place.

C. Hey, ring, ring! It's me. I'm your brother. It's all right. I was here before you, but come with me. Hey! Big boat and little boat say, "Please give me some power," and middle boat says, "O.K." Middle boat: "I'm going to get more power." Hey, Joe. Come on. I'll help you. We've got the best house in the world. We'll get some power. All we'll have to do is back right out and get it. We can get our power and gas easy. Linga, linga, linga. We can go now. When others come in, they'll be able to see that I built all this.

T. They'll see it right there where you built it.

After the third play session, which was very similar to the second, Tommy said he felt that he would not have to come back any more. He then went to his mother, she reported, and said: "Look here, Mother. There are some things that are mine, really mine. They belong just to me, and there are other things that I can share and will gladly share." His mother responded: "Of course, Tommy. That's the way it will always be."

The nursery school staff and Tommy's parents reported that Tommy had once again become the affable, free, expressive child they had known before.

The Case of Susan

The nursery school staff described Susan, three years old, as a charming youngster whose winning smile and understanding ways had made her popular with both children and adults. Her mother had considered Susan's relations with her parents and an older sibling excellent. When Susan was three years three months, a new baby arrived in the family. Two days after the mother and the new baby daughter arrived home, Susan became babyish, immature, and whining at home. This behavior became evident in the nursery school as well. Susan's mother frantically telephoned the nursery school one day to ask whether something could be done to stop Susan's constant whining, which had annoyed everyone in the family. She could not understand how so wonderful and confident a child could have become a whimpering, clinging one in so short a time.

The nursery school staff referred Susan to the play therapist, who conducted three play sessions with her. During the first two sessions Susan appeared to project her negative and hostile feelings for the new baby onto the human-like balloon figure in the therapy room, throwing it on the floor, stepping on it, squeezing its head and face, and crushing it inside the vise. Once her feelings were recognized, accepted, and at least partly clarified, she proceeded in the last session to pick up the balloon figure, kiss it, toss it in the air, and dance around the room while she held it in her arms.

A transcript of recordings of the three sessions follows.

First Session

T. You can use these in any way you like. [Mother starts to leave room, and C looks at her.]

C. No, you stay here for awhile.

**M.* Watch the watch. When this hand gets over here, I'll be back.

* *M*, mother.

C. O.K. I'll bounce two balls.

T. Two at a time you did.

M. I'll lay down the watch where you can watch it.

C. O.K. . . . It's not ticking.

M. Want me to put it on you? [Places watch on C's wrist.] Bye.

T. You can just keep your eye on that watch.

C. [Waves good-bye to mother.] Where's the baby?

T. Where do you suppose the baby could be?

C. Here? That's the baby. Lookit the big baby. This is a balloon head. Mr. Balloon Head. [Picks up a balloon in the form of a human figure. Squeezes balloon and cries, "Mommy, Mommy, Mommy."

T. That's what it cries. Mommy, Mommy, Mommy.

C. [Continues to squeeze balloon and cry, "Mommy, Mommy, Mommy." Looks at T and places balloon on table. Turns handle of vise.] What is it?

T. You want to know what it could be. It can be anything you want it to be.

C. A can opener.

T. Is that what it is? A can opener?

C. Lookit these soldiers. Are these cowboys or soldiers?

T. What do they look like?

C. Cowboys. See the cowboys. Those are all cowboys.

T. Mm-hm.

C. I'm gonna be a monkey.

T. That's what you're going to be.

C. [Puts on monkey mask.] Lookit me. I'm the monkey.

T. Susan is the monkey.

C. Now I'm gonna be a piggy. I'll say oink-oink. [Puts on pig mask.] Oink, oink, oink, oink, oink.

T. The piggy goes oink, oink, oink.

C. Oink, oink, oink, oink. [Takes mask off.] Now I'm gonna be a clown. This goes oink, oink, oink, too. Oink, oink.

T. The clown goes oink, oink.

C. Oink, oink, oink. [Laughs.] Now I'm gonna be a baby and drink from the bottle of water. Shall I?

T. That's up to you.

C. Should I sprinkle here? Here. Open your hand.

T. You want to sprinkle in my hand.

C. [Sprinkles water in T's hand.] Rub them together. [Drinks from the bottle and then replaces it on bench. Turns handle of vise again.] Now I have to can opener this. [Puts figure balloon into vise; it squeaks.] She doesn't want to be can openered.

T. She doesn't?

C. No. I heard my Mummy walking. Hey! It's almost up to here. This number right here. [Indicates number on wrist watch.] I hear her coming.

T. You hear her coming.

C. [Turns handle of vise. Shakes it back and forth. Looks at nursing bottles. Again turns vise handle and looks out window. Picks up figure balloon and squeezes it; drops it and steps on it.] I'm gonna throw the ball. You kick it like that.

T. Mm-hm. That's what you do to it.

C. See what you do? Rocky-rocky the baby to sleep. Where's the baby? Where is she? Here's a mirror.

T. Mm-hm.

C. [Peers in mirror of dresser.] Tick-tick.

T. That's the way it goes.

C. Tick-tock. Tick-tock. There's the baby in there. [Points to doll house.] Baby walking upstairs. One, two, three, four, five. Into your beds. They're in their beds. Into your bed you go, bad girl. [Baby doll.] And this one is a big girl.

T. A big girl.

C. With a round head. Walk, walk, walk. Here's the daddy going to bed now. Walky, walky, walky. Right next to the girl. [Middle doll.]

T. Mm-hm.

C. And here's the mommy. Walky, walky, walky. Right next to the baby. [Undresses male doll.] I'm taking his pantsies off.

T. Mm-hm.You're taking his pants off.

C. Walk, walk, walk. Walking up to bed, walking up to bed. Three little children.

T. Three little children and two big people.

C. And another little baby. Here's me. I'm taking her clothes off. I'm going to bed. Now he's up. [Male doll.] Up and up and up. [Dressing male doll.] Little up, little up. Put your pants back on. Walky, walky, walky downstairs. [Female doll.] Walky, walky, walky downstairs. [Male doll.] Walky, walky, walky. [Another male doll.] [Walks baby doll downstairs.] I'm climbing up this ladder. Let's climb up the ladders. Just climbing up the ladders.

T. Mm-hm.

C. And the little one on top of the bed. [Middle doll.] The little one sleeps under the bed. [Baby doll.]

T. One on top, one underneath.

C. Two underneath. Here's the bedroom. [Bends figure balloon and squeezes it.] I like that noise. Squeak, squeak, squeak. This is a big bed. Here's your bed.

T. That's my bed, huh?

C. Who sleeps in that bed?

T. Anyone you want.

C. Me. This is my little chair. [Crouches and sits on bed.] How come this doesn't go? [Points to watch on arm.]

T. You wonder why it doesn't go.

C. Oh. Supper is open. Here's your supper.

T. Quite a supper.

C. That's my mother's watch. Just pretend it's your supper. [Turns handle of vise.] Zoom, zoom, zoom, zoom. Here's your supper. Eat it up. Don't eat my mother's watch up. Just eat your supper up. Zoom, zoom, zoom. Here's your watch. Zoom, zoom, zoom. Here's your watch.

Second Session

C. [Talks to mother.] Are you gonna stay here? Here's a balloon. [Waves a balloon figure at T.] Good-bye. [To mother.] Mommy, leave your watch here. I want to see what time it is. [Looks at T's watch.] It will still be there tomorrow. [Puts balloon figure in upper part of doll house. Empties bag of dolls.] There. In the garbage can. [Walks to nursing bottles.] I'm gonna drink from this. [Drinks from large bottle and replaces it on bench.] He's gonna shoot you. [Cowboy figure.] Bang. Hoppy is gonna shoot you. Shoot and tie you up. All cowboys are shooting. [Handles soldiers and shoots T a few times.] Everyone is shot. [Squeees figure balloon and it squeaks. Walks figure balloon up the stairs of doll house.] Walk, walk, walk. [Throws figure balloon aside. Sits on floor, fingers stairway. Picks up figure balloon and whispers.] She's going to sleep. Shall I take her head off?

T. That's up to you.

C. [Places balloon in box with blocks.] That's a block. [Picks up figure balloon again, brushes it against T's face.] I wanta take your glasses off.

T. You'd like to do that, but that's one thing you can't do here.

C. Let's pretend to play school. O.K.? And you're the teacher. O.K.?

T. And I'm the teacher.

C. [Cuts a piece of paper and folds it in half. Cuts paper along folded line and into quarters, looks at T, folds paper again and shows it to T.] I'm gonna give these to my mother. That's for Mother's Day.

T. Is that a Mother's Day present?

C. Yeah. [Cuts another piece of paper in two.] This is my mother's present, too.

T. You have quite a few to give your mother. You like to give her things, huh?

C. [Holds papers in hand.] These are my mother's and my daddy's, too. Just for my mother and daddy. [Lifts come-back toy.] He's a big clown.

T. Mm-hm.

C. [Carries come-back toy to T.] There. Walk, walk, walk, walk, walk.

T. There you go.

C. [Leans against come-back toy, pushing it down.]

T. You want it to go down.

C. Yeah. [Pushes come-back toy into sandbox.] He's crying.

T. You're making him cry.

C. Yeah. [Finally succeeds in pushing come-back toy into sandbox.]

T. There, you have it.

C. He's crying. Nobody's taking him out.

T. He is just going to stay in there all the time.

C. [Hands T papers that she has cut.] Will you fold these for my mother? And my dad.

T. For no one else.

C. Not even you.

T. Not even me.

C. No. [Starts to cut paper again. Continues; folds one half sheet in two again and places it on top of the others.] See? Some's for my family, and not for you, either.

T. Not for me.

C. No. [Cuts more paper.] Only one is for you, and this is all you're getting. Here. None for your mother. No. It's all mine and my mother's.

T. Just yours and your mother's.

C. I'll be the teacher and gather up your things. O.K., honey. Let's, honey. Yes, honey. Where's that paper? And you, honey. Honey, honey. I'm gonna sprinkle some. [Drops a handful of sand from sandbox into pail of water. Watches it. Takes more sand and drops it into pail. Looks at T and laughs.] It's all getting brown, isn't it? [Throws more sand into pail.] The floor is getting wet. [Continues to drop handfuls of sand into pail.] It's getting brown water.

T. Yes, it is. It's getting to be brown water.

C. [Throws more sand into pail.] I splashed my shoe. See? [Sprinkles some sand over come-back toy. Drops more sand into pail and waves her hands in the air.] I wanta go wash them.

T. You want to wash them? O.K.

C. [Leaves room with T.]

Third Session

C. [Waves good-bye to mother and runs into the room. Drops a handful of sand into pail of water.]

T. It went right in, didn't it?

C. Look how much. [Drops another, larger handful into pail and laughs.] A big splash. Splash. The water's getting brown. [Drops two more handfuls of sand into pail.]

T. It's getting browner and browner.

C. Mmm. Now I'm making pie. [Plays in sandbox.]

T. So you're making a pie, that's what.

C. Here's your pie.

T. Is that for me?

C. Mm. Take a shovel and eat it. Take a spoon and eat it.

T. You want me to eat it.

C. [Throws more sand into pail and smiles at T.] O.K. Here. [Gestures toward T with shovel.]

T. You want me to eat with that, huh?

C. Not really.

T. You just want me to pretend?

C. Yes.

T. Mm-hm.

C. I'm throwing it all over the floor. [Throws sand on the floor.]

T. You are?

C. Swoosh, swoosh, swoosh.
T. You really like that.
C. [Continues to play with sand.] Now this is a little cookie, and I'll put it in a plate.
T. Mm-hm.
C. Here. And I'll give you some more. [Throws more sand into pail.] It's getting dark blue.
T. That's what it's getting to be. Dark blue.
C. [Fills mold with sand, pats it, and gives it to T.] Eat it.
T. You want me to eat it now.
C. And then I'll give you some more. Eat it up. O.K. Now eat it.
T. Now you want me to eat it. Suppose that I don't want any more?
C. Then you won't get any dessert. Now eat it all up. O.K., now take it. Now pick it up now. Hello, hello, hello, hello. [Dials telephone.] Pretend I hear the phone bell ringing and I say hello, and you talk.
T. Oh, all right, we'll pretend that.
C. Hello?
T. Hello.
C. Who is this?
T. Who is that?
C. This is Susan, and she's playing here. Good-bye.
T. Good-bye.
T. [Sneezes.]
C. God bless you.
T. Thank you.
C. [Picks up large bottle and drinks. Replaces it on bench.] I like to play here.
T. You like coming here and playing.
C. [Walks over to balloon figure and kisses it. Tosses it into air and catches it several times while dancing around the room.]
T. Well, our time is up for today, Susan.
C. One more bouncy and I'll go up.
T. O.K., one more bouncy and we'll go.
C. [Throws balloon figure into air one more time. Lets it fall on floor.] O.K. Good-bye, good-bye. Good-bye, Mister.
T. Good-bye.

Susan's mother came in after this last session to tell the therapist that she was very happy about Susan, who had again become a pleasant child; that she was no longer afraid to leave Susan with the baby; that Susan showed more affection for the baby and had assumed some responsibilities in the baby's care.

Benefits of Play Therapy for These Two Children

Both Tommy and Susan used symbolic forms—boats and balloon figures—to localize their anxiety about a new baby in the family. The gains in both cases were growth in terms of emotional insight, a feeling of security and comfort within themselves. What they needed was an opportunity to express their attitudes in an accepting relationship where they could feel respected as individuals, whatever their feelings and perceptions about themselves and their families might be.

Situational play therapy provided these children with an opportunity to work out temporarily disturbing feelings, and so removed the possibility that these feelings would be repressed, lose their identification to reality, and perhaps eventually seriously damage the self by pervading it with free-floating or systematic anxiety. Freed from these temporarily disturbing feelings, these children were able to use their psychic energies to express their real selves, thereby freeing these energies for a fuller utilization of their potentialities in both personal and social situations.

Accepting Regional Language Differences in School

LOREN R. TOMLINSON

Our language is not static, but living, developing, and changing. Neither is it uniform throughout the land at any specific point in time. Speech varies with the particular cultural background of the individual and in tone, accent, and rhythm according to the region in which he lives. These regional differences in speech can be identified in terms of large geographical areas, but the varieties within and among the areas are myriad. Although they are fairly distinct, regional differences in language have presented no significant barrier to communication. Actually, our language has been enlarged and enriched by these variations, rather than by duplication of some static standard.

Although schools have always had to contend with differences, by and large, schools in the past have had only infrequent direct contact with regional language differences and have been content to ignore them or to treat them incidentally. However, in recent years new developments in transportation and communication have brought the regions into a closer relationship. Moreover, population statistics show that great numbers of people are moving about the country from one region to another, some temporarily, others permanently.

These large scale migrations give rise to numerous social problems, many of which confront the schools. The school administrator must provide more classroom space and facilities, more materials of instruction, and additional instructional staff to meet the demands of increased enrollments. An even more crucial challenge confronts the classroom teacher,

REPRINTED FROM *ELEMENTARY ENGLISH,* 30, 7 (NOVEMBER 1953), 420-423, WITH THE PERMISSION OF THE NATIONAL COUNCIL OF TEACHERS OF ENGLISH AND THE AUTHOR.

since the children coming in from various parts of the country bring with them different backgrounds of experience which often cause them to contrast with the native children. Inasmuch as these children may differ somewhat in dress, sometimes in color, and almost always in speech, problems of adjustment on the part of both groups frequently develop. Each aspect of their differences may present problems with significant implications, and speech is no exception.

It is the responsibility of the classroom teacher to help both the native and the migrant children come to understand and appreciate each other's differences and develop those attitudes which are appropriate in a democracy. In his direct, daily relationship with the children, the classroom teacher plays the key role. The solution of the problem transcends curriculum design, for the most carefully planned curriculum is subject to the quality of the teacher's professional understandings and personal attitudes.

In the classroom where there are regional differences in language, it would seem to be of primary importance that the teacher create an atmosphere in which these differences are respected. In helping children achieve socially accepted standards of language, the teacher should keep in mind that these standards do not deny certain regional characteristics of tone, accent, rhythm, and idiom. As the teacher's attitude toward language variations becomes apparent to the children, it will do much toward influencing the attitudes that they take. The development of a desirable atmosphere requires more than passive acceptance or mere toleration of differences. The teacher can take the lead by encouraging all children to participate in language activities, particularly those involving oral language. At appropriate times interesting variations in pronunciations and usage can be explored on the children's intellectual level. In the lower elementary school, this may be done most effectively through simple discussions with the children. Older children can become quite interested in charting, for purposes of comparison, the major variations as they appear in speech and literature. Consideration of these language differences and their backgrounds not only increases the children's understanding, but also affords the teacher opportunities to emphasize, in a meaningful way to children, those common intergroup likenesses which underlie superficial differences. As the children discover the contributions of various regional groups to our living language, they develop the concept of cultural interdependence and are able to think more clearly about differences and likenesses on a broader scale.

Not all classrooms have members representing different regions or opportunities to contact the language of other regions firsthand. Fortunately, most normal children have a keen, innate interest in language. Unless their enthusiasm is destroyed by an unimaginative school language program, they express this interest in various ways. Early in the elementary school children become fascinated with words and their meanings. Later they seem to take particular delight in confounding adults with unusual words and expressions which they adopt or create. This is all a part of the process of growing up. Schools will do well to make effective use of this natural interest in helping children develop understandings related to regional language.

Children can have many satisfying experiences with language as they work in the social studies. In the middle and upper elementary school they frequently have occasion to undertake units of work closely associated with a particular region. In addition to a consideration of the geographical features and the way the people live, profitable study can be made of the language peculiar to the region. To the extent that the language reflects their characteristics, understandings of the people can be enriched. Later in the course of the unit of work, as children attempt to organize and clarify the knowledge that they have acquired, they may choose activities directly involving language. These activities may take the form of dramatics, original story telling, creative writing, singing, audience reading, and the like. Children enjoy using regional dialect in such activities and certainly its use can enhance the child's understanding and appreciation of both the people and their language.

With the exception of firsthand experience, the growing body of children's regional literature probably offers the best medium for helping children develop a sensitiveness to language differences. Well-written stories of this type have a strong emotional and intellectual appeal for children in the middle and upper elementary school. As the child reads and lives the story he frequently identifies himself with a sympathetic character. It is not unusual to observe children become so immersed in such reading that they assume for a time the speech and manner of their favorite personality. Skillful authors of regional literature can so expertly develop the background of the way of life of the region that the manner of speech and expressions used by the characters seem only natural and fitting to the reader. This kind of acceptance establishes the emotional tone for deeper appreciations and understandings which the teacher can help the children develop.

Unfortunately, regional speech is not always easily captured in writing. In an effort to convey a particular quality, authors sometimes resort to unusual devices which may confuse the inexperienced reader. Children who have heard the speech of a region have less difficulty with it in printed form. For those children who have no direct contact with speech variations, phonograph records done in regional language are available. The richest source for these children, however, is the teacher who reads regional dialect well. Not only can he further the children's interest in books in general, but he can also provide the background which they need for reading regional literature with a fuller enjoyment and understanding.

A less direct, but not less important, concomitant benefit which children may gain through the study of regional language has to do with the problem of prejudice. Just how prejudice develops in the child has not been thoroughly explored on a scientific basis. We do know that it is not a natural form of behavior and that children acquire if from adults. There is considerable evidence to support the idea that it can be effectively combated by increased understanding. One form of prejudice is directed toward regional language. As children become acquainted with differences in regional language and come to appreciate them, a long step is taken toward the elimination of that form of prejudice.

Meaningful experiences with regional language through firsthand contact, in the social studies, through regional literature, and in other ways can help children realize the value of diversity in a language and in a democracy. Just as our democracy looks to differences in individuals and groups for sources of wholesome growth, so does our living language. Geographical variations add considerably to the interest of our speech and they persist in spite of some rather constant forces against them. Traditionally, schools have attempted to standardize language on a formal level. Mass media of speech, especially radio and television, are working indirectly toward a less formal standard of language. Undoubtedly, both have done much toward improving the quality of speech in this country. However, neither should be regarded as an unmixed blessing. Ultimately they would standardize the tongue to a dead, awful sameness and have it become like a mass produced loaf of bread, near perfect in quality, but as devoid of flavor and distinctiveness.

The Case Study— A Means of Introducing Guidance Services

GAIL F. FARWELL
ANTHONY C. RICCIO

Although it is axiomatic that a good school provides guidance services for its pupils, there are still many schools in which organized guidance programs do not exist. Jones and Miller state that in the 1951-52 academic year, only 17.2 per cent of the 23,746 high schools they studied had at least a half-time counselor.[1] Historically, attempts to organize guidance programs at the elementary school level have lagged behind those at the secondary level.

If we assume that guidance services ought to be an integral part of all school systems, we must consider means of introducing these services into those systems where they do not as yet exist. The case study can often be used to establish a guidance point of view. Initiated by a principal, a part-time counselor, interested teachers, or a consultant from a nearby college or university, the case study might be employed to demonstrate how much it is possible to learn about a student. Teachers may possibly realize for the first time the tremendous amount of interest and knowledge that can be generated by a group committed to the task of learning more about an individual. Indeed, once materials have been organized, the classroom teacher may be truly surprised to discover how much he knows or does not know about a particular student.

This article is intended to offer a rationale for the case study and to demonstrate how it might be employed as a vehicle through which to introduce organized guidance services into a school system.

REPRINTED FROM *THE NATIONAL ELEMENTARY PRINCIPAL,* 40, 7 (MAY 1961), 38-40, BY PERMISSION OF THE PUBLISHERS AND THE AUTHORS.

Rationale of the Case Study

The case study is an endeavor to focus all the school's facilities on the task of understanding an individual student. It represents an attempt to understand a student in terms of his self-concept, his environment, and his interpersonal relations. It aims at the development of self-insight and self-realization on the part of the student.

Like most other concepts in the field of guidance, the case study concept rests upon these basic principles: (1) Human behavior is caused; (2) Behavior can be modified; (3) Teachers can be provided preparation which will help them in working with students to modify their behavior; and (4) The integrity and sacredness of the individual demand that he be considered a subject worthy of study and assistance.

With these principles in mind, it may be stated that the case study concept is comprised of three interrelated processes. First, an attempt is made to assemble the necessary meaningful data about the individual. Second, means of helping the subject are considered and followed through. Finally, there is positive action and self-direction on the part of the subject. In its most complete sense, the case study is a unified attempt by the school staff to assist a given individual to realize his optimum potential. As such, it is applicable to all students—the normal as well as the atypical.

The Case Study Procedure

As a basic first step in conducting a case study, an interested person has to take the initiative. This person might be a teacher, administrator, counselor, or school psychologist.

His initial job is to develop a case history of the individual pupil who is to be studied. If there is a good cumulative record available, the case history will be rather easy to up-date. If no comprehensive cumulative record has been maintained, information will have to be gathered about personal identification, pre-school experiences, home background, significant school experiences, the testing record, and the academic record. As a step toward initiating a guidance program, the person conducting the case study should keep a log of activities necessary to the development of the case history. In this way, the school staff can see the complexity of doing a case study from the beginning and learn to appreciate the value of an organized inventory service in simplifying the case study procedure.

In collecting information and establishing a case study, we should keep in mind that to load the case study with irrelevant information is a waste of time. We should include only useful information. Many times during the process of a longitudinal case study, it will be desirable to delete, rather than add, information. To fail to delete out-dated information is to deny the individual the right to change, to deny his right to *become.*

After the assembling of data, the action phase of the case study begins. A case conference should be arranged, involving appropriate members of the school staff, the parents, and other persons concerned with the child's development. From it should come a tentative appraisal of the current situation and an uncovering of background information not previously revealed. The next action would be the recommendation of steps directly associated with the pupil. This helping relationship might involve home consultation with the family, counseling with the boy or girl, intensive therapy by an agency equipped to provide such a service, or remedial work. An adjusted program of studies, a recommendation for further or lesser involvement in activities, or the procurement of a part-time job might be suggested. The nature of the specific case would dictate the choice of the action techniques.

The case study is never completely terminated. At the close of the action phase, the pertinent data becomes a part of the child's longitudinal developmental record. To reopen the case study then becomes a rather easy task.

If members of a school staff attempt some selected case studies and understand the steps necessary to develop a comprehensive case study, if they understand the scope and activities of an organized guidance program, and if they see a longitudinal developmental portrait of growth and development as desirable in assisting the pupil, the case study procedure can provide guidelines for initiating and maintaining a guidance program.

An Example

In Jenkins School, a newly employed counselor received a referral from a fourth-grade teacher. A case study seemed desirable. The new counselor was conscious of the fact that organized guidance procedures had not been a characteristic of this school's program. The counselor went to the record file to seek information about Billy. The cupboard was bare of significant information other than simple identifying information, the school levels enrolled in, the academic record, and grades received.

Mr. Brown, the counselor, then proceeded to gather data for a case history. He made a home visit to determine familial status and impact, preschool experiences, and current viewpoint of both parents. Mr. Brown's log showed the necessity of three visits involving six hours and 30 miles of driving. Billy had been given standardized tests but the results had not been recorded and the tests could not be located. Billy was then subjected to several standardized tests. The time involvement was 13 hours, counting administration and scoring.

There were no anecdotal reports from Billy's teachers so summary reports were requested from his current teachers—total time involved for all staff, nine hours. His previous teachers were also consulted but they could only make generalizations; specific observations were now clouded because of the passage of time and valuable insights were lost forever. Soliciting this information took four hours. The family physician and clergyman and Billy's club director were consulted, requiring four and one-half hours for Mr. Brown.

All told, it took thirty-six and one-half hours of staff time during a two-week period to assemble the case history. The case conference and action phase with Billy were not yet accounted for. If this school had had an organized guidance activity, the case history would have been assembled over a four-year period. This skeleton example should provide some clues to the value of guidance organization.

Value of the Case Study

If guidance services are to be introduced into a school system, they must be deemed worthwhile by the administrator and his staff. Since the case study utilizes so many of the techniques characteristic of a good guidance program, it might well be employed to demonstrate the efficacy of a host of guidance techniques. A case study could reveal how the results of a school-wide testing program, which were not formerly utilized, might be applied to gain a better understanding of a given individual. A case study might also point up dramatically how the curriculum pattern followed in a school either fails or succeeds in meeting the most basic needs of the individual being studied. It can also result in professional growth for the principal and his staff. The case study often helps to focus attention upon the relationship between home and school and clarifies the reasons for a student who must reside in these oftentimes disparate environments performing the way he does. Indeed, the case study is a means of evaluating the school program as it affects the lives of given individuals.

Although the case study is an intensive organized study of one individual, it can easily be employed to make thorough studies of the entire student body. If each teacher conducts one case study a month, there will be data on each child in the school after a period of three or four years. It is then not too difficult a matter to continue the procedure and prepare studies on new pupils. If case studies are begun in the elementary school and continued throughout the years a child is in school, they will become the basis for a pupil inventory service. The action phase of the case study has implications for the information, counseling, and placement aspects of the guidance program.[2]

For the case study technique to be successful, certain conditions must be present: (1) Teachers must become skilled in collecting, interpreting, and acting upon data; (2) The school administration must support the activity and provide time for its operation; (3) The school staff must recognize this procedure as a means of promoting a developmental picture of the individual and as the common thread to which a developmental program of guidance services may be attached.

Pressey and Robinson have pointed out that the child falling within the wide range of normalcy is the most neglected child in our public school system.[3] Teachers have a tendency to give attention, positive or negative, to the atypical child. Oftentimes, students of average achievement can become superior students if they are understood and encouraged on an individual basis to excel. The case study is a most desirable means of motivating the average achiever to abdicate mediocrity.

The case study is a means of making our schools better through a thorough and intensive study of the most important product of our schools—our children. In the case study concept is found the culmination of the services and developments that the guidance movement has contributed to the modern American school.

REFERENCES

1. A.J. Jones and L.M. Miller, "The National Picture of Pupil Personnel and Guidance Services in 1953," *The Bulletin of the National Association of Secondary School Principals,* **38** (February 1954), 119.

2. Gail F. Farwell and Herman J. Peters, "Guidance: A Longitudinal and Differential View," *The Elementary School Journal,* **57** (May 1957), 442-445.

3. Sidney L. Pressey and Francis P. Robinson, *Psychology and the New Education* (New York: Harper and Brothers, 1944), p. 329.

❧ Part Three

THE ELEMENTARY SCHOOL CHILD AND THE WORLD OF WORK

Vocational Guidance in the Elementary School

WALTER M. LIFTON

The swell in the number of textbooks written for people involved in guidance in elementary schools is but one indication of the increasing concern of professional workers with their responsibility for providing help at this level. Counselor Trainers find an increasing proportion of their classes contain students working in the elementary schools. This article is devoted specifically to a discussion of the role and use of vocational guidance in the elementary grades.

The Growing Concern

For some time now writers in the field have pointed out the marked discrepancy between children's concerns and the manner in which the textbooks and teachers meet them. Specifically Bennett[1] in evaluating the results of the Midwest Conference of State Supervisors of Guidance Services and Counselor Trainers[2] held in 1950 as well as the results of the SRA Junior Inventory points up the real and growing concern of youngsters over their academic and vocational future. She documents clearly the fact that, based on SRA Junior Inventory responses, their answers to the question "I'd like to know what I'm going to be when I grow up" remained approximately the same from grades 4 through 8 accounting for 38, 41, 38, 36, and 40 per cent respectively of responses for each grade.

Hoppock[3], beyond suggesting ways occupational concepts could be introduced into the schools, points up the need to integrate the presen-

REPRINTED FROM *THE VOCATIONAL GUIDANCE QUARTERLY,* 8 (WINTER 1959), 79-81, BY PERMISSION OF THE PUBLISHERS AND THE AUTHOR.

tation of the material into the existing curricula of the schools. Certainly the incorporation of any data into the curriculum today is dependent on both parent and teacher attitude. With this in mind two studies are worth reviewing.

Shores and Rudman[4, 5] surveyed 270 communities to see how closely parent's, teacher's, librarian's, and children's evaluation of children's reading interests and informational needs (grades 4-8) coincided. A few of their results are cited. They found that girls more frequently than boys wanted to ask about horses, dogs, vocations, boy-girl relationships, ethics, values, and religion. Parents show a particularly strong desire for children to ask questions about vocations. Teachers are more concerned with social skills. It is also possible that teachers consider the elementary school years as inappropriate for serious concern with vocations.

They also found that children are not necessarily interested in asking about the same things that they wanted to read about.

An Exploratory Study

The second study was conducted by the author. It was concerned with the implication that teachers might not be aware of the early age at which attitudes and values about the world of work begin to crystallize. It was also concerned with the emphasis on vocations, in terms of career planning, rather than utilizing the elementary grades as a place where curiosity about the world might help broaden a youngster's perspective.

Two beginning classes in guidance provided subjects for the survey. The students in these classes were primarily teachers in the elementary schools and did not plan on professional guidance careers but wished instead to increase their classroom effectiveness. Each teacher was asked to consider which occupations they could use as illustrations of classroom concepts. To insure real occupational sophistication they were restricted to only those jobs in which they knew training requirements, salary levels, and job opportunities. Using the *Dictionary of Occupational Titles* categories their responses were tallied. Professions led the list by far, followed by sales and clerical tasks, with skilled trades barely showing. The job distribution was in *almost exact* reverse to the distribution of jobs resulting from census data.

The teachers were then asked to go through all of the books used in their classes and to make a list of any occupation used as an illustration. Again the results were fascinating.

In the primary grades there was a heavy emphasis on service occupations. There was then a rapid shift in the upper grades to the professions, with the skilled trades again being barely represented. In other words, from both their teachers and their texts youngsters were receiving a distorted picture of the importance and types of jobs available.

Realizing that these teachers could not help youngsters secure a true picture of the world of work if their own experiences and textbooks did not offer help, the author then began a survey of books available in the area of occupations to develop a list teachers could use to supplement their background. Again the results were surprising. From a series of books for the early primary grades published by Children's Press there appears to be a complete vacuum until books for junior high school youngsters like the Dodds Meade series occur. To verify this finding the author approached several major book publishers to explore their interest in books describing the world of work and designed for grades 3-6. Repeatedly the answer given was that they do not have, nor do they plan to publish books of this type because "children are not interested in vocations."

Serious Questions Arise

All of these results raise for guidance counselors several serious questions. If these results based upon small samples hold true in more controlled studies several avenues are available to the profession to improve the situation. Guidance supervisors might encourage teachers to engage in more field trips where the emphasis of both pupils and teacher would be directed on the workers and the skills they utilize. Parents might be encouraged to come to school and share with the children information about their jobs. Teachers could be encouraged to seek different types of employment during summers. Publishers could be encouraged to put out materials which they then could be sure of selling.

The above material suggests a rather negative picture. There are several recent advances, however, worth noting. Several of the leading encyclopedias have completed major revisions of their entries on careers and vocations. In almost all cases the number of pages allotted has been vastly increased. At least two publishers utilize a guidance consultant to insure that all articles in their encyclopedias present a more realistic picture of the world of work and job opportunities. One anthological encyclopedia[6] has introduced a vocational game which appears throughout the volumes. The game is designed to help children see how their interests persist from one industry to another. They also are given a chance to think about work activities on several hundred jobs. Recently a social studies series on the third grade level focused on "Working Together"[7] utilized skilled trades among their many examples. There is a book[8] on the world of work for use in grades 4-5 now being given a pilot run in three cities to test children's interests and the correct placing of this kind of material. One city system[9] has developed a course for use in grades 7-8 to help children who may not be continuing on to high school.

It is obvious that many questions requiring research have been raised. Equally necessary is the development of texts to meet the developing needs of schools for vocational guidance materials. If the age old concept of guidance as a lifelong process is to remain true, greater attention to the role of the elementary school can no longer be delayed.

REFERENCES

1. Margaret Bennett, *Guidance in Groups* (New York: McGraw-Hill, 1955), 54, 246.

2. National Association of Guidance Supervisors and Counselor Trainers, *A National Study of Existing and Recommended Practices for Assisting Youth Adjustment in Selected Elementary Schools of the United States* (Ann Arbor, Mich.: Ann Arbor Publishers, 1953), pp. 40-44.

3. Robert Hoppock, *Occupational Information* (New York: McGraw-Hill, 1957), p. 351.

4. Harlan J. Shores and Herbert C. Rudman, *What Children Are Interested In* (Champaign, Ill.: Spencer Press, 1954), p. 16.

5. Herbert C. Rudman, "Interrelationships Among Various Aspects of Children's Interests and Informational Needs and Expectations of Teachers, Parents, and Librarians" (Doctoral dissertation, University of Illinois, 1954).

6. Walter M. Lifton, "Ask Yourself," throughout 18 volumes of *Our Wonderful World* (Chicago: Spencer Press, 1957).

7. Alta McIntire and Wilhelmia Hill, *Working Together* (Chicago: Follett Publishing Co., 1954).

8. Walter M. Lifton, *What Could I Be?* (Chicago: Science Research Associates, 1960).

9. Martin Burack (unpublished course materials for City of Chicago elementary schools course on vocations, Grades 7-8).

The Roots of Careers

ROBERT P. O'HARA
Boston College

Mothers, fathers, and teachers often wonder what children will be when they grow up.

During the past half-century this wonder has been translated into efforts to predict occupational choice by statistical methods. More recently the choice of an occupation has been thought of as a process of development.

In 1951 Ginzberg and his associates set forth the theory that occupational choice is a process that progresses through three stages: fantasy choice, tentative choice, and realistic choice.[1]

In the first stage, boys and girls make choices that are not related to the adult world of work in a logical fashion but rather in an imaginative, dream-world fashion.

The second stage, which Ginzberg called the tentative stage, has three substages. In the first of these, the interest stage, boys and girls, speaking of the work they want to do, may say, "It's an interesting job," "I like the work," "It's exciting."

Children at the second substage, the capacity stage, may make such statements as, "I'm good at math," "French is my best subject," "I've won several medals in swimming."

Children at the third substage base their choices on values. They may say: "It's a good paying job," "I'd like to be able to stay in one place and have lots of friends," "I'd like to travel," "This kind of work gives you the satisfaction of doing something for others."

REPRINTED FROM *THE ELEMENTARY SCHOOL JOURNAL*, 62, 5 (FEBRUARY 1962), 277-280, BY PERMISSION OF THE UNIVERSITY OF CHICAGO PRESS AND THE AUTHOR.

During the realistic stage, the child considers all the factors involved simultaneously, while he explores and arrives at the final choice.

Ginzberg reported that boys and girls pass through the substages in the order stated within fairly regular age limits: interest, at eleven to twelve years of age; capacity, at thirteen to fourteen years of age; value, at fifteen to sixteen years of age. A pilot study led us to wonder whether these three substages might not have earlier starting points.[2]

In the Ginzberg study, the existence of the stages was determined by the fact that boys in the sixth and seventh grades based their choices primarily on interest, while in Grades 8 and 9 the basis for choice was capacity and in Grades 10 and 11 the choices were based largely on value.

To search for the use of similar bases for choice in public elementary school, 829 boys and 750 girls from a suburban-industrial community of Greater Boston were asked two questions: "What sort of person do you want to become?" And "Why do you want to be that kind of person?" The written answers were gathered in May, 1959.

TABLE 1 Bases for Occupational Choices of 829 Boys and 750 Girls in Grades 4-6

GRADE	PUPILS	CHOICES	BASES	INTEREST		VALUE		FAMILY		CAPACITY		OTHER	
	No.	No.	No.	No.	%	No.	%	No.	%	No.	%	No.	%
Boys:													
4	286	308	352	155	44	123	35	56	16	7	2	11	3
5	257	305	349	171	49	112	32	52	15	7	2	7	2
6	286	327	389	206	53	132	34	31	8*	12	3	8	2
Girls:													
4	248	275	315	110	35†	170	54‡	13	4	6	2	16	5
5	211	252	287	100	35†	141	49‡	26	9	6	2	14	5
6	291	369	434	161	37†	226	52‡	17	4	8	2	22	5

* Significantly different from the fourth grade at the .01 level of confidence.
† Significantly different from the corresponding *interest* base for boys at the .01 level of confidence.
‡ Significantly different from the corresponding *value* base for boys at the .01 level of confidence.

The Boys' Choices

For our content analysis we classified the statements into the categories suggested by the Ginzberg study. The findings are presented in Table 1.

Between boys of high intelligence and boys of average intelligence there were no significant differences or even trends in the data within grades or from one grade to another. For boys in Grades 4, 5, and 6, interests were clearly the dominant basis for choice by the sixth grade.

Values as a base remained relatively constant throughout the three grade levels, about a third of the choices having values as a base. The decline in family influence was significant beyond the .01 level. Family here included uncles and aunts.

At each grade level, capacity was mentioned very infrequently. This finding makes us curious about what happens in Grades 7, 8, and 9. If the capacity stage occurs, as Ginzberg reports, in Grades 8 and 9, then a relatively spectacular surge of emphasis on this factor must occur in Grade 7 and in the early part of Grade 8.

If such a surge occurs, we wonder whether it is developmental, as Ginzberg implies, or whether it can be attributed to pressures in the school system, as Tiedeman hypothesizes.[3]

Ginzberg says that consideration of values in occupational choice starts at the age of fifteen or sixteen. For about 25 per cent of the boys in our sample, values entered into decisions as early as fourth grade.

The Girls' Choices

The data showed no significant differences or trends between girls of high intelligence and girls of average intelligence. For the girls, Grades 4, 5, and 6 clearly constitute a value stage. The differences between boys and girls on both interest and value factors are significant at every grade level.

Ginzberg presents a tentative conclusion on the work choices of girls in Grades 4, 5, and 6: "the girls . . . think of the adult's world of work in terms of their immediate desires without much concern for the feasibility or appropriateness of the work which they have chosen."

At all three grade levels, four occupations accounted for about two-thirds of all choices made by the girls. The choices were teacher, nurse, secretary, and mother. It would seem that these choices are not only feasible but appropriate for girls. It is also clear that the predominance of these choices explains the emphasis on value orientation in the girls' career development. The values they express are characteristically nurturant and appear to be quite appropriate for the majority of the girls' choices.

The girls were highly altruistic, the boys less so. About 13 per cent of the boys based their choices on money. Only 2 per cent of the girls' bases had this orientation.

How Close to Reality?

At each grade level for the boys about 15 per cent of the choices and bases were pure fantasy. For example, boys said: "I would like to be a bissness man and sit and work big deal." "I would like to be a cop and have adventurs."

The number of fantasy choices for girls was negligible. The bases in the girls' responses gave evidence that they had already played in real life the roles of teacher, nurse, and mother. They had taught their younger brothers and sisters. They had helped the teacher in school. They had taken care of babies at home. They had helped Mother when someone was sick. One girl had helped massage her brother's polio-stricken arm. The girls had swept, cooked, washed dishes, and made clothes.

All these experiences gave the girls a concrete understanding of their future careers that was far superior to the boys', and this realistic understanding had developed as early as fourth grade.

For the boys, choice was not restricted. For them the world was wider. But they did not have the intimate, concrete contact with the world that the girls had.

The problem is one of the degree of realism. In answering our questions, the boys in the sixth grade were more realistic than the boys in the fourth grade. One sixth-grade boy said, "When I grow up I would like to be an architect. When I am sixteen I will work in a playground as an instructor, and in the winter I will try to go to college and study about being an architect. I want that kind of job because it is a creative kind of job." This kind of statement seems realistic.

Our analysis of the reasons why 829 boys and 750 girls in Grades 4, 5, and 6 chose certain occupations showed clear-cut differences between reasons reported by boys and reasons reported by girls. The results confirm the Ginzberg finding that by sixth grade boys make choices based on interests. Values appear to be more important for boys than had been thought, however. The slight attention paid to capacity as a basis for choosing an occupation makes us curious about the existence of a capacity stage in Grades 8 and 9, a stage Ginzberg suggested.

For the girls in Grades 4, 5, and 6 there is evidence of a stage when values are of primary importance with interests secondary. Girls as well as boys paid little attention to capacity in making their choices. Girls, like boys, showed a decrease in family influence on vocational choice.

Finally, girls, because of the nature of their choices and their childhood experiences at home and in school, seem to have a more realistic understanding of their future work world than boys do.

REFERENCES

1. Eli Ginzberg, Sol Ginsburg, Sidney Axelrod, and John L. Herma, *Occupational Choice: An Approach to a General Theory* (New York: Columbia University Press, 1951).

2. Robert P. O'Hara, "Talk about Self," Harvard Studies in Career Development, No. 14 (Cambridge, Mass.: Harvard Graduate School of Education, 1959. Mimeographed).

3. David V. Tiedeman, "Occupational Choice: An Approach to a General Theory: A Review," Harvard Educational Review, **22** (1952), 184-190.

Occupational Information in Elementary Education

GOLDIE R. KABACK

Providing educational and occupational information for junior and senior high school boys and girls is now an accepted service of most school guidance programs. It would appear that information about occupations in elementary education might also do much to develop respect for the worth and dignity of all types of labor and provide a base for later vocational choice and planning.

The following suggestions in the area of occupational information are offered with the hope that they may serve to stimulate further investigation and experimentation by elementary school counselors.

Children View Work World

Children are continually learning and forming impressions about the activities which surround them. Their attitudes toward the world of work are already beginning to take shape when they enter school. The mother in her role as homemaker, the father or older sibling in the role of office or factory worker—each serves as a model to imitate or with whom to identify.

The child, however, makes his own evaluations of the vocational experiences about him. The grocer may be that "nice man" who offers cookies to little girls when they accompany their mothers or he may be that "awful man" who chases little boys when they loiter too close to the apple stand. The policeman at the school corner may be regarded as a trusting friend who stops oncoming traffic so that children are able to

REPRINTED FROM *THE VOCATIONAL GUIDANCE QUARTERLY,* 9 (AUTUMN 1960), 55-59, BY PERMISSION OF THE PUBLISHERS AND THE AUTHOR.

cross the street safely or he may be the enemy to outwit, to escape, and to hide from.

In answer to questions regarding parental occupations, children usually answer that father works downtown, in an office, a factory, a mill, a department store, and so on, but not many children are able to describe the nature of the work in which their parents engage. Attitudes about work, however, are inculcated quite early in the home, often without parental awareness. The frustrations of unemployment, conflicts with one's supervisor, and the hazards of particular occupations color a child's feeling about the work of his parents.

Children express these feelings in the following statements: "I don't have money for the bank this week because my daddy is not working." "My mother's check from welfare hasn't come yet." "My daddy says that teachers don't earn enough money." "Our house is cold because the oilmen are on strike." "My mother is working again because daddy was fired from his job."

Early Biases Are Few

Children seldom regard unskilled or semiskilled occupations as undesirable forms of labor. They admire the man who has just cleaned the walk in front of the school and they imitate the work of the sanitation department worker as he sprinkles and sweeps the street. They have as much praise for the classmate who completes an attractive potholder as for the classmate whose beautiful painting adorns the place of honor on the classroom wall. They are no more excited about interviewing the school principal, the school nurse, or the school doctor than they are about interviewing the lunchroom workers and the service people who deliver milk and food to the school. The bus driver or the train conductor are much more important people to them than is the local banker or the school superintendent.

The very games that children play suggest some identification with vocations that they see about them. "Doctor, lawyer, Indian Chief . . ." have served many generations as have the play kits of nurse, doctor, chemist, and the toy blocks of more recent years. It takes little effort to get children to talk about the work of the doctor, the nurse, the salesclerk, and the factory worker. They have little hesitation about indicating what they like or dislike about the activities to which these people are committed.

First Graders Study Work

Recently a first grade teacher in a graduate class entitled Educational and Vocational Opportunities described the following method that she had used in her classroom in order to have her pupils become more aware of the world of work. One of the legs from one of the toy chairs had broken off. After some discussion the children decided that they needed a carpenter to repair the chair. A unanimous "yes" went up as the teacher asked whether they wished to play carpenter. The children decided that a pair of pliers, a saw, a hammer, and a long nail were needed. The necessary steps were listed on the blackboard: (1) remove the broken piece of wood, (2) cut a new piece of wood, (3) nail the new piece of wood onto the chair. With the list in hand the group went off to the woodworking shop. The record of the work done was later discussed in class. John had pulled the old nail out with the pliers; Ben had sawed off the required piece of wood; Mary had handed the proper nail for Henry to hammer in. The children also talked about the qualities needed to perform a good job. They decided that they needed strong arms and hands to saw, hammer, and to pull out the old nail; good sense and a cautious approach were needed in order to use tools; good judgment was needed in order to select the proper nail and to know when to stop hammering so as not to break the wood.

The toy chair experience led to a discussion about other work activities of the carpenter. The class became so interested in "real work" that they began to talk about the occupations of their parents. Helen told the class about the various things that her mother did as a housekeeper. The children decided to play "doing housework" and asked Helen to play the role of her mother. As Helen dusted the room the teacher drew a picture of a woman on the blackboard. Each child observed the physical activity involved and colored a part of the blackboard picture that he felt was important to the job being done. Soon the children had colored the woman's eyes because "she had to see what she was doing"; her arms and hands because "she needs them to sweep and dust"; her legs because "she needs to get around"; her waist because "she needs to bend." One of the children colored the top of the woman's head because "she needs brains to know what to do next"; and another colored her mouth because "if she is working for a lady she must tell her when she is finished." The completed blackboard picture was a riot of color.

The class has since "analyzed" the job of the milk monitors, the clean-up squad, and the work of Eleanor's mother who works in an office and must therefore "know her alphabet in order to file letters." The teacher ended her report to the graduate class by saying, "The children just love this kind of game. Frankly, I'm so excited myself that I find myself thinking of new ways all the time to present material about jobs related to what we are doing in class. I am certainly looking forward to developing materials for other classes when I am appointed School Counselor."

A Second Grade Project

In the same graduate class a second grade teacher discussed a three week unit on "What I would like to do when I grow up," in which her pupils had participated. She indicated that her major goals in this project had been to instill a respect for all types of work and for the children to understand how the various workers in the community served the children themselves.

First she had suggested that each child ask his parents to describe to him the nature of their work. As each child reported on his parents' occupations in class the other children asked questions and began to explore ways in which the occupations contributed to the welfare of the people in the community. Finally the children selected one of the occupations as a class project. A story was written about the occupation and then several of the children acted out the work involved. Group discussions, oral reports by individual children, questions and answers, and the writing of the story were grouped under the language arts section of the curriculum by the teacher.

The children counted the number of different jobs that had been reported on and added the number of jobs that were represented in the school—teachers, principal, clerks, school nurse, physician, custodian, and so on, as well as other occupations in the community that had not been mentioned. Approximate weekly, monthly, and yearly wages for each occupation were apportioned in various amounts for food, rent, clothing, and the like. The teacher grouped these class activities under the mathematics section of her lesson plans.

The children in this particular class developed a newspaper in which they listed the occupations that had been discussed and a brief statement as to the nature of the work. Each child then indicated which one of the occupations he preferred and the reasons for his choice. The newspaper also included the children's explanations for selecting indoor or outdoor occupations and whether they liked to make things or whether they liked to read about things. The majority of the children stated that they liked to work with others on class projects but one boy wrote, "I like to make something by myself and then show it to the others." All of the children were eager to read the newspaper and to talk about the particular occupation in which each was interested.

As the occupation project progressed, each child was asked to cut out pictures in newspapers and magazines that portrayed some phase of the occupations listed in the class newspaper. The children prepared attractive covers for the folders that contained pictures that they themselves had drawn. Finally, the children hung the folders on the classroom bulletin board, arranging the occupations as to whether the work was performed indoors or outdoors.

There was no status value attached to any one occupation that had been discussed. The chief lesson learned was that it did not matter what kind of work one engaged in as long as it was well done and contributed to the welfare of others. The determinates of later vocational adjustment had been planted—pride in workmanship and achievement and respect for the work of the other man.

4th Grade Teacher Reports

A fourth grade teacher described how she had related the study of occupations to the Social Studies Curriculum. For "Our Working City" unit the children in her class investigated the work of their parents in relation to the welfare of the community and to themselves. For the unit on "We Build Homes" the children discussed the work of the bricklayer, the carpenter, the plumber, the electrician, the painter, and others. The class visited a new housing development under construction and learned that the work of the man who dug the hole or shoveled the sand was as important to the completion of the housing project as the design of the skilled architect. In the units on "Transportation" and "Who Works to Clothe Us" the children talked with the bus driver, the elevator operator in a local department store, and with sales clerks. They interviewed parents and neighbors regarding various types of work activities and finally arranged the following outline in their notebooks entitled "Investigating Jobs in Our Community."

1. How many different jobs are there?
2. How many people are employed in each job?
3. What is the nature of the work done?
4. Are different jobs declining or expanding?
5. Is it indoor or outdoor work?
6. Is the work seasonal?
7. What are the educational and training requirements? How long does it take to learn to do this kind of work?
8. How does one get a job of this kind?
9. How old must one be to get a job of this kind?
10. What are the physical requirements for the job?
11. How many hours a week does one work on the job?
12. Are there opportunities for advancement?
13. What are the weekly or monthly earnings?
14. Is union membership required? Why?
15. How much vacation time?
16. Is there health insurance and a retirement or pension plan for the workers?

The fourth grade teacher's evaluation of the occupation project was as follows: "It is not only what the children learned and talked about in class or during our field visits to different industries that is important. I believe that they also learned something about the value of work and the right attitudes toward work. I hope to be able to do much more in this area when I become a School Counselor."

Seasons, Holidays, and Jobs

Columbus Day, Thanksgiving, Christmas, winter, summer, spring, fall. How many pots of paste and crayons and sheets of paper are used up by busy kindergarten and elementary school children to picture ships with sails for Columbus Day, plump yellow pumpkins for Thanksgiving, and bright shiny toys for Christmas! How many easels are spattered with paint to show the bright green and yellow of spring, the rich reds of fall, and the white star shaped flakes of winter!

Yet each holiday and each season of the year too can be related to what men do. Cotton, wool, and warm clothing are seasonal topics that involve the work of the farmer, sheep shearing, cotton mills. Toys for holidays are made and sold and delivered by men and women. Christmas cards are placed in mailboxes and picked up by postmen who take them to the post office so that other postmen can deliver them to homes. These and other work roles are easily dramatized through play activities in order to bring children closer to the ways of the world in which they live.

Along with knowledge of actual work performance, however, must come respect for the dignity of every work effort. For it is the present elementary school child who will man the machnines in an age of automation whose wonders are just beginning to touch the horizon of our economy.

REFERENCES

1. Max Baer and Edward C. Roeber, *Occupational Information,* Rev. ed. (Chicago: Science Research Associates, 1958).

2. William Davey *et al., Everyday Occupations* (Boston: D.C. Heath & Company, 1950).

3. Eli Ginzberg *et al., Occupational Choice: An Approach to a General Theory* (New York: Columbia University Press, 1951).

4. Walter J. Greenleaf, *Occupations and Careers* (New York: McGraw-Hill, 1955).

5. Robert Hoppock, *Occupational Information* (New York: McGraw-Hill, 1957).

6. Harry D. Kitson, *How to Find the Right Vocation* (New York: Harper and Brothers, 1946).

7. Harry D. Kitson, *I Find My Vocation* (New York: McGraw-Hill, 1954).

8. National Society for the Study of Education, *Social Studies in the Elementary School,* 56th Yearbook, Pt. II (Chicago: University of Chicago Press, 1957).

9. Sarah Splaver, *Socio-Guid-dramas Series* (New York: Occu-Press, 1954-1960).

10. Donald E. Super, *The Psychology of Careers* (New York: Harper and Brothers, 1957).

11. Jerry M. Weiss, *Guidance Through Drama* (New York: Whiteside Inc., 1954).

Occupational Choice of Twelve-Year-Olds

DONALD A. DAVIS
NELLIE HAGAN
JUDIE STROUF

A proposed theory of occupational choice postulates that it is an orderly process involving many years and many decisions.[1]

Ginzberg theorizes that the process of occupational choice can be analyzed into three periods: fantasy choices before 11 years of age; tentative choices between 11 and 17 years of age; and realistic choices between 17 and young adulthood when the choice is finally crystallized.

The purpose of this study was to investigate the validity of parts of this theory of occupational choice. Do 12-year-olds make more tentative choices than fantasy ones? Are these choices a function of age only or are such factors as socio-economic environment, sex, race, intelligence, and reading retardation influential?

Method

All sixth graders from the three elementary schools in Muskegon Heights School District, Michigan, were sampled. School A is in a medium socio-economic neighborhood, while Schools B and C are in a low socio-economic locality. School A has all white children; School C has all Negro children; School B has students about equally divided between the white and Negro race. The average age of the 116 children in the study was 12 years. None was below 11 or over 16 years of age and, thus, all fitted within Ginzberg's tentative stage of 11 to 16.

REPRINTED FROM *THE PERSONNEL AND GUIDANCE JOURNAL*, 40, 7 (MARCH 1962), 628-629, BY PERMISSION OF THE PUBLISHERS AND THE AUTHORS.

All the children were asked to write paragraphs telling what they would like to be when they grew up and why they had made that particular choice. These papers were then submitted to two judges for classification and tabulation according to Ginzberg's definitions.

Relationships were found by contrasting the boys with the girls; the whites versus the Negroes; the low socio-economic level with the medium group; the total sample with a group which showed reading retardation; and each school with the other.

Fantasy occupational choices were defined as translations of simple needs and impulses into occupational goals. Tentative choices indicated those decisions based upon capacities, interests, and values of the individual.

Race means either Negro or white; reading retardation refers to children of normal intelligence who were retarded in reading as shown by standardized tests; socio-economic environments were arbitrarily classified as low and medium; and intelligence quotients were based upon standardized tests given at the various schools involved.

Results

It was found that in School A, 22 of the 29 girls made tentative choices, while only 6 of the 18 boys did so. In School B, 13 of the 18 girls made tentative choices and 8 of the 16 boys made similar choices. School C supported the tendency of girls to choose more maturely, as 11 of the 14 girls were in the tentative category, in contrast to 8 of the 15 boys. In the total sample, 74 per cent of the girls were in the tentative classification, while only 41 per cent of the boys could claim this maturity. Table 1 shows these data, according to school, sex, and tentative or fantasy choices.

TABLE 1 Tentative and Fantasy Choices in Schools A-B-C

		School A	*School B*	*School C*	*Total*
T*	g	22	13	11	46
	b	6	8	8	22
F	g	7	5	4	16
	b	13	8	11	32
	Total	48	34	34	116

* T indicates tentative choice, F indicates fantasy choices; "g" is girls in the sample; "b" is boys in the sample.

Interesting, too, were the relationships found between intelligence and occupational choice. Results showed that children who have less than 90 IQ made fantasy choices more often than tentative choices. However, the children whose IQ's ranged from 100-129 made over twice as many tentative choices as fantasy ones at the same average age. Table 2 shows the percentage in each IQ group that made tentative and fantasy choices.

TABLE 2 Relationship of Occupational Choice Maturity to IQ

IQ	*70-79*	*80-89*	*90-99*	*100-109*	*110-119*	*120-129*	*Total*
T	0	3	14	28	20	3	68
F	1	10	13	14	10	0	48
Total	1	13	27	42	30	3	116
%-T*	0	23	52	67	67	100	

* %-T indicates per cent of total sample making tentative choice in each IQ group.

When all 116 sixth graders from schools A-B-C were contrasted with 41 with reading retardation, it was found that while only 40.9 per cent of the total sample made fantasy choices, more than 51.0 per cent of the retarded group did so. This indicates that reading retardation may be related to immaturity of occupational choice.

A comparison of School A with the combined totals for Schools B and C showed 58.3 per cent tentative choices and 59.7 per cent tentative choices respectively. Socio-economic level apparently has little or no relation to the occupational choice maturity of the children.

When School A (all white), School C (all Negro) and School B (mixed) were compared, the percentages were: A, 58 per cent tentative, 42 per cent fantasy; B, 62 per cent tentative, 38 per cent fantasy; C, 56 per cent tentative, 44 per cent fantasy. It is difficult to draw conclusions from these last data, because the intelligence level of the students in School A was considerably higher than that of the other schools and there were more girls (proportionately) in School A than in Schools B and C, but it does not seem that race is related in any significant degree with maturity of occupational choice as indicated in this study.

However, much speculation could be made about School B, with the highest percentage of tentative choices of either the white or colored, since School B had almost equal amounts of boys and girls and 68 per cent of the students fell into the normal IQ range (90-110).

Conclusion

It was found that of the 116 12-year-old sixth graders studied, tentative choices were made by 60 per cent of the students. More mature choices seem to correlate positively with intelligence and the feminine sex, and inversely with reading retardation, but not with race or socio-economic environment. On the whole, this study seems to substantiate Ginzberg's theory of occupational choice.

REFERENCE

1. Eli Ginzberg, "Toward a theory of occupational choice," *Occupations,* 30 (1951), pp. 491-494.

Vocational Guidance—How and When

DONALD E. KITCH

Some assumptions upon which a sound program of vocational guidance is based are examined in this article. Procedures which may be of assistance to school people in developing such a program are also suggested.

Each year some two million young people graduate from high schools throughout the United States. Approximately an equal number of youth leave school annually without finishing high school. Each of these individuals faces the task of finding a place for himself in the adult world, a task that grows increasingly difficult as the nation's economy becomes more complex. The future of the nation and the happiness of the individuals themselves depend to an important extent upon the success with which these youth solve the problems associated with finding and undertaking suitable adult roles.

A democratic society makes certain demands upon its youth. It expects each to assume a shareholder's responsibility for the conduct of government at the local, state and national levels. It expects that most of them will undertake the obligations involved in the establishment of a home. It anticipates that each will be willing and able to perform his share of the work that society needs to have performed. To the home and the school are delegated the major share of the responsibility for making certain that each young person, as he approaches adulthood, is prepared to undertake successfully these and other appropriate roles.

Statements of educational objectives have recognized the responsibility of the schools for assisting youth to achieve a satisfactory occupational

REPRINTED FROM *EDUCATIONAL LEADERSHIP,* 10, 6 (MARCH 1953), 364-369, BY PERMISSION OF THE PUBLISHERS AND THE AUTHOR.

adjustment. Recent studies of public opinion indicate that the public expects this type of service from its schools. A public opinion study completed in Pasadena in connection with a recent survey of the schools in that community shows that 84 per cent of the citizens expect the four-year junior high schools to provide assistance in the selection of an occupation and that 85 per cent believe that these schools should offer training for a job or vocation.[1] Recently the Palo Alto Education Council, a citizens' group, studied the opinions of parents in that community as to the services desired from their schools. Two-thirds of the parents believed that the schools should be responsible for helping students select a vocation and 45 per cent felt that every student should be prepared to earn a living by the time he graduated from high school.[2] Indications are that the public is inclined to go along with the educators in respect to the responsibility of the schools for helping young people to work out a satisfactory occupational adjustment.

How can the public schools increase their effectiveness in helping young people to develop sound occupational objectives? In the past, efforts in this direction have been based upon the apparent assumption that decisions concerning occupational goals are arrived at largely through an intellectual process. Efforts have been directed toward helping individual students to gain a better understanding of their interests and abilities, to gain a broader knowledge of their educational and occupational opportunities, and then, through counseling and appropriate group activities, to integrate the two sets of facts into a program of occupational selection and training. Most activity of this type has been developed at the high school and college levels because decisions have to be made at that time as to specific programs and because the intellectual nature of this process seems more suited to that level of maturity.

Assumptions Underlying Program

Perhaps the time has arrived to examine with a critical eye the assumptions upon which such a program of vocational guidance is based. Such an examination need not imply that the procedures are altogether ineffective, but rather that it might be possible to improve upon them. Certainly an important step in the strengthening of the occupational adjustment services provided by schools can be taken if a satisfactory theory as to how occupational choices are made can be stated and tested.

A beginning in this direction has been made by a team of workers at Columbia University. Team members came from the fields of economics, psychiatry, sociology and psychology. The report of their study was published in 1951.[3] A long-term study of a somewhat similar nature is now being carried on under the direction of Donald E. Super, professor of education, Teachers College, Columbia University. It is too early to formulate specific conclusions concerning the exact nature of the occupational choice process, but, on the basis of reports from the above studies and the experiences of persons who have engaged in vocational guidance work, it is possible to suggest certain principles or assumptions that should be considered by curriculum and guidance workers in connection with the development of vocational guidance programs in schools.

1. *The selection of an occupation is the result of a series of decisions that are made over a long period of time rather than the result of a single decision.* These decisions are cumulative in effect in that they tend to limit or condition later decisions. They occur as the result of experiences that are a part of the total growth and development process. Ginzberg and his associates tentatively identify three stages in the decision-making process: fantasy, tentative and realistic.[3, p. 186]

2. *Decisions concerning occupational objectives are strongly affected by nonintellectual factors that frequently exert a subtle and unrecognized influence.* The child who learns to avoid situations that result in dirty hands or clothing does not do so because of intellectual choice. Yet this particular aspect of his personality pattern will limit his later choice of an occupation. The attitudes he acquires from other individuals with whom he identifies strongly may exercise important influences upon his ultimate selection.

3. *The range of occupational choices possible for any particular individual is limited by his knowledge of the possible choices open to him.* From the standpoint of an individual, it may not be important that he know of occupations with which he is not familiar. He can fit into any one of a number of jobs because of his inherent adaptability. From the standpoint of society, it is important that young people be helped to explore the great variety of jobs that make up the labor force. It should be added that knowledge of possible occupational choices must be accurate knowledge if it is to form the basis for a sound decision.

4. *The ability to make an occupational choice is significant evidence of a desirable degree of maturity.* The adolescent who is able to see him-

self as a future adult worker indicates that he has the ability to recognize and accept for himself a socially acceptable adult role. He thinks of himself as the kind of person who can meet the demands of his culture.

Procedures Can Aid Adjustment

From principles such as these, it is possible to draw implications as to procedures that can be followed by curriculum and guidance workers in the development of learning experiences that will help individuals to develop sound occupational goals.

1. *The school's program for promoting occupational adjustment should begin when the pupil first enters school and should continue as long as he remains in school.* This does not mean that something new should be added to the curriculum. It does mean that present curriculum experiences should be examined for the purpose of determining how they can contribute to the objective of occupational adjustment. Many social studies experiences might be reoriented in such a manner as to provide more information concerning occupations or to promote the development of more wholesome attitudes toward certain groups of occupations. "Community helpers" units in some primary grades now make valuable contributions in this respect. Sometimes units in the upper grades tend to emphasize things and processes and to overlook possible opportunities to learn about the people who use the things and carry on the processes. Units on coal or steel, for instance, provide an excellent opportunity to give attention to the many workers involved in these industries and to develop information about the manner in which they carry on their work.

In general, the objective of such experiences in the elementary grades should be the development of a "readiness" for making occupational choices. Expected outcomes might be: (a) the recognition that all citizens of a democratic society are expected to be workers and therefore must select an occupation; (b) the recognition of the social values of all necessary work; (c) a familiarity with the different occupations followed by people in the pupil's own community; (d) an understanding of how different jobs affect individual and family living patterns; (e) an understanding of the relationship of individual interests and abilities to the types of activities involved in different jobs; and (f) some understanding of the individual pupil's own interests and abilities.

2. *Pupils should be given an opportunity to identify positively with*

individuals representing a variety of occupations. Attitudes toward occupations are frequently a reflection of attitudes toward individuals. Parents of pupils or other persons from the school's community might be used as resource persons at appropriate times in order to give children an opportunity to become personally acquainted with individuals following a variety of occupations. Since teachers tend to come from middle-class groups, they probably should control their own tendencies to display attitudes that label some occupations as desirable and others as undesirable. The early development of emotionalized attitudes toward certain occupations tends to limit later choices.

3. *More effective use should be made of non-reading methods of giving youngsters information about occupations.* The development of large industries located in special areas of communities tends to restrict the opportunities of children to make firsthand observations of adults at work. Much of society's necessary work is now carried on in walled buildings or within fenced yards. In suburban bedroom communities many children have no opportunity to observe the work performed by their own mothers and fathers. Young people, therefore, find less opportunity to actually see how work is done by adults while at the same time the work being performed is becoming more complex. The schools should be concerned with the development of a rich fund of concrete experiences in observing adults at work and in carrying on activities that represent samplings of actual work experiences. Such a supply of sensory experiences will help youngsters to develop the ability to derive meaning from symbolized experiences such as those involved in listening, talking and reading. Schools should make more effective use of means of giving occupational information such as the following: planned work experience programs; contrived work experience such as "work days"; role playing and dramatic play; relating class activities to appropriate occupations; providing planned opportunities for observing people at work on jobs; using sound movies, slides, etc.

4. *Parents should be directly involved in educational and occupational planning.* Studies of how young people determine their educational and occupational objectives reveal that parents play an important role in these decisions. Many such studies indicate that adolescents rely upon the advice of parents more than upon the help of teachers and counselors. Undoubtedly the attitudes of parents toward possible alternative choices, conveyed in many ways, have a more important effect in determining choices than even the adolescents are aware. It would seem

wise, therefore, for the school to involve parents directly in important conferences concerning the plans of their students. Such an arrangement provides an opportunity to assist parents as well as students in arriving at sound decisions. A strategic time for an important conference of this type would seem to be just prior to or during the ninth grade when students in many secondary schools are expected to make decisions that influence the remainder of their educational experiences. The effectiveness of such planning conferences for adolescents will be increased if they have been preceded by a regularly conducted series of parent-teacher conferences during the elementary years.

A Basic Program

In summary, the following might be considered a desirable basic program for the development of sound occupational adjustment:

1. *Elementary Grades (1 through 7 or 8)*

(a) Appropriate emphasis, especially in social studies, on learning experiences that give children realistic and concrete knowledge of occupations followed in their own communities. Direct observation and dramatic play are especially suitable techniques.

(b) Learning experiences designed to give children an understanding of their own interests and abilities.

(c) Experiences that result in wholesome attitudes toward all necessary work and a readiness for making an occupational choice when the time comes to do so.

(d) Regular conferences of teachers and parents that will help both to develop a more complete understanding of individual children and the factors that influence their behavior.

2. *Upper Elementary or Junior High Grades (7 through 9)*

(a) Continuation of (a), (b) and (c) above.

(b) Emphasis in all classes upon exploratory values with a special attempt to relate the activities carried on in class to appropriate occupations. Development of courses offering an exploration of important fields of work such as industrial arts and general business.

(c) A special unit in the 8th or 9th grade intended to provide more specific and complete information about educational and occupational opportunities.

(d) A special unit designed to aid each student in developing an understanding of his own values, interests and abilities.

(e) Continuation of conferences with parents and scheduling of a major planning conference for teacher or counselor, parent and pupil during 8th or 9th grade.

3. *Senior High Grades (10 through 12)*

(a) Individual counseling at appropriate intervals concerning educational and occupational plans. Parents should be included in counseling conferences when that is desirable. At least one additional major planning conference should be held with the parents during the 11th or 12th grade.

(b) Continued emphasis in all classes upon the relationship of class activities to occupational opportunities. Provision of needed broad field courses in order to supplement those offered in junior high grades.

(c) Arrangement whereby appropriate courses can be used as try-out experiences by students who have made tentative decisions concerning occupational objectives.

(d) A work experience program through which students can be helped to secure exploratory and try-out experiences in an actual working situation.

(e) Vocational courses suitable to the school and the community through which students can develop skills that will enable them to secure beginning jobs.

(f) A special unit in the 11th or 12th grade in which students who need to do so can reconsider and revise their educational and occupational plans.

REFERENCES

1. Clyde M. Hill and Lloyd N. Morrisett, *Report of the Pasadena School Survey, 1951* (Pasadena, Calif.: Pasadena Board of Education, 1952), p. 72.

2. Wilford M. Aikin, "What Do People Want From Their Schools?" *The Kiwanis Magazine* (May 1952).

3. Eli Ginzberg, Sol W. Ginsburg, Sidney Axelrod, and John L. Herma, *Occupational Choice: An Approach to a General Theory* (New York: Columbia University Press, 1951).

Part Four

COUNSELING WITH THE ELEMENTARY SCHOOL CHILD

Differential Factors between Elementary and Secondary School Counseling[1]

HERMAN J. PETERS

Paradoxical though it may seem, society as a whole must come to the aid of the individual—finding ways to identify him as a unique person, and to place him alongside his fellow men in ways which will not inhibit or destroy his individuality. By its educational system, its public and private institutional practices, and perhaps most importantly, by its attitude toward the creative person, a free society can actively insure its own constant invigoration.[2]

Interest in guidance, and in particular counseling, at the elementary and secondary school has prompted me to raise questions as to either one's singularity of distinguishing hallmarks. It is in the pupil's school career that many of the pristine encounters with one's individuality form patterns of the self. The foundation and direction of a vigorous adulthood of productivity has so very often its nurturing in the school years.

For too long, many of us have been so busy in the doing that we have had little time to challenge our guidance activities. Perhaps more fundamental to our activities is a concern for thinking through the rationale for our guidance procedures. The importance of an intellectual look at our work is well emphasized by the Pepinskys': "Theoretical Approaches, which have the function for gaining and accounting for the

[1] An address given at the American Personnel and Guidance Association Convention, March 25, 1959—Cleveland, Ohio.
[2] "The Rockefeller Report" on Education. Quoted in the U.S. Office of Education Circular No. 553—Guide to the National Defense Education Act of 1958.

REPRINTED FROM *THE SCHOOL COUNSELOR,* 7, 1 (OCTOBER 1959), 3-11, BY PERMISSION OF THE AMERICAN SCHOOL COUNSELOR ASSOCIATION AND THE AUTHOR.

behavior of clients, can serve as useful guides to counselor activities with clients, as in the broad field of scientific endeavor, or behavior science in particular, a theoretical approach to the behavior of clients calls for conceptual rigor."[9, p. 19] With this set, let us proceed to look at some of the differential factors between elementary and secondary school counseling.

The Question

Should we accept the current thinking and research findings in counseling as being fully or partly applicable to the elementary and/or secondary school? Should we be encapsulated in the college and clinic approaches, as excellent as some of them are? Too, are there differences between counseling in the elementary school and counseling in the secondary school? Might we do a better job in counseling in the elementary and secondary schools, if we better understood the distinguishing characteristics that define the counseling relationship?

At this point, it is well to give my definition of counseling. Counseling is a one to one psychological relationship where in privacy a competently trained counselor assists a pupil to think through his concerns. The focus of this paper is on differential factors in counseling rather than the larger area of guidance. Of course, any consideration of differences will overlap with other phases of guidance work. It is hoped that this discussion might serve as a stimulus for research in the area of counseling in the elementary or secondary school.

Some Major Differences

One of the major differences between counseling in the elementary and secondary schools lies within the general framework of the central purpose of guidance in each school level. "Guidance in the elementary school should assist the pupil to develop a harmonious and integrated personality core through carefully planned school experiences which reflect the integration of the forces impinging on the individual. This is in contrast to guidance services in the secondary school which assist adolescents to extend themselves to the optimum in all the various aspects of adolescent and adult living, such as educational planning, career choice, personal relationships, and living with one's self."[6 p. 445] The integration of the various aspects of living begins to change to differentiation during the junior high school years. Thus, this becomes a crucial period for effective counseling of the pupils. The pupil has become accustomed to correlating his behavior with the group during the elementary school years. Then with seemingly disconcerting suddenness the high school student must differentiate his life plans in terms of his unique abilities and interests.

The impact of the organizations of the elementary and secondary schools defines very often the possibilities in counseling. The extended and intensive relationship with one teacher or at most two or three in the elementary school is in contrast to the brief and often superficial relationship with school staff in the secondary school. Unless the elementary school is large, the opportunities for environmental manipulation as an outcome of counseling are non-existent. The flexible structure within the day long elementary classroom permits possibilities for counseling through activity interviews and conferences. The comparatively unstructured time sequence may permit a teacher to engage in his secondary role of counselor with a child in helping him look at his behavior as he progresses through a class activity which allows for differential performances by the many pupils. Other aspects of the organization have their impact on counseling, e.g. the limited or non-existent course choices in the elementary grades versus the increasing number of courses for possible selection in senior high school. Thus, *course* choice is not a problem of counseling in the elementary school. However, should not there be concern for *subject* matter choice in the elementary school? Is it not here that interest must begin for the almost irreversible choice of high school? How may this difference be reconciled in counseling the pupil?

A third major difference is the significantly greater dependency relationship involving parents of elementary school children. Not only the approbation of behavior but also the support of the counseling relationship by the adult is almost a universal when counseling with elementary school children. Although the parental rights continue throughout high school, the very nature of the growing adolescent in our culture reduces the adolescent's concern about what parents think. The paradox of this situation is that in many ways the elementary child has more freedom to act and thus fewer problems for counseling. The adolescent is on the search for maturity and to the dismay of his elders breaks through the limits of behavior as set by the adults. Thus, counseling on the search for meaning is unique to the adolescent and adult as contrasted to the elementary child. Jersild states that, "As they grow older, children tend to become somewhat subdued in their quest for meaning. By the time they have reached adolescence, there are many who have learned that it is not good to inquire too much into the meaning of things. It is this attitude that makes it possible for many adolescents to learn what is assigned at school even when it has little or no personal significance. There are many who do not have as much freedom as they had when they were small to ask questions of what, where, whether, and why? Yet in all adolescents, as in all human beings, this search for meaning is an essential quality and it goes on in various ways."[7, p. 25] Do we through counseling activity help the adolescent in his search for meaning?

Fourth, the nature of the elementary curriculum usually focuses on subject matter which is non-personal in the sense that it does not require a close look at one's abilities and past performances. The secondary curriculum is similar, but because of the parcelled organization of the secondary schools, there are a number, often many, of discrete school events where the pupil is encouraged to look at himself in relation to a program of studies to be selected. This in itself assists some pupils to be in a state of readiness for counseling. Blair and Burton state that in pre-adolescence "if school subjects were so organized as to include the personal and social problems of these children rather than chronological organization of history or the logical organization of geography, opportunity could be provided for these boys and girls to use their abilities to be realistic and begin to see the casual relations in human behavior." [3, p. 73] Does the curriculum make a difference for counseling purposes?

A fifth difference overlaps with the nature of the school and may be tersely stated in terms of the core of psychological development. The focus of childhood psychological functioning is on security, especially in his family relationships. In the junior high school pupil, self-expression seems to be the core from which spring phases of behavior. The senior high school student centers his behavior in terms of peer relationships. Should not many counseling concerns be considered in terms of these key factors determining behavior? More specifically, we will look at the junior high school pupil. Piaget, Isaacs, and Gruenberg[3] report in their individual studies that it is in pre-adolescence that the individual begins to seek reality, objectively, and a concept of self distinguishable from the outer world. Thus, the reports indicate, this gives us some basis for the counseling of junior high school pupils involving dissemination of facts and materials, e.g. vocational information. Insight is also approaching a high level of development, thus affording a more verbalized counseling relationship.

Before discussing more of the differences relating specifically to the counseling process, it is in order to reflect for a moment on who does the counseling in the elementary and secondary schools.

The responsibility for counseling varies greatly between the elementary and secondary schools. Currently, the organizational pattern of the elementary schools gives the teacher the counseling role, secondary only to the instructional assignment. The benefits of this secondary type of counseling must be limited. The high school counselor has counseling as a primary function. Also, the worker usually is strongest in his major role. Therefore, too often the counseling function in the elementary school often becomes a burden rather than an important secondary function. Too many teachers today may do effective counseling by chance rather than on a basis of sound training. Thus, a sixth difference lies in the primary responsibility for counseling in the elementary and secondary schools.

Specific to the counseling process is motivation to seek or to refer one's self for counseling. The adult who seeks counseling comes with a concern. The adolescent may voluntarily seek an appointment with his school counselor. The elementary school child does not come to the counseling setting ready to work on a concern. Probably the child comes sensing that it is he upon whom the counselor (teacher to him) will work. The referral of self would subsume a state of readiness to begin counseling on the individual's concern. Thus, the extrinsic motivation most always required for starting counseling with the elementary school child distinguishes it from the many voluntary self-referrals by adolescents.

As we look more closely at the counseling process, we shall see some areas of profound differences as relates to elementary and secondary school counseling. Although guidance is primarily concerned with normal pupils, we may gain from considering the thinking of those who deal with severely disturbed boys and girls.

Bijou states that "Historically, Anna Freud initially attempted to apply the techniques developed for the neurotic adult to the child. It soon became apparent to her that the child treatment situation differed from that of the adult in many significant details and that techniques applicable to adults would have to be modified. Many other therapists recently concurred with her impressions."[2, p. 611] Perhaps nowhere else is this statement substantiated as in the variance between the child and the adolescent in the capacity to relate feelings and concerns. The child cannot verbalize as extensively as the adolescent nor is he inclined to do so if he does have an unusual verbal capacity. Also, the child is beginning to think through the nature of problem solving but maturationally and experimentally, he has far to go. Too, the capacity to relate feelings is clouded by the child's inability to discern with clarity the differences in his fantasy concerns and those which are fantasy but have the additional ingredient of trouble. Thus, the counseling function in the elementary school runs into a barrier, a rather typical one, of the child's minimal ability to relate his feelings. Too, the emotional tones of adolescence may give pressure to an adolescent to relate his feelings.

A ninth difference is the child or adolescent's concept of time. The younger child views time as NOW. The adolescent can view actions not only in the present but also in the future. He also begins to think back to "When I was a little boy." Thus, the adolescent has a number of reference points other than the immediate present. It is difficult to counsel when one has few conscious time reference points. Behavior as viewed primarily in the present may not seem to the pupil to need revision or change. Behavior viewed as a basis for future action does imply the need for at least a consideration of change to meet the continuing demands of daily living—now and in the future. For the younger pupil, contiguity of behavior with time makes both almost congruent. With the adolescent years there comes a pulling apart of the circle of behavior and its contiguous time dimensions. Thus, there may be an adolescent need to think through next steps in daily living.

The therapeutic relationship in the counseling interview is considered by many to be the vital force for change in the counselee. Certainly it is this phase of counseling, above all others, that the elementary teacher can and often does employ in individual work with boys and girls. The firm yet permissive, the free yet limited, the just never punitive, the authoritative never authoritarian climate can foster changes, often imperceptible, in the sensitive, albeit not fully developed, rational young child. The same might apply to the adolescent in the counseling interview but unless one has unusual artistry in blending the above qualities into the classroom, an overdose can cause bedlam in the secondary school. The adolescent may misinterpret these qualities as boundless freedom. Of course, this does not mean to go toward the negative end of the continuum of teacher control. It does mean that the latitude for positive aspects of the emotional climate may not be as wide in the secondary school as in the elementary grades.

Fully aware that so many of the differences between counseling in the framework of this paper may be a matter of degree, it is, nevertheless, important to consider each because degree of the quality or aspect under consideration may be so slight or great as to preclude its effectiveness in counseling. Counselee responsibility also falls into this category. Robinson in his scholarly work states that "An important goal in counseling is developing willingness in the client to take responsibility for attacking his problems. That is, the client should be able to meet NEW problems on his own or at least need less help than he did before he came for counseling. Growth in such maturity might be measured by judging the degree to which the client takes on responsibility, in successive interviews for clarifying his problems and planning what to do about them."[12, p. 110] Counseling the elementary school may help to give the child more self responsibility but it is certainly not of the magnitude one finds in Robinson's statement which is applicable for older youth and adults. Perhaps in the elementary years, the counselor needs to give reassurance and support, procedures which are polemic in a discussion of counseling of youth and adults.

A twelfth difference may be seen in the adult's perceptions of certain kinds of behaviors in the child which may be referred to as annoyances and which the child may or may not view as hurdles. These same kinds of behaviors in the adolescent become obstacles as they grow in proportion to the individuals fantasying about them. Thus, it becomes difficult at the child level to know whether the child will *grow out* of these annoying behaviors or *grow into* a contumacious individual. Here is but another challenge for the counselor.

At this point let us look, briefly to be sure, at what may be done to think through the counseling function in the elementary grades. Granted that much more needs to be done at the high school level, one can safely argue that more of the adult procedures will work here and that we are lagging behind in investigating counseling for the elementary school boy or girl. Whether one accepts in full, in part or not at all, the psychoanalytic theories, one must give due consideration to the ideas presented by some of its proponents. What Slavson says in the following quotation surely has implications for counseling of children. Slavson states that, "There is a sharp difference between psychotherapy for adults and psychotherapy for children.

"The most outstanding characteristics of a child are his comparatively weak ego organization and his limited ability to deal with inner impulses and external demands. The second difference, which is a direct outgrowth of the first, is the basically narcissistic quality of the child's libido organization, his lack of ego control, hence impulsiveness, his still narcissistic character, hence self-indulgence and feelings of omnipotence. The third distinction is the surface nature of his unconscious. One is impressed with the readiness and almost complete unself-consciousness with which young children act out and speak about matters that are embarrassing to an older person. This can be attributed to the incomplete superego development, the lack of repressive forces (ego), and undeveloped sublimation channels. Finally, the child's identifications are in a fluid state."[13, p. 143]

To me this offers a sound base for re-emphasizing the need for support, reassurance and adult initiative in helping the child. Initiative in the sense of helping the child gain a sense of direction is intended; certainly not blind submissiveness of the child. Thus, the counselor of children asumes more responsibility, not so much for the children's actions as he does for deciding the direction of what is acceptable behavior. To help the child see his purpose in what he is doing is a far better approach than to try, and that's about all one would be doing, to help him see the raison d'être for his behavior. Dreikurs states it well when he says, "An effective discussion with the child should not be concerned with WHY the child misbehaves or fails, why he acts as he does: it should lead to an explanation of the PURPOSE for which he does it."[5, p. 46] Dreikurs continues by emphasizing that it is more important to look at the child and what he wants—than to look at what caused this behavior. "Such interpretations of his true intentions evoke, if correct, an immediate and characteristic reaction. This automatic reaction consists of a roguish smile and a peculiar twinkle of the eyes, a so-called 'recognition reflex.' The child need not say one word, or he may even say 'no'; but his facial expression gives him away."[5, p. 47] Although the sincere and earnest relationship is required in all counseling, it is in this recognition reflex that one may see a different action in elementary counseling than in senior high school. By the time of late adolescence, the boy or girl has learned to a more or less degree to wear the mask of personality. If the relationship exists, the teacher in his counseling function in the elementary or secondary setting may say, "I wonder whether you would like to talk more about. . . .", "Could you be doing this because. . . .", "Perhaps you are trying to do. . . .".

As one reflects on the differences between elementary and secondary school counseling, as one tries to see several steps or ideas that might improve counseling in these boys and girls, the basic question of WHO NEEDS COUNSELING? arises. Do elementary teachers and secondary teachers look in similar ways upon similar kinds of students in terms of guidance help needed. Using the Robinson questionnaire "What Should Be Done?"[11, p. 500] and a modification of it for the elementary school child[11, p. 501], Mangan and I decided to search for similarities and differences. A comparison of the combined participants of 222 elementary and secondary school teachers and the results by elementary and secondary school teachers were made. The teachers were from a variety of schools with a variety of cultural frameworks.

It was interesting to note that a trend existed for more secondary school teachers to recommend intensive counseling and elementary school teachers to recommend special non-conference methods out of the four categories given for rating on the questionnaires.

Each questionnaire contained 14 paragraph descriptions of 14 typical yet hypothetical pupils. The rater then indicated which of the following types of guidance might be best for each pupil:

0 Probably no need for guidance program to work with this student.
1 Routine use made of conferences and activities; nothing especially planned for student at this time.
2 Special plans made to fit this student's needs with particular emphasis placed on non-conference personnel methods, e.g., activities, readings, change of grade, work experience, etc.
3 Special plans made to fit this student's needs with particular emphasis placed on the school providing intensive counseling help.
4 Refer the student to some agency outside of the school for help.

Full realization was made of the fact that these were severely brief character portraits.

In this paper some of the differences between elementary school and secondary school counseling have been set forth. These were differences based on the purposes of guidance.

Several basic points for a reconsideration of the elementary school counseling function were presented: (1) the need to study the theory of the ego organization of the child, (2) the need to use the procedure of explaining the "purpose" rather than the "why" of the child's behavior to the child, and (3) a look at teachers responses to the questionnaire involving who needs what kind of guidance.

In closing let us think of Kowitz and Kowitz's statement pertinent to the topic and as given in their 1959 book, *Guidance in the Elementary Classroom:* "Although there have been a number of advances in therapy with children, few of these are within the area of counseling. The effectiveness of the counseling process with elementary school children is a field which deserves careful study and thorough research."[8, p. 142]

REFERENCES

1. Alfred Adler, *The Education of the Individual* (New York: Philosophical Library, 1958).

2. Sidney W. Bijou, "Therapeutic Techniques With Children," *An Introduction to Clinical Psychology,* eds. L.A. Pennington and Irwin A. Berg (New York: Ronald Press, 1954), pp. 608-631.

3. Arthur W. Blair and William H. Burton, *Growth and Development of the Preadolescent* (New York: Appleton-Century-Crofts, 1951).

4. *Guidance of Children in Elementary Schools* (New York: Board of Education, 1956).

5. Rudolph Dreikurs, *Psychology in the Classroom* (New York: Harper and Brothers, 1957).

6. Gail F. Farwell and Herman J. Peters, "Guidance: A Longitudinal and a Differential View," *The Elementary School Journal,* **57,** 8 (May 1957), 442-445.

7. Arthur T. Jersild, *The Psychology of Adolescence* (New York: McGraw-Hill, 1959).

8. Gerald T. Kowitz and Norma G. Kowitz, *Guidance in the Elementary Classroom* (New York: McGraw-Hill, 1959).

9. Harold B. Pepinsky and Pauline Pepinsky, *Counseling Theory and Practice* (New York: Ronald Press, 1954).

10. Arthur H. Polster, "Counseling in the Elementary School," *California Journal of Elementary Education,* **4,** 1 (August 1935), 51-54.

11. Francis P. Robinson, "Guidance for All: In Principle and Practice," *The Personnel and Guidance Journal,* **31,** 8 (May 1953), 500-504.

12. ———, *Principles and Procedures in Student Counseling* (New York: Harper and Brothers, 1950).

13. S.R. Slavson, *Child Psychotherapy* (New York: Columbia University Press, 1952).

14. Marian Wells, "Counseling the Elementary School Child," *The National Elementary Principal,* **27** (February 1948), 44-45.

Pupil-Teacher Conferences

JOSEPH MORAY

Parent-teacher conferences are now used in many school districts to replace or augment report cards. When our school initiated a conference method of reporting to parents, some of the children in my classroom seemed concerned about what would be discussed with their parents.

"How about having pupil-teacher conferences too?" I suggested.

The children approved. As one child put it, "I want to see what it feels like to have a conference."

When conference week arrived, I found that the pupil-teacher conference had a great many unforeseen advantages. As I conferred with each child, I noted items to discuss with the parents. This procedure saved time in preparation for the parent-teacher conference, which was to come later. I was able to get a picture of the child's view of his relationship with his parents. In addition, some sources of confusion, which I had not been able to discern under regular classroom procedures, were brought to light.

Light on Spelling and Subtraction

As a part of each interview I went over the work that had been saved in the child's cumulative folder. During one conference, a boy and I examined subtraction examples on a test in arithmetic. The boy explained exactly how he had done one example and, at the same time, revealed that he did not understand what to do when there were several consecutive zeros in the minuend. I took time to explain the process. There was a flash of understanding and the exclamation, "Oh, now I get it!"

At another conference the pupil and I observed that long words and

REPRINTED FROM *THE ELEMENTARY SCHOOL JOURNAL*, 58, 7 (MARCH 1958), 335-336, BY PERMISSION OF THE UNIVERSITY OF CHICAGO PRESS AND THE AUTHOR.

long names were often misspelled on his papers. I asked the child to say several of the words slowly, dividing them into syllables. Then I had the child spell the syllables separately. The child was amazed to discover how simply long words could be spelled by this method. The method had been taught before, but apparently the child had not grasped the idea.

A Look at Doubts and Distractions

Sometimes during a conference a child revealed other causes of difficulty. One girl mentioned that the girl who sat next to her was a constant source of distraction. Another pupil disclosed that he was afraid of making mistakes because his parents seemed so critical. Some children showed a lack of self-confidence. The teacher's reassurances in the conference resulted in more relaxed attitudes.

In several conferences I could sense that unexpressed doubts and fears were troubling the children. I made a mental note to try to get these children to feel more at ease in the classroom so that they would be able to express themselves.

A number of conferences brought out no special difficulties but gave an opportunity for the children to learn the levels at which they were working, as revealed by achievement tests. While we went over the test booklets we talked over strengths and weaknesses. The children were greatly concerned when scores appeared to be too low, and they were interested in knowing what they could do to make faster progress. The conference afforded an opportunity to give such information confidentially and to make suggestions to fit individual needs.

When the conferences with pupils and with parents were over, I had the feeling that the interviews with pupils had been just as important as the interviews with the parents. As far as I know, there has been no widespread movement for pupil-teacher conferences. Perhaps we teachers are expected to have such conferences as a matter of course during the school day or before or after school when we feel some special need for them.

Setting a Conference Schedule

It is difficult, however, to concentrate with a child on a specific problem when thirty or forty other children are demanding attention. How can time be set aside during school hours for conferences with children?

I discussed this matter with the children when we were planning our conferences. First we decided that, as far as possible, each child would have a conference on the same day that his parents were to come for their after-school conference. We then decided on the schoolwork that was to be done during the week when most of the conferences were to be held. I duplicated an assignment sheet for all subjects for the week. We arranged our assignments so that there would be several study periods each day. During the week of conferences our class time together was very short, so we had to work on a close schedule.

We agreed that, after the explanations were made for each assignment and while a conference was in progress, no child was to interrupt the conference. Time was allowed at the end of each period for checking or collecting work. There was an extra strain on the children, for they were not used to having so many study periods in one week. Most of us felt, however, that the results were worth the effort.

In the primary grades, where there is a staggered reading program, conferences might be planned during morning and afternoon reading periods. In the upper grades, if regular school time is not available, it is better to hold the conferences before school rather than after classes are dismissed; children may not be in a mood for a conference after school.

We have parent-teacher conferences because we feel that a report card, in itself, does not give a complete picture to the parents. Why not have regularly scheduled pupil-teacher conferences and complete the evaluation picture for the pupils as well?

Teachers will benefit from discovering difficulties of individual pupils and from a confidential exchange of information. During the interview with the pupil the teacher can select material to be used later at the conference with the parents. Children like their conference with the teacher. It gives them a feeling of importance because they are getting individual attention. It also removes the mystery of what happens at parent-teacher conferences.

One girl expressed the feeling of many of the children when she said, "I feel better now that I know what you're going to say to my parents. I was worried before I had my conference."

Play as a Counselor's Tool

GEORGE W. MURPHY

The intent of this article is to summarize psychological literature in an attempt to determine the value of play as a technique for understanding the child, and as a tool for the elementary and junior high school counselor.

The study of play as a means of understanding the child is a comparatively new approach in the field of psychology. It is a technique whereby the child can express his feelings and emotions with something he is familiar.

Rousseau was the first to advocate that the child be educated through play. He offered the suggestion that the teacher himself enter into the play activity.[10] Although Freud used play as a means of therapy, he only touched the surface of its possibilities. Only in the last thirty years have people become interested in play as a technique for better understanding the emotions of a child.

Prior to 1919 little work was done with children, because of the difficulty of utilizing free association as is achieved in adults. Prior to this time no work was done with children under six years of age.[9] After 1919, Melanie Klein and Anna Freud began to employ the technique of play as a means of analyzing children. Melanie Klein feels that the super-ego is highly developed in the child under six years of age, and Anna Freud feels that the child at this age has not developed a complete super-ego.[10]

Since the first use of play as a technique in understanding the child, much has been written about the use of toys, the type of toys, and techniques that should be used. The tools employed have broadened to in-

REPRINTED FROM *THE SCHOOL COUNSELOR,* 8, 2 (DECEMBER 1960), 53-58, BY PERMISSION OF THE AMERICAN SCHOOL COUNSELOR ASSOCIATION AND THE AUTHOR.

clude all types of toys, psychodrama, drawings, fingerpaintings, clay, music, and almost everything that is known to the young child.

Before one can fully understand the use of play as a technique, it is important for him to understand the development of play in the child. Play involves all types of activity, beginning in the very young child. He passes through sequential developmental stages including motor activities of grabbing, picking up objects, and placing special meanings to things. As the child progresses in age, so do his play activities. He begins to incorporate what he has learned in the past to carry out present activities. As he matures his realm widens, first it includes friends in the neighborhood, and then those at school. With each new group of friends his scope of play activities increases.

Many types of play rooms have been described in the literature. In the beginning, Melanie Klein used play in the home of the child as a technique. She felt that the child would relate better in an environment with which he was most familiar After experimentation she found that the child would relate much better outside the home in a setting which was geared for play. By this means the child was removed from the many threats the home offered to his security.[9]

The play room should be kept as simple as possible. With the exception of the basic furniture, the only things which should be there are toys. There should be a sink, and the floor should be washable. The toys should be the type that would instill the child to use his imagination as much as possible to reveal his emotional needs.

It should be emphasized that the type of toy used in therapy is not really important. It is far more important that it be something that will motivate the child to structure as well as endow the materials with conceptional and functional content.[14] Toys used should be inexpensive, for during acts of aggression it is not uncommon for the child to break the toy. It has been suggested that the child's toys be kept locked, allowing only the same child to use the toys each time. This offers the child a sense of security, feeling they are his own and no one elses.[9] Another suggestion is that the child be allowed relative freedom in selecting the toys with which he desires to play.

Studies have been made of the type of toys which are available for the use as tools in therapy with the child. The supply of such toys is practically unlimited, and new ones are coming on the market each day. The following toys are examples of those used to demonstrate motor activity, pattern activity, mechanical activity, and unstructured activity: guns, soldiers, farm animals, baby dolls, telephone, doll family, furniture, trucks, planes, balls, nok-out bench, goose, clay, scissors, plate, pencil, crayons, and paper. The child was then observed to see which toy she picked to best express her needs. It was found that the doll family was chosen most by the child. The conclusion was that she seemed to be able to best express her feelings through this medium.[2]

There are two schools of thought with regard to the manner in which play therapy should be carried out. The first is unstructured play. The child is given complete freedom in his choice of toys, and in setting his own stage for play. In this approach, the therapist becomes an observer, watching what the child does. He may enter into the play on the request of the child, taking whatever part the child desires. The second, is the structured plan. The therapist sets the stage for play, gives the child the toys, and asks him to act out what would happen. The main advantage of this plan is that it enables the patient and the therapist to get to the root of the problem more quickly. It also enables the therapist and child to join forces in order to reach a common goal.[8]

There are certain facts to be kept in mind in dealing with play as therapy. The person should have a genuine respect for the child as a person. At all times he should display patience and understanding. As in any work with a child, the therapist should first understand and accept himself. The therapist should allow himself sufficient objectivity and intellectual freedom in understanding the things the child is attempting to tell him. Sensitivity, empathy, and a good sense of humor are essential qualities demanded of the personality of the therapist.[1]

The child should be helped to understand that he can do anything he likes in the room—that this is his play room. He should also understand that the therapist will not tolerate any physical violence to either himself or the child. Under no circumstances should the adult display any emotion when the child shows aggression and destroys a toy. At the same time, the therapist should not try to force the child to play with a certain toy. He will return to it when he is ready.

In periods of aggression, the child will often destroy the toy with which he is playing. The child will completely ignore the toy for a while, but eventually come back to play with it. Once the child has expressed his aggression and again plays with the toy, he shows the therapist that he has mastered the cause of the aggression and is accepting it in a new light. The child will often discuss how he feels using the doll family to show his emotions.[13]

Often in play therapy the child takes the part of the adult and asks the therapist to take the part of the child. Transference takes place between the child and the therapist. Through his role-playing as a child, the therapist can feel with the child in his dealings with the world of adults. Through this medium the child is given an opportunity to learn about himself in relationship to the therapist.[1]

The statement made by Lawrence K. Frank in his article *Play In Personality Development* sums up the theory behind this technique: "This approach to personality development emphasizes the process whereby the individual organism becomes a human being, learning to live in a social order and in a symbolic cultural world. Thereby we may observe the child from birth on, growing, developing child play as a means to exploring the world around himself." [4]

One of the basic factors reported in the literature was that the toys used with each child should be within his realm of play. A child should not be exposed to toys that are too old for him because he would not be able to express his true emotions through them. By using toys he is used to playing with, the child will feel freer to play and enter into the world of make-believe. The adult observing him will also obtain a truer picture of what the child is experiencing.

In order to do any work with children it is necessary for the person (psychologist, analyst, or a school counselor) to understand children and have a desire to work with them. The qualities of acceptance and empathy are the most important qualities. It is essential that the person working with the child accept him as he finds him—advancing the child forward from that point toward mutual understanding of the problem. It is also necessary that the adult understand, as well as feel, what the child is experiencing if he is to be enabled to help the child.

In general all the authors were in agreement concerning the type of toys that can be used. The writer found two main differences of thought expressed in the literature. First, there is disagreement regarding the importance of the strength of the super-ego in the young child. Second, authors do not agree on the merits of using the structured techniques or the unstructured. In the case of the first, this writer feels, the therapist will be guided by his own psycho-analytical theories. This should not produce a disagreement. Basically it is a difference in ideals and training. The second difference involves the technique employed, and this will be determined by the amount of training of the therapist, as well as his ability to understand what the child is trying to say through play.

It was a general fact that the doll family was considered the best means of getting the child to express his true feelings about the home situation. When this device is used, it is important to keep the doll family limited to the size of the child's family. Quite often the child will destroy the person within the family that is causing the problem. This may be done by either breaking the doll, completely ignoring it, or stating that he is going to send him away. It is not uncommon for feelings of guilt to follow the removing of the threat to his security. Eventually, the child will again include the doll that had been left out of the play. When this happens the therapist knows that the child is showing acceptance of the problem, and is ready through the world of make-believe to attempt to cope with his personality conflicts.

Everyone agrees that it is extremely important for the person in therapy to be non-emotional. He should not show any display of emotion if a toy is destroyed. By keeping control, the therapist helps the child feel that the room is a place he can do as he pleases. Usually the first time the child destroys an object, he will look at the adult for rejection. When this is not forthcoming, it will give the patient the security of acceptance. This is one of the basic factors in the use of play therapy. It helps the child understand his personality, and its relation to himself as well as the world around him.

Play therapy is a comparatively new and underdeveloped field. Its scope is wide—ranging from toys to art and music. This paper has dealt only with the use of toys employed to help the therapist better understand the child.

The three objectives of the study were to determine: (1) the value of play in understanding the child, (2) the possible use of play by the school counselor, (3) the extent to which it could be applied to the junior high school.

Due to the child's lack of ability to understand himself and the world around him, play therapy is an invaluable tool. It allows a trained person to observe the child in a certain setting. In adults this is done through talking and reasoning, using past experiences. Due to his limited experience, the child is not capable of doing this. Through the use of play, he can accomplish what the adult does by talking.

The use of this technique in our schools can be very helpful to the counselor in his efforts to aid the child to understand himself. However, it is important that the counselor *always* keep in mind that he is *not* a trained psychologist, or therapist. It should never be used to analyze a child, for that is not the counselor's job. With training, this technique could become a valuable tool to the school counselor as he endeavors to help the child achieve maturity and self realization.

The use of toys in the junior high school guidance program is not advisable. The main objection is that chronologically the majority of junior high school pupils have little interest in toys. At this age, the child has the power to reason. Play can be used in the junior high school through such techniques as music, draw a person, draw a house—a tree —a person, finger painting, scatter drawing, and psycho-drama.

REFERENCES

1. Virginia M. Axline, "Play Therapy Procedures and Results," *American Journal of Orthopsychiatry,* **25** (1955), 618-627.

2. Helen R. Beiser, "Play Equipment for Diagnosis and Therapy," *American Journal of Orthopsychiatry,* **25** (1955), 761-771.

3. J.H. Conn, "Play Interview Therapy of Castration Fears," *American Journal of Orthopsychiatry,* **25** (1955), 747-755.

4. L.K. Frank, "Play in Personality Development," *American Journal of Orthopsychiatry,* **25** (1955), 576-591.

5. L.K. Frank, R.M. Goldenson, and Ruth Hartley, *Understanding Children's Play* (New York: Columbia University Press, 1952).

6. Gesell and F. Ilg, *The Child From Five to Ten* (New York: Harper and Brothers, Publishers, 1946), 359-374.

7. T.F. Graham, "Doll Play Phantasies of Negro and White Primary School Children," *Journal of Clinical Psychology,* **11** (1955), 11-25.

8. G. Hambridge, "Structured Play Therapy," *American Journal of Orthopsychiatry,* **25** (1955), 601-618.

9. Melanie Klein, "The Psychoanalytic Play Technique," *American Journal of Orthopsychiatry,* **25** (1955), 223-283.

10. D. Lebo, "The Development of Play as a Form of Therapy," *American Journal of Psychiatry,* **12** (1955), 418-442.

11. C.E. Moustakas and H.D. Schalock, "An Analysis of Therapist-Child Interaction in Play Therapy," *Child Development,* **26** (1955), 143-157.

12. Jean Piaget, *Play, Dreams, and Imitation in Childhood* (New York: W.W. Norton, 1951), 147-168.

13. J.C. Soloman, "Play Technique and the Intergative Process," *American Journal of Orthopsychiatry,* **25** (1955), 591-601.

14. A.G. Woltman, "Concepts of Play Therapy Techniques," *American Journal of Orthopsychiatry,* **25** (1955), 771-784.

A Day in the Life of an Elementary School Counselor

BARBARA QUILLING

What does an elementary school counselor do? I have been asked this question a number of times and have always had difficulty giving a simple but satisfactory response. I decided that one way of describing my work was to keep a diary of my activities. What follows is a chronological statement of my activities on January 29, 1962, a typical school day.

8:15 In school—discussed with third grade teacher that we found a visual difficulty in testing one of her students last week and suggested that she might want to change his seat in class.

Obtained from seventh grade teacher a physical exam report on counselee.

Picked up cumulative records on teacher referrals.

8:45-9:00 Went into sixth grade class—teacher ill, substitute on her way.

9:00-9:15 Regular Monday A.M. discussion with principal on referrals, parent contacts, testing, etc.

9:15-9:30 First grade boy—4th contact. Superior intelligence, counseling for acceleration to 2nd grade this Wednesday—culmination. Groundwork has been laid with counselee, his parents and present teacher.

9:35-9:50 First grade boy (teacher and parent referral)—2nd contact—aggressive behavior in class, not adjusting to move into new

REPRINTED FROM *GUIDANCE JOURNAL*, 1, 3 (WINTER 1961), 59-61, BY PERMISSION OF THE PUBLISHERS AND THE AUTHOR.

house and riding school bus. Became ill and could not sleep nights for fear he would miss school bus. Seems to be improving about bus situation and home adjustment—classroom behavior still disturbing.

9:55-10:25 Two seventh grade boys (self-referrals) discussed separately their results on the *Henmon-Nelson Tests of Mental Ability* in relation to school subjects, high school and vocational plans.

10:25-10:35 First grade boy (teacher referral). Problem: lack of cleanliness.

10:35 Call State Department of Guidance and Testing to reserve film on *Iowa Tests of Basic Skills* to be used for seventh grade parents night on February 7.

10:40-10:50 Coffee break with intermediate teachers.

10:50-11:00 Fifth grade boy—4th contact—has not been completing home assignments or class work. With his permission, I had talked to his mother by phone about a stated study period at home. Mother had not mentioned call or study! He feels he is doing better!

11:00-11:15 Sixth grade girl (teacher referral)—new student, an underachiever, her teacher feels. Will schedule her for next *Henmon-Nelson.*

11:15-11:30 Eighth grade boy (self-referral) study help in American Democracy.

11:30-11:40 Eighth grade boy (self-referral) seeking help in writing to colleges about missionary study.

11:40-12:10 Fifth grade boy—2nd contact (teacher referral). Living in trial home for adoption. Has had very poor home in past. Teacher is trying to help him adjust to new home and school. Counselee is constantly disrupting class to brag about his new material wealth. Likes school very much and is achieving.

12:10-1:00 Lunch

1:00-1:15 Seventh grade boy (teacher referral). Very nervous—achieving but acting out in class. Teacher has counseled with effectiveness so far this year—but feels child now needs new face!

1:20-1:35 Seventh grade girl (self-referral). Desired further explanation of *Iowa Test of Basic Skills* profile and study helps.

1:35-1:50 Sixth grade girl (self-referral). Peers are calling her names and refusing to play with her.

1:55-2:10 Third grade girl (teacher referral). Under-achiever—second contact.

2:10-2:20 Conferred with second grade teacher about first grade boy coming to her class on Wednesday.

2:30-2:50 Eighth grade girl (self-referral). For ability evaluation.

2:50-3:05 Called to principal's office to talk with eighth grade female counselee who is receiving 4 F's out of 6 subjects.

3:10-3:15 Eighth grade pupil in to return and discuss career pamphlets.

3:20-3:45 Recorded data on interviews. Returned records to teacher. Closed shop for the day.

❧ Part Five

GUIDANCE AND THE LEARNING SITUATION IN THE ELEMENTARY CLASSROOM

Special Part-Time Classes for Emotionally Disturbed Children in a Regular Elementary School

An Experimental Project of the Willowbrook School School District, Los Angeles County[1]

JOHN W. HOWE

THE PROBLEM: EMOTIONALLY DISTURBED CHILDREN IN REGULAR PUBLIC SCHOOLS. Where are the future patients of our mental hospitals and inmates of our jails? Today many of them are in our public schools. They are the children who are overly angry and aggressive, overly fearful and withdrawn, overly confused and bizarre. Their teachers refer to them as emotionally disturbed.

Harried as these children are, they cannot profit fully from education. The emotional disturbance makes it impossible for them to get along well with teachers or other children, or to work well at their studies. These children need help. Our schools have legal provisions for taking care of children's *physical* needs. Schools can even give children free food, for we know that "you can't teach a child when he is hungry." But

1 Administrative and supervisory personnel of Willowbrook School District at the time of this study, 1953-54 and 1954-55, were: Mr. Ronald C. Henderson, Superintendent; Mr. Arthur E. Prince, Assistant Superintendent; Mrs. Lillian K. Commons, Director of Special Services; Dr. Earl F. Carnes, University of Southern California, Director of Guidance (part-time); Mr. Stanley M. Brozovich, District Psychologist and Special Class Teacher; Mr. Lloyd D. Dickey, Principal; Mr. Charles W. Depue, Principal; Mr. James G. Faustina, Principal; Mrs. Geneva B. Daniel, Principal; Mr. Tom W. Evans, Special Class Teacher; and Mr. Louis King, Special Class Teacher.

REPRINTED FROM *THE SCHOOL COUNSELOR,* 5, 2 (JANUARY 1958), 26-33, BY PERMISSION OF THE AMERICAN SCHOOL COUNSELOR ASSOCIATION AND THE AUTHOR. THE AUTHOR IS CONSULTANT IN RESEARCH AND GUIDANCE, LOS ANGELES COUNTY SUPERINTENDENT OF SCHOOLS OFFICES.

what about *emotional* needs? Can you teach a child when he is angry? . . . Frightened? . . . Confused? . . . When he is hungry, not for food, but for emotional security? What provisions should the schools have for meeting children's emotional needs?

APPROACH IN WILLOWBROOK. A new school approach to the problem of emotionally disturbed children has been tried out in the Willowbrook School District of Los Angeles County. It is essentially a modification for use in an educational setting of the activity group therapy techniques of S.R. Slavson.[1]

Following is a brief narrative account of how the Willowbrook School District embarked on this project in October, 1953, and carried on the special class sessions from March, 1954, to June, 1955.

HOW THE PROJECT STARTED. A copy of the Slavson film [2] "Activity Group Therapy," was reviewed and purchased by the Office of the Superintendent of Schools, Los Angeles County. From this office a consultant brought the film to the Willowbrook School District where it was studied and discussed by the forward-looking Superintendent and administrative staff. After much careful study, they concluded that the method could probably be adapted for use in a regular public school setting. As far as could be learned, this clinically-developed method had not been used previously in an ordinary non-specialized elementary school. It seemed worthy of trial, despite some risks and uncertainties.

TEACHERS' OPINIONS SOUGHT. After the administrators had concluded that such a project might be possible, a meeting of the third, fourth, fifth and sixth grade teachers was held to see whether they also favored the experimental project. They were given a chance to see the film, ask questions, make suggestions, and approve or disapprove of the tentative research plans. Almost unanimously the teachers favored the project. They seemed heartened by the prospect of more systematic help for the emotionally disturbed children in their classrooms. They expressed the feeling that some such help was generally needed throughout education, and that it was perhaps overdue.

CONFIDENTIALITY OBSERVED. All parties agreed to keep the project confidential at first so as not to prejudice the outcome by premature comments from inside or outside the school district. No breach of this professional confidence ever occurred during the entire research period.

TEACHERS REFER CANDIDATES AND PERTINENT DATA. The teachers were then invited to suggest a list of possible candidates for the "Activity Clubs" (the name given to the special classes to suggest pleasant connotations rather than stigma—an *extremely* important point). Along with the names of selected pupils, the teachers submitted educational data and anecdotal records to give a picture of the child as possibly emotionally disturbed. Teachers were helped in making their selections by a suggested list of symptoms for which they could be watchful.[2] Additional data on each child was furnished by principals, nurses, the district psychologists, the director of welfare and attendance, and the school physician[3] either by examination or from files already on hand. Psychiatric advice on the planning of the project was furnished by a psychiatrist from the State Department of Mental Hygiene.[4]

SELECTION AND COMPOSITION OF THE CLASSES. When all the data had been assembled, the administrative and supervisory staff very carefully drew up the lists for the first classes. As a safety factor, and in order to aid in comparison, interpretation and evaluation, it was decided to begin the program with at least *two* such classes and two teachers. A third class under a third teacher began in September, 1954. In order to escape or minimize possible misunderstandings or criticisms, it was also decided to include in each class at least one child from each ethnic group in the community (Negro, Mexican and Anglo) and one child from each of the four elementary schools in the district. Ages ranged from approximately ten to twelve years at time of entrance to the class. Boys only were accepted. (It was planned to add two girls' groups in the future.) The children were drawn from the third, fourth, and fifth grades so that they could remain in the program *at least two years* before graduation to junior high school. Educationally retarded children were accepted, but not mentally retarded.

"MOST SERIOUSLY DISTURBED" SELECTED. Since there was room in the first two classes for a total of only twelve children, the most seriously disturbed children were chosen for the program. This probably constituted the least ideal operating condition and the most severe test for the program.

COUNTERBALANCING THE PERSONALITY TENDENCIES. Each class was purposely overweighted at first with more of the withdrawn, shy children

[2] Dr. Earl F. Carnes, Associate Professor, Department of Educational Psychology and Guidance, University of Southern California, prepared a "guide sheet" of symptoms or behaviors to help teachers observe and identify possible cases of emotional disturbance.

[3] Dr. Andre R. Tweed, psychiatrist, Los Angeles, served as school physician for the project.

[4] Dr. Simon J. Conrad, Director, Los Angeles State Mental Hygiene Clinic, very kindly gave this valuable aid.

than of the aggressive, hyperactive types. This was done in order that later on the necessary number of hyperactive children could be *added* (rather than having to eliminate any child) in order to achieve satisfactory *counterbalancing* between underactive and overactive tendencies in the group.

Therefore, at the first meeting of each "club," only four boys were present: two withdrawn, one "miscellaneous" or effeminate, and one hyperactive-aggressive. At the second, third, or fourth meeting, one or two more hyperactives were added, care being taken not to overbalance the group in this direction.

DURATION AND SCHEDULES. The clubs met *once a week* for a *two-hour session* over a *two-year period*. The sessions were purposely scheduled for the last hours of the school day, 1:30 to 3:30 P.M., in anticipation of the fact that the hyperactive-aggressives might find it difficult to return immediately from the club activities to the more restricting limits of the regular classroom.

ANTICIPATED DIFFICULTIES. Much possible trouble was anticipated in connection with the activity clubs:

1. *Parental opposition rare.* It was thought that some parents might object to placement of their child in the project. After candidates had been selected, the principals conferred with the parents individually and confidentially, explained the nature of the project, and allowed the parents to *request* placement of their child if they so desired. In all except one instance, parents were already aware of their child's special needs, and requested such placement.

2. *"Bad name."* It was thought that it would be very difficult to prevent the spread of rumors that this was a club for "bad boys" and that the pupils themselves might tend to resist placement. This prediction *was* well-founded. Several of the boys made remarks in the first few weeks such as: "We know you are trying to help us," "Joe S—— should be in here. He's about the worst boy in our school." The presence of the "good" withdrawn boys and the permissiveness of the "Club," however, counteracted these ideas effectively in time. Within a few months, the administration found it had successfully cultivated the notion that the "Activity Club" was a privilege; the number of requests by pupils to get into the clubs was seen to rise steadily. In each room which was to have a boy in the program, teachers announced the plans for the Club, mentioned that it would be necessary to get the principal's permission, and managed to "select" the pre-determined candidate and one or two oth-

ers from the numerous enthusiastic volunteers. The principal then "selected" the candidate from among the teacher's "selections."

3. *Leaving class.* It was feared that a great deal of guarding would be necessary to keep the boys from running wild *outside* of the room, etc. In order not to have the non-directive teacher step out of his role, some consideration was given to installing a concealed buzzer by which the principal might be alerted to look for "unauthorized visitors in the hallway." The buzzer was never installed, but the principal happened to be present in the hallway and was useful in this capacity on a few occasions. In one class the teacher solved this problem early by saying "Let's not go outside, boys. It'll get us all in Dutch with the office." The teacher of the other class held off mentioning the problem for several months and had a little more trouble; he finally made a similar statement, with similar good results.

4. *Bodily harm.* Mayhem was the first and worst of the anticipated fears. It did not actually develop in any group. This is perhaps the more noteworthy and meaningful in view of the plentiful baiting and scuffling that did ensue, especially in the earlier sessions. There were numerous occasions when the teachers were fearful about possible injuries, though they did not show it. But the boys seemed to set their own limits short of any real injury, for none occurred.

PHYSICAL EQUIPMENT, ROOM, MATERIALS, TRANSPORTATION, ETC. The room and materials chosen for the activity clubs were of the simplest, crudest, and least expensive kind. A large storeroom, somewhat apart from neighboring classrooms, was fitted up with a circular drop-leaf kitchen table, two work benches, scrap lumber, scrap sheet metal (copper), woodworking tools, paints, clay, plaster, paper, crayons, games, etc.

The children were brought from the surrounding schools either by the assistant principal, the principal, or by the director of welfare and attendance. The conversations among the boys on their trips to or from the class often provided valuable additional clues as to their personal problems, feelings and thoughts.

ONE-WAY VISION SCREEN "HOMEMADE." A one-way vision screen was placed *high* in the wall near the ceiling, at one corner of the room. It looked like the covering of an ordinary ventilator. The screen was "homemade" from very fine mesh copper wire, purchased at a local hardware store, sprayed lightly with aluminum paint on one side and dark paint on the other. The observation niche behind this screen was kept darkened at all times and observers in this niche were never discovered by the pupils. This screen is cheaper than one-way vision glass; and it is unbreakable. It also permits *sound* as well as sight to reach the concealed observer, so that remarks can often be heard. Optically, it is not quite as satisfactory as one-way glass.

TEACHERS OF THE SPECIAL CLASSES: QUALIFICATIONS, ROLE IN THE GROUP. In addition to the regular teaching credential, the teachers chosen for the special classes possessed previous experience of a psychological nature. All three had done counseling with young adults and teen-agers. It was agreed ahead of time that they would strive to follow as nearly as possible a neutral, non-directive, and non-verbal role within the group. If the situation were to get out of hand and correctional measures were needed, it was agreed that these would be undertaken by the building principal. In two years, nothing occurred which necessitated sending for the principal, or sending anyone to him. His presence in the hall was helpful in returning boys to the room on one or two occasions, as has been mentioned.

BASIC THEORY AND ASSUMPTIONS. The underlying theory or assumptions behind this experiment were as follows:

The emotionally disturbed children were given a chance to employ or abandon their behavior patterns of withdrawal or aggression and their other symptoms in a group of peers so selected that the opposite behavior tendencies *counterbalanced* each other as nearly as could be arranged. The *interaction* between the children with opposite behavior patterns tends in time to oppose or "level off" the extremes, so that the withdrawn become more active and stimulated, and the hyperactive become more conforming and less impulsive. All the children, including the effeminate or otherwise disturbed child, tend in time to *identify* with the other group members and to adopt their more "regular" patterns of behavior. In addition, all the group members tend in time to identify also with the calm, mature, matter-of-fact *adult* teacher.

ROLE OF THE SPECIAL TEACHER. The teacher tries to remain as calm, neutral, permissive, acceptant, uninvolved and casual as possible, without being so aloof as to appear cold or unnatural. His presence undoubtedly is somewhat restrictive and tempering for the hyperactives, but facilitative and supportive for the withdrawns. He does not strive for deep rapport, nor does he employ highly verbal methods. This would immeasurably complicate *his* job, and probably interfere with therapy by the *group*.

LIMITED CONSCIOUS EFFORT. The behavior changes in the group

characteristically take place slowly through time, and by "acting out." They take place more or less *unconsciously* (little or no conscious effort being demanded of the student), rather than by verbal-conscious-insight methods. It is to be noted that many of the children in the special classes were relatively non-verbal and non-achieving in academic subjects in the regular classroom; verbal-conscious-self-examination is not their strong forte, nor a good avenue of therapy for them.

During the two-hour period, the boys were given little or no direction, instruction, or suggestion. They were left almost entirely on their own to select any or no particular activity. Some structuring of their activity did occur in the form of materials left exposed to view by the teacher. There was some evidence that when restlessness was high in the class, it was channeled constructively by the presence of semi-structured materials, such as boards pre-cut to make racks or boxes, patterns traced on sheet copper ready for tooling, etc.

REFRESHMENT PERIOD: VALUES FOR TEACHER'S OBSERVATION AND FOR GROUP ACTION. The last half-hour of the class was spent around the small circular kitchen table where inexpensive refreshments were furnished from the school cafeteria, such as peanut butter, graham crackers, orange juice, milk, etc. This had the value of creating a situation where interaction of each member with all the others was possible. It provided an opportunity for the group to act or plan as a total group if it wished. Also the teacher was enabled to observe the total group from a somewhat better vantage point and to hear meaningful verbal exchanges.

TEACHERS KEEP NOTES. After each meeting of the special class, the teacher wrote up the highlights of the activities he had been able to observe and remember. These were rich in detailed personal and interpersonal observations. Like all good anecdotal records, they attempted to give an *objective* account of the observed speech or behavior, *before* making interpretations based on this data. Mimeographed charts of the room were sometimes used to graph the positions or movements of the boys during five-or-ten-minute intervals. The teacher's anecdotal records became the chief source for studying and/or evaluating the development of the individuals and the group over the period of time.

MONTHLY OR SEMI-MONTHLY STAFF MEETINGS. Semi-monthly staff meetings were held to review the teachers' records, consider variations of routines, replacement of those boys who had moved with their families to another district, etc. Rather full notes and records were kept of all staff meetings from the time the project was first contemplated. Copies of these records are available in limited supply for confidential loan to other school districts interested in similar experimentation.[5]

EVALUATION. A complete clinical evaluation of each case, before and after the therapy experience, was recognized as desirable and necessary for scientific evaluation of the effectiveness of the program. Unfortunately, the entire project had to be accomplished without any special budget and it was impossible to secure such definitive pre-study and post-study data. In lieu of such data, though certainly not as a sufficient substitute, the following brief subjective impressions of the staff and the teachers are mentioned.

WITHDRAWN CASES APPEAR IMPROVED; HYPERACTIVES LESS SO. The workers on the project who observed the groups from the beginning, and who studied the weekly anecdotal records, believed they noted a definite increase in activity and confidence on the part of the "withdrawns" in all cases. Hyperactives appeared still noticeably active, though less hostile, less inclined toward serious fighting, and more inclined to engage in good-natured horseplay. Perhaps this represented a socialization of the hostile impulses into more acceptable channels of humor and sports. The regular classroom teachers also reported a seeming improvement in the withdrawns in most instances; in a few instances they reported improvement for the hyperactives also. In one case, a worsening of the hyperactive condition was suspected, but the teacher was not certain of this, nor was the staff.

CONCLUSION. From the fact that three special classes were carried on with no known untoward effects, it would appear that at least one definite conclusion may be drawn from this project at the present time:

It *is* possible within the *ordinary educational setting* of a regular public school, and with the aid of certain specialized personnel, to *employ the group activity techniques* developed and utilized for more than twenty years by S.R. Slavson[6] and known to be successful for many emotionally disturbed children.

It was the opinion of the research team that the results of this pilot project warrant further study and replication. There is little doubt that Slavson's methods are effective with emotionally disturbed *school children at the clinic.* Why not *at the school,* if employed there?

[5] These notes were kept and compiled by Mrs. Lillian K. Commons, Director of Special Services, to whom inquiries should be addressed, at Willowbrook School District, 1855 East 126th Street, Willowbrook, Los Angeles County, California.

[6] As examples of related methods and investigators, see References 3, 4, 5, and 6.

Future replications should tackle at least two important considerations not dealt with here: (1) *How* effective is the method in each individual case at school? To determine this, full clinical data will be needed on each child *before* and *after* the two-year period in the special class. (2) How feasible, effective, and advisable is it, in the school setting, to set up and maintain monthly group therapy meetings or other regular contacts with the parents of the special class children?

REFERENCES

1. S.R. Slavson, *An Introduction to Group Therapy* (New York: International Universities Press, 1943).

2. ———, "Activity Group Therapy" (film), Nathan Hofheimer Foundation (New York: Columbia Communication Materials Center, Columbia University, 1950).

3. August Aichorn, *Wayward Youth* (New York: Viking Press, 1935).

4. Bruno Bettelheim, *Love Is Not Enough* (New York: Free Press of Glencoe, 1950).

5. Gisela Kenopka, *Therapeutic Group Work with Children* (Minneapolis: University of Minnesota Press, 1949).

6. Fritz Redl and David Wineman, *Children Who Hate* (New York: Free Press of Glencoe, 1951).

Classroom Teacher Guidance in Relation to Learning Activities

FRANCES G. KOENIG

The classroom teacher is rapidly becoming a guidance counselor and group leader of the children who live with her on an average of five hours daily for ten months each year. What does this mean in terms of the classroom situations that call for learning? New insights into the dynamics of child behavior and personality must become an integral part of the teacher's philosophy if she is to be instrumental in the educative process.

The major strivings, the goals, which each individual hopes to achieve, and the purposes and ambitions of all of us stem from our more or less forgotten childhood dreams and aspirations. In the process of becoming culturized, of being accepted by our peers, and of being impressed by customs and mores, we face frustrations, tensions, coercions, and inhibitions. The emotional tone with which we live is often set for us in our school days and earlier. Whatever the forces that impinge upon us, we become the personalities that we are. Whatever the stresses in childhood, we carry with us the end-result into our adulthood.

Teachers are often faced with problems which demand solutions quickly so that the children in their classes can learn at a fairly normal pace. Here is the case of Arthur, in the fourth grade, nine years of age, failing in reading and refusing to play games with the other children. His mother, called in by his teacher, came to realize that he was not a dull boy, but that he had something disturbing him. She saw a consultant psychologist, who helped her understand that the boy had developed a fear of his father. He had constantly been criticizing the boy's reading

REPRINTED FROM *UNDERSTANDING THE CHILD,* 20, 2 (APRIL 1951), 40-46, BY PERMISSION OF THE PUBLISHERS AND THE AUTHOR.

aloud at home, telling him that he "mumbled" his words and that Arthur would do better if he were to listen to his father's reading. Along with this came the fact that the father was an avid baseball fan and would go to games very often.

With an intensive period of psychotherapy, Arthur began to feel that he did not have to be like his father and that he could develop his own interests and aptitudes. The psychologist had several sessions with his father and mother. The father then began to take Arthur to ball games and to show an interest in his son's activities. His teacher guided him toward the security he needed in school and soon he was eager to tell his classmates about the games he had seen. He was also given every opportunity to read to the others and soon became a reader all wanted to hear. His general feeling of belonging and of being liked rose to a marked degree.

Paul, seven and a half, in the third grade, is the kind of boy frequently misunderstood. He had been complaining of pains in the knee joints for some time. The teacher, again the guide, and this time toward better health, called his mother to school to discuss this problem. When she was told by the mother that he often had these pains at home while being prepared for bed, they both realized the pressing need for medical examination. His physician found nothing organically wrong. The mother, meanwhile, had been rubbing Paul's knees with, if you please, cold cream, and, to her amazement, the pains always left him upon application. He was taken to a child psychologist who discovered that he has felt rejected by his parents ever since his little sister was born (then two years old). His parents were induced to change their methods of handling the children; as a consequence, Paul's pains disappeared completely in six months. He now felt that he did not need this method of getting affectional security from his mother. With great interest on the part of his teacher, with frequent words of praise, and with classroom chores for him to perform, he is becoming a well-liked boy. He enjoys school and home and is eager for accomplishment.

It was the fine insight of their teachers that saved these two boys from frustrations and emotional tensions that would have become stumbling blocks to normal learning and to healthy personality.

The teacher at once becomes a catalyst and an inhibitor in a learning situation. She can encourage many natural reactions as well as retard those which are frowned upon in social living. She can reduce to a shorter time element the period required for developing the skill subjects, the group activities, the creative experiences inherent in the child but needing a creative and well-trained teacher to help him express those qualities within him. On the other hand, she can retard those reactions which may be anti-social, explosive, egocentric and pre-delinquent so that socially acceptable inhibitions may function without any ill effect and with preventive force. The school influences the mental health of the next generations and promotes better social understanding when the teacher is oriented toward a satisfactory resolution of the conflict between personal desires and social standards. It devolves upon the teacher, then, to support the ethical conventions of the school system which employs her. She should consciously guide the children toward emotional security through affection and educational direction.

It must be remembered also that while the child may be considered lazy, lacking in persistence, irritable, or passive, it is essential for the teacher to look for physical and/or emotional causes. These factors are, in reality, symptoms, rather than behavior patterns.

Initiating Group Activities

In various group situations teachers often ask themselves why some children begin an activity with eagerness, interest, and zest only to lose the cooperative effort required to complete a task. Do some children evince spasmodic or superficial interest in the different activities? Often it seems as if the child has physical or emotional discomfort; more cooperation has been asked for in the particular group situation than such children are emotionally or socially able to give. The alert and understanding teacher will guide toward better social relations by permitting a child to work within the group which contains his closest friends.

The egocentric child finds great difficulty in submerging himself in a group. Contrary to popular opinion, he is in reality not self-confident, but overbearing and inadequate. He hopes that by centering attention upon himself his basic insecurities will be overlooked. The neurotic child will create disturbances in the classroom because of his lack of security within himself and lack of normal experiences with other children.

There is a tremendous need of extra guidance time and facilities to redirect and reeducate, to find the causes and to enlist the aid of the parents of such children so that they can become better adjusted to group living with its give and take. The classroom teacher cannot be expected to treat such children, but she can take cognizance of these possibilities and assist where she can.

Creative Activities

The teacher is told much concerning the child's adjustment to school life in his response to music, poetry, dancing, color, form, and the plastic arts. The tense, inhibited child, fearful of letting himself go in aesthetic experiences, and more greatly in need of them than the mentally healthy child, tries to ignore his feelings by tightening his control over them by repressive measures. Here is the case of Michael, eleven and a half years of age, who not only is the child of a broken home, but also has epileptic seizures. He constantly refused to partake in any learning experiences through aesthetic means. He would insist on doing arithmetic drill work when the children were working with puppets, dancing, or painting. At such times he became extremely pedantic and compulsive and insistent upon the teacher's attention toward him. Betty began by being class housekeeper and expressed a desire to clean up after the groups had completed their handwork and construction so that everything would look clean and neat once more. Both children had to repress their emotions so much that they could not enter into freedom of motion for a long time.

Puppetry, peep shows, scroll stories, and music often call out reasoned or intellectual responses in children. Where this is so, the emotional nuances are lacking. However, with teacher stimulation of individuality and spontaneity, as in the use of puppetry in the language arts, in dancing and rhythms, emotional responses come far more easily and with greater relaxation and friendliness. It must be remembered that creative expression often appears crude, unimaginative, or prosaic at the outset and seems to be lacking in educative values. Yet this very permissive environment and self-expression brings to the fore the status and role of the children in the classroom. This is shown in the characters and the words and actions the children choose. They give insight into the present mood. If the child feels at ease in the teacher's presence or if he needs more time to thaw out, the teacher should be aware of the possibilities for more active participation. She should slowly inculcate the desire on the part of those children who ask to be the backdrops for various dramatic forms of expression to step out of this passive role into a more active and personal one.

Recent experiences have pointed up the fact that children who can experiment with color seem to adjust with greater ease to other learning situations and can relax and enjoy themselves. On the other hand children who are inhibited or frustrated, anxious or unhappy at home, express themselves by smears, muddiness, daubing of one color over another with no organization or representation. It has been noted that after several such experiences these children seem more relaxed and more easily integrated into the group. Repetition of the same mood in color and form gives the teacher a clue to the dominant emotional tone in the child. It may even expose some serious mental disorder. Here is the case of Manuel, seven years of age, who smeared finger paints daily for two months. He used the green color only. Each day when asked by his teacher to tell the story of his picture, he would give the same answer in Spanish, "Tripa" (meaning *intestines*). The teacher recommended investigation and study of this boy. He was taken to the mental hygiene clinic of a city hospital and then hospitalized for observation. Shortly before entering the clinic the teacher had him join a group therapy situation in the school. Later, institutional care was advised by the psychiatric division of the hospital. This shows one of the possibilities toward discovery and care, prevention and direction, which can be fostered through the use of free expression in painting.

It has also been found that freedom of choice in the type of story or composition the child writes in class reveals individual differences in interests, style, and content. It is advisable for the teacher to write impersonal comments on the child's composition paper in order to reassure him that he is safe in developing his own honest thoughts, that he will not be ridiculed, that what he says is wholly acceptable to her.

Guiding Intellectual Development

It is known that the ability to follow directions in learning situations grows with the years in school. Normal six-year-olds should be able to follow three directions when the task at hand is made concrete and when the directions are to be carried out immediately. However, when there is to be a delay between the directions and the carrying out of the job, single directives should be given; one order should be carried out at a time.

Academic achievement cannot stand alone. It must be coordinated with the physical, emotional and social development of each child. All of these phases integrated into a whole must be included in the measuring rod used for grade norms. Studies have shown that those children with greater intellectual ability are able to pursue more interests with greater intensity than those with lower intelligence. In spite of this fact, some of them perform their tasks with great unevenness in accomplishment. This may be due to physical discomfort or to some disturbance in the emotional life of the child. The teacher must constantly be aware of this possibility.

It is also known that the ability for abstract thinking is not developed in younger children. All ideas and concepts must be concrete. Slower learners must have such concrete experiences throughout the grades. In fact, many normal children have been found to prefer concretized learning through the sixth grade. The ability for abstract thinking seems to come with quickening maturity. Thus children in the upper grades are able to weigh facts, to choose from two or more plans and to reserve judgment. As he grows older, the child will see more details through the broadening of his experiences. This affects his ability to speak, to take part in plays and assembly programs, to dramatize, to write more fluently and to tell a tale. He has a sounder memory system which he utilizes through cues that aid him in the recall of learned facts. It is not necessary to teach older children through concrete memory experiences. Children in the upper elementary grades can recall accurately, even after several weeks have elapsed, facts which had been learned in the classroom. Some factors in the lack of recall, however, are the lack of attention in the initial learning situation, a below-normal average in intelligence, or an unconscious avoidance of retention in what may have been a painful experience. On the other hand, there are children who find security in facts and build a large memory system on them.

Guiding Emotional Development

Many teachers have found children in their classrooms who seem to need constant reassurance from adults in order to create confidence in their own ability. Some children depend on personal approval to such an extent that they even attach themselves to the more autonomous members of the class. Others are handymen or housekeepers and do many simple chores so as to be rewarded by the approval of the teacher or classmates. There are still others who collect, distribute, and return play equipment while the other members of the class are participating in the games.

Our culture seems to demand a levelling down of emotional expression. Yet we do not realize that many children of school age have an extremely warm feeling tone toward others. It is too bad that in the process of becoming culturized many children learn to repress more and more. If the teacher can capitalize on the various gradations of emotional responses in her children she will find them happier and more eager to learn and participate in group work.

In problem situations there are many children who are emotionally immature. Some evade or deny the problem. They should be assisted by the teacher in developing self-confidence and assurance in attacking problems and trained in the skills of handling them.

We have heard a great deal about freedom and flexibility in classroom programming. It is true that children like an ordered day for personal satisfaction and security, but there is no need for rigid time allotment. It is best to shift from one activity to another with ease. Some egocentric children become so absorbed in what they are doing that they are not conscious of group needs. On the other hand, there are children who are emotionally so immature that a much shorter time span should be planned for each activity than would be considered average for the grade and age. The individual differences of the children then become the constants rather than the 15 or 30 minute periods set aside for each phase of learning.

Some Principles

The child will have a thrill of pride in his own achievement when a small word of praise is given by the teacher and when he is given approval by his own group. It is important for the teacher to remember to stress the child's progress in relation to his own past achievement so that neither the bright nor the dull child will feel discouraged. It is imperative to remember to use the standard of the child himself as a standard of comparison. In her attitude toward him, the teacher can elicit a sense of wellbeing from him in some athletic skill, in the neatness of the room, in a hobby, in his management of a chore, or in his part in a program for the assembly.

In order that the child may achieve affectional security in the classroom, it is important for him to have legitimate opportunities for gaining attention. For example, the particularly aggressive child can enter into dramatic play or into a "Show and Tell" period. Through this means a need for "the center of the stage" can be gratified and a release of deep-seated emotional attitudes can be achieved. Many such children are rejected at home. The teacher becomes a mother substitute and the school a family substitute. Emotionally insecure children gain social recognition and attention through these helpful surrogates for parental love that is often lacking.

Strangely enough, many teachers maintain a strict barrier between themselves and their children. A good principle for the teacher to follow is one in which she can become personal and confidential and one in which she is not afraid to lay aside her professional mask. However, some children must be made to realize that their classmates also have her interest and that they must share in the cooperative living. The teacher realizes, of course, that this affectional security should come from a normal family life. However, since this is often denied to these children at home, and since they are constantly seeking for it, the substitute home (the classroom) functions in this direction.

In assisting the day-dreaming child who escapes from difficult problems, the teacher can gather the content of his phantasy life through various types of composition and themes, such as "Things I Dream of Doing" and "My Three Wishes." She can encourage imaginative storytelling to reveal the direction of the child's phantasy life. She can encourage him to talk and write about his ideas of himself. It is a sound mental hygiene principle to let the child know the requirements and training necessary in order to become the grown-up person of his dreams. It has been said that one does not have to become Cinderella in order to have a moderately enjoyable time at a classroom party. This principle, which leads him toward the reality world, is one which will carry him through many trying periods.

Beginning Early

Since we must all face some type of authority in society at one time or another, it is important for the child's training to begin early. First, he must adjust to school situations where he will learn to accept the authority of the teacher, not because she is the "superior" figure, but because she is the guiding factor in his learning. He must learn to accept the competition of others in his classroom and to find satisfaction in doing things for himself. The weight of the group in democratic living can be utilized to overcome violent reactions to school authority because of over-indulgence or neglect or unwise authority at home. It is advisable to use as few commands as possible with children who have repressive authority at home, as well as to ignore the defiance of an egocentric child. A choice of action may be given him and a reasonable explanation offered for any request made of him.

Many teachers have been known to offer objections against treating the individual child in the classroom. It is true that all of us resent emotional favoritism, but if we are aware of the needs of such children and offer them differential treatment with a rational basis for it, the other children will understand this and often offer help for children requiring this special care. We are well aware of the differences in the children in our own classrooms. Let us then maintain sound attitudes toward those children who have problems.

The relationship that is built between the teacher and the individual child is the most important factor for sound mental health. In spite of the many evaluations made pro and con concerning progressive versus traditional education, the indications are that while progressive education has many advantages over the traditional type, something has been lacking in both in regard to achieving sound mental health for all the children. In a healthy relationship between the teacher and her children, there appears a permissiveness in the environment—a permissiveness to be themselves, a permissiveness to be understood, to be accepted, to have their feelings recognized, to have their thoughts clarified—permissiveness to help children retain their self-respect. The derisive term "Let the little dears express themselves" had become an insulting byline for those people who lacked the understanding of child development or who lacked the appreciation of the value of self-expression.

❧ Fundamental Drives

It is known that all children, like all normal adults, have fundamental drives and urges which, if fostered through mental hygiene principles and practices leading toward sound mental health, will result in feelings of belonging, being liked, knowing that they are wanted, and creating out of their own experiences. It is also true that certain aspects of frustration are desirable. It was J.F. Brown who said, "Without any blockage, the individual remains a mediocrity, stupid, unimaginative, with 'cow-like content.'" It must also be remembered that the culture of a particular society constantly impinges upon the personality development of each child. He arrives in school with an already accumulated pattern of thinking, feeling, and acting. He already is dependent on a social group. He already has been exposed to the stresses and strains of living in a society. When the teacher is truly a guiding factor in learning activities, she can help the aggressive child displace his aggression onto inanimate objects through group activities, through aesthetic experiences, and through spontaneous play. She is never afraid of "wasting" time. It is in such situations that the child releases his frustrations and reduces the tensions which weigh him down. The child who is fast developing introverted features in his personality will be drawn into expressing himself with greater ease. Extremes in either direction, passivity or aggressivity, which lead to neurotic patterns, are slowly but surely eradicated under the able and expert guidance of a creative teacher.

Behavior Problems of Children as Viewed by Teachers and Mental Hygienists

A Study of Present Attitudes as Compared with Those Reported by E.K. Wickman

GEORGE A.W. STOUFFER, JR.

In 1928 a study was published which has been described both as "a classic investigation"[1] and as "one of the most illuminating and interesting studies in the field."[2] This was E.W. Wickman's *Children's Behavior and Teacher's Attitudes.*[3] The study has been widely quoted and, as the author of this paper discovered, it is also very often misquoted, or variously interpreted. Even though it was conducted twenty-five years ago, the inclusion of data from it in recent books in the field of mental hygiene indicates that it still exerts considerable influence on contemporary thinking in that field.

So influential has Wickman's study been in shaping public and professional opinion that it was thought worth while to repeat it, in an attempt to ascertain whether the passage of twenty-five years had produced any measurable change in teachers' attitudes toward children's behavior, and whether any new problems of child behavior confronted today's teachers.

In the present study, which follows the pattern established by Wickman, rating scales were submitted to teachers in elementary schools and to mental hygienists—psychiatrists, psychologists, and psychiatric social workers—in child-guidance clinics. On these scales teachers and mental hygienists recorded their judgments as to the degree of seriousness of each of 50 behavior problems of children. The raters were directed to

REPRINTED FROM *MENTAL HYGIENE,* 36, 2 (APRIL 1952), 271-285, BY PERMISSION OF THE PUBLISHERS AND THE AUTHOR.

make their ratings at any point on a scale that was descriptively captioned to indicate an ascending degree of seriousness, from minimal concern on the part of the rater to judgment of the problem as a grave one. The calibrated rule contained twenty equal divisions, to facilitate statistical treatment of the data obtained.

One questionnaire—Form A—was administered to teachers, with a set of directions for completing it. This form duplicated in every respect the one completed by the teachers in Wickman's original study. A second questionnaire—Form C—was rated by the mental hygienists who coöperated in the study, duplicating the one submitted by Wickman to his group of mental-hygiene experts. The mental hygienists were furnished with their own set of directions and conditions under which they were to rate the various problems. These were different from those given the teachers. A third questionnaire—Form B—was administered to the same teachers who had completed Form A. In this form the directions and conditions for rating were the same as those under which the mental hygienists had made their ratings on the 50 problems.

A brief explanation may be in order as to how the directions and conditions for rating differed for the various forms. The conditions for rating the behavior problems on Form A included a time limit, and the directions were worded with the aim of obtaining the rater's immediate impression and, perhaps, emotional reaction to a current situation. On Forms B and C, which were identical, there was no time limit for completing the ratings and the wording of the directions was aimed at getting the raters' intellectualized attitude toward a problem, not as to its effect at the moment, but as to how they thought it would affect a child's future development. This modification of Wickman's procedure was made to meet criticisms of his findings growing out of the lack of uniformity in the directions and conditions for the rating of the scale by teachers and by mental hygienists. In brief, an attempt was made to find out whether the teachers' ratings differed when they used the two different sets of directions and conditions.

The 481 male and female elementary-school teachers who coöperated in the study were chosen as a representative sample of teachers from all parts of the country, teaching pupils of various racial extraction and socio-economic status, in rural and urban schools, with a variety of educational philosophies. The 70 mental hygienists participating included psychiatrists, psychologists, and psychiatric social workers on the staffs of thirteen child-guidance clinics throughout the country. The over-all sampling closely approximated the one used by Wickman.

When the data were collected and evaluated, the relationship between the rating of the 50 problems of child behavior by the teachers of Form A and by the mental hygienists on Form C was recorded as shown in Table 1. Table 2 shows a rank-order comparison of today's teachers' ratings (Form B) and those of the mental hygienists when both groups were using identical questionnaires.

The results both of inspection and of statistical treatment showed that today's teachers, psychologists, psychiatrists, and psychiatric social workers were in much closer agreement as to the seriousness of certain problems of children's behavior than they were twenty-five years ago. This appears in our first comparison, Table 1, in which we used Wickman's procedure of furnishing the teachers and the mental hygienists each with their own set of directions and conditions for rating the behavior problems; and an even greater similarity in attitude is found when both groups were given the same directions and conditions for rating.

The data on the ratings by teachers and by mental hygienists were organized to appraise the agreement of these two groups of people who are concerned with child behavior and mental hygiene. This was done by three methods of examination. First, we considered the relative position, in the rank-order arrangement as to seriousness, assigned respectively by the teachers and the mental hygienists of today to the various problems of children's behavior. Little in the way of agreement seems apparent in an examination of Table 1. No item of behavior in the teachers' column is in juxtaposition with the same item in the mental hygienists' column. Of the ten problems rated the most serious by the teachers, and, therefore, appearing as the first ten in the rank-order arrangement, only two are found in the ten rated most serious by the mental hygienists. At the other end of the rank-order arrangement of the problems, of the ten rated least serious by the teachers, only four are found in the last ten positions in the rating by the mental hygienists.

Further examination of the problems ranked in order of seriousness by the teachers and the mental hygienists reveals that the most marked differences in the ratings are in the following behavior items:

Disobedience	Smoking
Impudence, rudeness	Masturbation
Impertinence, defiance	Heterosexual activity
Disorderliness in class	Obscene notes, talk
Profanity	Unsocial, withdrawing

TABLE 1 A Rank-Order Comparison of the Ratings by Today's Teachers (Form A) and Mental Hygienists of the Relative Seriousness of 50 Behavior Problems of Children

	Teachers (Form A)	*Mental Hygienists*
1.	Stealing	Unsocial, withdrawing
2.	Cruelty, bullying	Unhappy, depressed
3.	Heterosexual activity	Fearfulness
4.	Truancy	Suspiciousness
5.	Unhappy, depressed	Cruelty, bullying
6.	Impertinence, defiance	Shyness
7.	Destroying school material	Enuresis
8.	Unreliableness	Resentfulness
9.	Untruthfulness	Stealing
10.	Disobedience	Sensitiveness
11.	Resentfulness	Dreaminess
12.	Temper tantrums	Nervousness
13.	Unsocial, withdrawing	Suggestible
14.	Obscene notes, talk	Overcritical of others
15.	Nervousness	Easily discouraged
16.	Cheating	Temper tantrums
17.	Selfishness	Domineering
18.	Quarrelsomeness	Truancy
19.	Domineering	Physical coward
20.	Lack of interest in work	Untruthfulness
21.	Impudence, rudeness	Unreliableness
22.	Easily discouraged	Destroying school materials
23.	Suggestible	Sullenness
24.	Fearfulness	Lack of interest in work
25.	Enuresis	Cheating
26.	Masturbation	Selfishness
27.	Laziness	Quarrelsomeness
28.	Inattention	Heterosexual activity
29.	Disorderliness in class	Restlessness
30.	Sullenness	Inattention
31.	Physical coward	Impertinence, defiance
32.	Overcritical of others	Slovenly in personal appearance
33.	Sensitiveness	Tattling
34.	Carelessness in work	Obscene notes, talk
35.	Shyness	Laziness
36.	Suspiciousness	Stubbornness
37.	Smoking	Attracting attention
38.	Stubbornness	Thoughtlessness
39.	Dreaminess	Imaginative lying
40.	Profanity	Disobedience
41.	Attracting attention	Carelessness in work
42.	Slovenly in personal appearance	Masturbation
43.	Restlessness	Impudence, rudeness
44.	Tardiness	Inquisitiveness
45.	Thoughtlessness	Disorderliness in class
46.	Tattling	Tardiness
47.	Inquisitiveness	Interrupting
48.	Interrupting	Profanity
49.	Imaginative lying	Smoking
50.	Whispering	Whispering

TABLE 2 **A Rank-Order Comparison of the Ratings by Today's Teachers (Form B) and Mental Hygienists of the Relative Seriousness of 50 Behavior Problems of Children**

	Teachers (Form B)	*Mental Hygienists*
1.	Unreliableness	Unsocial, withdrawing
2.	Stealing	Unhappy, depressed
3.	Unhappy, depressed	Fearfulness
4.	Cruelty, bullying	Suspiciousness
5.	Untruthfulness	Cruelty, bullying
6.	Unsocial, withdrawing	Shyness
7.	Truancy	Enuresis
8.	Impertinence, defiance	Resentfulness
9.	Cheating	Stealing
10.	Easily discouraged	Sensitiveness
11.	Resentfulness	Dreaminess
12.	Destroying school material	Nervousness
13.	Suggestible	Suggestible
14.	Heterosexual activity	Overcritical of others
15.	Domineering	Easily discouraged
16.	Temper tantrums	Temper tantrums
17.	Selfishness	Domineering
18.	Nervousness	Truancy
19.	Disobedience	Physical coward
20.	Laziness	Untruthfulness
21.	Impudence, rudeness	Unreliableness
22.	Lack of interest in work	Destroying school material
23.	Fearfulness	Sullenness
24.	Sensitiveness	Lack of interest in work
25.	Carelessness in work	Cheating
26.	Masturbation	Selfishness
27.	Overcritical of others	Quarrelsomeness
28.	Quarrelsomeness	Heterosexual activity
29.	Obscene notes, talk	Restlessness
30.	Enuresis	Inattention
31.	Slovenly in personal appearance	Impertinence, defiance
32.	Sullenness	Tattling
33.	Physical coward	Slovenly in personal appearance
34.	Shyness	Obscene notes, talk
35.	Suspiciousness	Laziness
36.	Inattention	Stubbornness
37.	Stubbornness	Attracting attention
38.	Tardiness	Thoughtlessness
39.	Disorderliness in class	Imaginative lying
40.	Dreaminess	Disobedience
41.	Thoughtlessness	Carelessness in work
42.	Profanity	Masturbation
43.	Attracting attention	Impudence, rudeness
44.	Inquisitiveness	Inquisitiveness
45.	Restlessness	Disorderliness in class
46.	Imaginative lying	Tardiness
47.	Tattling	Interrupting
48.	Interrupting	Profanity
49.	Smoking	Smoking
50.	Whispering	Whispering

It would appear that these problems, all of which seem to represent an objective type of behavior, might be thought of as problems that outrage the teachers' moral sensitivities and authority, or that frustrate their immediate teaching purposes. According to the ratings by the mental hygienists, however, only the "unsocial, withdrawing" behavior could, with reasonable certainty, be considered as representing a serious future to the school child's stability.

Since this first appraisal of the relative seriousness assigned to the behavior problems of children by the two groups did not seem to be too productive, an examination of the data in a more precise fashion was made.

An evaluation for agreement or disagreement between the teachers and the mental hygienists was made by examining the means of their ratings on the same items of problem behavior for statistically significant differences. This technique revealed that today's teachers and mental hygienists were in substantial agreement as to the importance of the following behavior problems of children:

Resentfulness
Nervousness
Domineering
Easily discouraged
Suggestible
Sullenness
Physical coward
Restlessness
Imaginative lying
Thoughtlessness
Lying

In Wickman's original group of teachers and mental hygienists, only two problems, "cruelty" and "temper tantrums," were assigned about the same degree of seriousness by the clinicians and by the teachers. Of the eleven items about which the mental hygienists and teachers now find themselves in agreement, in Wickman's study there was complete disagreement as to the seriousness of "resentfulness," "easily discouraged," "suggestible," "physical coward," "imaginative lying," and "domineering." All of these problems, with the exception of "lying" and "thoughtlessness," were characterized by Wickman as "problems describing the withdrawing, recessive personality and behavior traits"[3, p. 126] or as "extravagant, overdetermined personality and behavior traits."[3, p. 128]

The behavior problems that the clinicians rated as more serious than did the teachers include:

Unhappy, depressed
Unsocial, withdrawing
Overcritical of others
Sensitiveness

Fearfulness	Shyness
Enuresis	Suspiciousness
Dreaminess	

Again it would appear that overt, objective behavior is rated as more serious by the teachers, and a subjective type of behavior by the mental hygienists. However, more agreement between the two groups than was found in Wickman's original inquiry seems clearly to emerge.

In a third method of evaluation correlations were obtained by arranging the means of the ratings by the mental hygienists of the respective behavior problems of children in order of seriousness from the highest to the lowest, and listing opposite the corresponding values for these behaviors as judged by the teachers. The matched means were then converted into ranks, which in turn were converted into per-cent positions. The per-cent positions were changed to "scores" by the use of Hull's table. In computing the coefficient of correlation between the above matched scores, Pearson's product-moment formula was employed.

Wickman reported a coefficient of correlation of minus .11 between the rank-order arrangements as to seriousness of the problems of child behavior as rated by the mental hygienists and by the teachers. In the present study a coefficient of correlation of plus .52 was secured when Wickman's original procedure was duplicated (teachers' Form A and mental hygienists' Form C), and a coefficient of correlation of plus .61 was obtained when Wickman's procedure was modified to provide both groups with the same directions and conditions for rating the problems (teachers' Form B and mental hygienists' Form C).

In a comparison of the ratings by today's teachers and by the teachers of twenty-five years ago, shown in Table 3, it was found that problems relating to honesty, sex, truancy, and to classroom order and application to school tasks are rated among the most serious of the 50 problems of behavior by today's teachers, as they were by the teachers of Wickman's study. However, several of the problems concerned with withdrawing, recessive personality traits—*i.e.,* unhappiness, depression, unsociability, and withdrawing—have moved toward the top of the list as rated by today's teachers. Masturbation has dropped sharply in the teachers' estimation as a serious behavior problem. Interesting changes in position downward as to seriousness are those of smoking and profanity, in which there were striking shifts in position.

On the ratings for obscene notes, masturbation, and heterosexual activity there were large standard deviations of the means, indicating con-

TABLE 3 **A Comparison of the Rank-Order Arrangement of 50 Behavior Problems of Children as Rated by 481 of Today's Teachers (Form A) and 511 Teachers in E.K. Wickman's Study**

	Wickman's Study	*Present Study*
1.	Heterosexual activity	Stealing
2.	Stealing	Cruelty, bullying
3.	Masturbation	Heterosexual activity
4.	Obscene notes, talk	Truancy
5.	Untruthfulness	Unhappy, depressed
6.	Truancy	Impertinence, defiance
7.	Impertinence, defiance	Destroying school material
8.	Cruelty, bullying	Unreliableness
9.	Cheating	Untruthfulness
10.	Destroying school material	Disobedience
11.	Disobedience	Resentfulness
12.	Unreliableness	Temper tantrums
13.	Temper tantrums	Unsocial, withdrawing
14.	Lack of interest in work	Obscene notes, talk
15.	Profanity	Nervousness
16.	Impudence, rudeness	Cheating
17.	Laziness	Selfishness
18.	Smoking	Quarrelsomeness
19.	Enuresis	Domineering
20.	Nervousness	Lack of interest in work
21.	Disorderliness in class	Impudence, rudeness
22.	Unhappy, depressed	Easily discouraged
23.	Easily discouraged	Suggestible
24.	Selfishness	Fearfulness
25.	Carelessness in work	Enuresis
26.	Inattention	Masturbation
27.	Quarrelsomeness	Laziness
28.	Suggestible	Inattention
29.	Resentfulness	Disorderliness in class
30.	Tardiness	Sullenness
31.	Physical coward	Physical coward
32.	Stubbornness	Overcritical of others
33.	Domineering	Sensitiveness
34.	Slovenly in personal appearance	Carelessness in work
35.	Sullenness	Shyness
36.	Fearfulness	Suspiciousness
37.	Suspiciousness	Smoking
38.	Thoughtlessness	Stubbornness
39.	Attracting attention	Dreaminess
40.	Unsocial, withdrawing	Profanity
41.	Dreaminess	Attracting attention
42.	Imaginative lying	Slovenly in personal appearance
43.	Interrupting	Restlessness
44.	Inquisitiveness	Tardiness
45.	Overcritical of others	Thoughtlessness
46.	Tattling	Tattling
47.	Whispering	Inquisitiveness
48.	Sensitiveness	Interrupting
49.	Restlessness	Imaginative lying
50.	Shyness	Whispering

siderable variance of opinion among today's teachers as to the seriousness or importance of these three problems. Wickman's teachers had disagreed most markedly on "smoking" and "nervousness," as judged by the size of the standard deviations.

A separate evaluation of the ratings of the male elementary-school teachers was made. When the ratings of the male teachers were matched against those of the entire group, including these male teachers, no item was rated by the male teachers as being more serious than by the entire group of teachers. However, the following behavior problems were rated as less serious or less undesirable:

Heterosexual activity	Impertinence, defiance
Masturbation	Unreliableness
Physical coward	Disobedience
Smoking	Temper tantrums

This may indicate that there are measurable sex differences between male and female teachers in attitude toward certain problems of behavior.

It was discovered that while teachers have changed their attitudes toward the behavior problems of children in the past twenty-five years, there has been little change in the attitude of mental hygienists, as shown in Table 4. The change, however, can best be determined by examining the statistical significance of the difference of the means of the ratings of the two groups of clinicians. When this was done, it was found that the psychiatrists, psychologists, and psychiatric social workers of today's child-guidance clinics rated 37 of the 50 problems of child behavior exactly as had the mental hygienists of twenty-five years ago. On the remaining 13 items, there were few marked reversals of attitude or shifts in opinion, as measured by the evaluation of the seriousness or importance of certain problems. Of the 13 changes, Wickman's mental hygienists rated the following problems of more importance than did the mental hygienists of today:

Suspiciousness	Physical coward
Resentful	Sullenness
Overcritical of others	Selfishness
Easily discouraged	Stubbornness
Domineering	

Problems regarded as more serious by today's clinicians are:

Enuresis
Destroying school materials
Restlessness (overactivity)
Disorderliness in class

The increased importance of enuresis might possibly be explained upon the basis of the increased psychological significance attached to it as an evidence of underlying emotional maladjustment, rather than as a purely medical problem. It would seem that the problems that the mental hygienists of twenty-five years ago found more important than do those of to-day largely represent subjective behavior. Behavior that the present-day group thought more important than did the group of twenty-five years ago would seem to represent objective behavior. The coefficient of correlation between the rating by the mental hygienists in Wickman's study and those in the present study was found to be a plus .87.

To determine whether today's teachers were confronted with any new behavior problems of children, other than those reported by the teachers of twenty-five years ago, 232 of today's teachers, of all grades, were asked to report and rate the undesirable behavior of their pupils. The only new problems of behavior were "reading comic books" and "watching television." When teachers were asked to evaluate the problems they had listed as to seriousness or importance, it was found that their ratings of the problems were uniformly similar to the rating of the same problems supplied by the investigator.

The majority of the items listed by teachers as undesirable represented what children do rather than what they fail to do. In analyzing the lists of problems, it would seem that the behavior-problem child in school is still, as he was twenty-five years ago, identified chiefly by annoying, disorderly, irresponsible, aggressive, untruthful, and disobedient behavior. Teachers of today, however, are not so oblivious to behavior indicative of social and emotional maladjustment as were those reported in Wickman's inquiry.

All the evidence would seem clearly to indicate that the passage of years has brought changes in teachers' recognition, understanding, and practice in the area of the mental hygiene of the social child. The teachers' changed attitudes might be attributed to a change in the total social and, in particular, school situation as it exists today. If we accept the judgment of the psychologists, psychiatrists, and psychiatric social workers as an adequate criterion, we can authoritatively say that teachers

TABLE 4 A Rank-Order Comparison of the Ratings by the Mental Hygienists of Wickman's Study and Those of the Present Study on the Relative Seriousness of 50 Behavior Problems of Children

	Wickman's Study	*Present Study*
1.	Unsocial, withdrawing	Unsocial, withdrawing
2.	Suspiciousness	Unhappy, depressed
3.	Unhappy, depressed	Fearfulness
4.	Resentfulness	Suspiciousness
5.	Fearfulness	Cruelty, bullying
6.	Cruelty, bullying	Shyness
7.	Easily discouraged	Enuresis
8.	Suggestible	Resentfulness
9.	Overcritical of others	Stealing
10.	Sensitiveness	Sensitiveness
11.	Domineering	Dreaminess
12.	Sullenness	Nervousness
13.	Stealing	Suggestible
14.	Shyness	Overcritical of others
15.	Physical coward	Easily discouraged
16.	Selfishness	Temper tantrums
17.	Temper tantrums	Domineering
18.	Dreaminess	Truancy
19.	Nervousness	Physical coward
20.	Stubbornness	Untruthfulness
21.	Unreliableness	Unreliableness
22.	Truancy	Destroying school materials
23.	Untruthfulness	Sullenness
24.	Cheating	Lack of interest in work
25.	Heterosexual activity	Cheating
26.	Lack of interest in work	Selfishness
27.	Enuresis	Quarrelsomeness
28.	Obscene notes, talk	Heterosexual activity
29.	Tattling	Restlessness
30.	Attracting attention	Inattention
31.	Quarrelsomeness	Impertinence, defiance
32.	Imaginative lying	Slovenly in personal appearance
33.	Impudence, rudeness	Tattling
34.	Inattention	Obscene notes, talk
35.	Slovenly in personal appearance	Laziness
36.	Laziness	Stubbornness
37.	Impertinence, defiance	Attracting attention
38.	Carelessness in work	Thoughtlessness
39.	Thoughtlessness	Imaginative lying
40.	Restlessness	Disobedience
41.	Masturbation	Carelessness in work
42.	Disobedience	Masturbation
43.	Tardiness	Impudence, rudeness
44.	Inquisitiveness	Inquisitiveness
45.	Destroying school materials	Disorderliness in class
46.	Disorderliness in class	Tardiness
47.	Profanity	Interrupting
48.	Interrupting	Profanity
49.	Smoking	Smoking
50.	Whispering	Whispering

have grown in their knowledge of how the school child develops and behaves.

While we may be gratified by the increased degree of similarity in attitude toward the behavior problems of children by the teachers and clinicians of today, we cannot ignore the fact that a difference still does exist. In comparing the attitudes of the mental hygienists and the teachers, one must recognize the differences in professional interests. The psychologist, the psychiatrist, and the psychiatric social worker are interested solely in the social and emotional adjustment of the individual child. Society has caused the chief interest of the teacher to be the educational achievement of the child. Does the public think that the teacher's job is that of a social engineer, engaged in promoting the all-round growth and development of pupils, or that of a filling-station attendant whose job it is to fill the tank in the child's mind with subject matter? All persons connected with schools know that children are sent to school to be "educated." Social pressures seem to operate to the disadvantage rather than the welfare of the child. The teacher cannot escape this pressure in determining his or her chief interest; and it is important to remember that no such pressure is brought to bear upon the psychologist, the psychiatrist, or the psychiatric social worker, who usually works in the seclusion of his office, isolated from the many potent and influential forces of the community.

In interpreting the comparative ratings in a study of this sort, it should be remembered that the teachers, in rating behavior items like "masturbation" and "truancy," were probably making their evaluations, particularly on our Form A of the rating scale, in terms of a larger perspective than the more restricted professional horizon of clinicians. Teachers are undoubtedly aware of the dire consequences for the child, the school, and the teacher if community opinion is outraged by a violation of conventional sexual taboos. Similarly, their concern about truancy is understandable. How can you reach the goals of education, largely community prescribed, if the pupils fail to attend classes?

In assessing the total picture of the attitudes of teachers and those of mental hygienists toward the behavior problems of children, one cannot but wonder if there are not in conventional school practices certain things that aggravate and promote the development of behavior problems. It would appear that our present tradition-bound school, with its regimentation and its regimented teachers, of necessity fosters behavior that is pathological from a mental-hygiene point of view. If this is true, who is to accept the responsibility for the teacher's attitude? The teachers in question make the natural mistake—owing, no doubt, to practical schoolroom conditions—of evaluating children's behavior in terms of good order and recognition of authority. On the other hand, the psychologist, the psychiatrist, and the psychiatric social worker think in terms of the effects of behavior in the long run. Teachers are expected to maintain reasonable order, and in doing this, at times make the mistake, from a mental-hygiene point of view, of favoring withdrawing behavior and ruthlessly suppressing overtly aggressive (symptomatic) behavior without thought of the consequences thereof.

Are the differences between the attitudes of teachers and mental hygienists toward certain problems of children due to social pressure rather than to a wide gulf between them in knowledge of the principles of mental hygiene and understanding of the child's welfare?

Considerable emphasis has been placed by Wickman and other investigators in similar areas upon the amount and significance of the disagreement between teachers and clinicians as to the importance of the symptoms of "shyness," "sensitiveness," "unsocial," and other withdrawing behavior in children, but the trend, the data would tend to indicate, is in the direction of eventual agreement or similarity of attitudes in the two professional groups. This, by the way, is not to imply that all shy, unsocial, sensitive, withdrawn children are of necessity headed for the neuropsychiatric hospital.

Certain implications for teacher-training institutions would seem to grow out of the findings of a study of this nature. The increased emphasis upon an understanding of child growth and development on the part of these institutions has undoubtedly been reflected in the changing attitudes of teachers. However, an increased fusion of the twin disciplines of education and psychology in the training courses of prospective teachers might conceivably increase their over-all knowledge and understanding of the physical, mental, social, and emotional life of the child.

There must be continued instruction of the teacher in the dynamics of child behavior. New knowledge must continuously be made a part of the teacher's understanding and approach to the child. Some teachers undoubtedly will need reeducation and eradication of fixed attitudes in regard to the emotional and experiential factors that produce behavior problems in children.

The public—and parents in particular—must be reoriented, where necessary, as to the rôle of the school and the teacher in the education of children and they must constantly be given information to assist them in understanding what could and should be accomplished in the best interests of the child.

Psychologists, psychiatrists, psychiatric social workers, and teachers need to exchange ideas and experiences in regard to the behavior problems of children. It would appear that these professional people have much to offer one another, and from their mutually increased knowledge would come marked advances toward the goal of complete understanding of the child. Continued and cooperative research in the multiple issues of child behavior is important. If education for life is to become a meaningful concept, we will need to know more about and constantly to investigate the social and emotional dynamics of behavior as well as the intellectual development of the child.

REFERENCES

1. Norman Fenton, *Mental Hygiene in School Practices* (Stanford, Calif.: Stanford University Press, 1948), p. 164.

2. J.M. Lee and D.M. Lee, *The Child and His Curriculum* (New York: Appleton-Century-Crofts, 1940), 76.

3. E.W. Wickman, *Children's Behavior and Teacher's Attitudes* (New York: The Commonwealth Fund, 1928).

Part Six

GUIDANCE RESEARCH AT THE ELEMENTARY SCHOOL LEVEL

The Functions of Successful Discipline

ROBERT J. HAVIGHURST

Recently a group of us at the University of Chicago finished an eight year study of the development of moral character in a group of children whom we observed from the time they were 10 years old until they reached the age of 17 or 18. At the end of our study we made ratings of these young people on all-round moral competence. These ratings were compared with facts about these boys and girls to find out what traits and what things in their experience were closely related to good character.

Among the characteristics which we studied in relation to character development were severity of discipline and consistency of discipline in the family. We found that severity of discipline which these young people had received as children bore no relation to their moral character. Some who had been severely disciplined had very poor character; others with a history of severe discipline had very good character. Some who had been very lightly disciplined had very good character; others with lenient discipline had poor character.

But consistency of discipline was very closely related to moral competence. The coefficient of correlation of consistency of discipline with moral competence was .62. This was one of the characteristics most highly related to good character. The child who had received consistent discipline, whether severe or light, was very likely to have good character.

Discipline can be successful or it can be unsuccessful, but it is essential. Meaning by discipline a control exerted over a child by an older person through punishment or threat of punishment, discipline is essential in the rearing of children. It can be a power for good in the child's

REPRINTED FROM *UNDERSTANDING THE CHILD,* 21, 2 (APRIL 1952), 35-38, BY PERMISSION OF THE PUBLISHERS AND THE AUTHOR.

life, or a power for evil, but it is essential to the relation of the child to the older person or persons who take responsibility for rearing the child. Nobody can rear a child from babyhood without at least occasionally slapping the child's hands, or spanking him, or confining him to a play-pen or a room, or scolding him, or withdrawing one's love from him. These are all types of punishment, for they make the child feel uncomfortable because of what one has done to him, which is the characteristic of punishment.

While discipline is essential, it is not always successful. Sometimes it does good, but sometimes it does harm, or at best no good. If we wish to use discipline more successfully it is useful to think of the various functions of discipline; some of them wholesome and some unwholesome. By distinguishing wholesome from unwholesome functions of discipline it may be easier to manage discipline so that it functions wholesomely.

☙ The Wholesome Functions of Discipline

There are three wholesome uses or results of discipline.

1. *To teach the child that the world responds in orderly fashion to his actions.* The only kind of control that anyone can achieve over his world is the control of being able to predict what will happen when he does something. In a world which contains dangers as well as pleasures and satisfactions, it is necessary for survival that the child learn to predict danger as well as pleasure. This he does partly by suffering from burns by hot radiators, bumps from falls, scratches from kittens, and bad tastes from putting certain things in his mouth. But he also learns to predict some dangers from the punishments his parents give him, and these could hardly be learned in any other way.

This is why consistency of discipline is so important in the formation of character. Through consistent discipline the child learns that certain behavior will always be followed by punishment, even though it may be light punishment. He learns to expect the world to punish him for what is wrong (and also to reward him for what is right, provided his parents have consistently rewarded him for doing "good" things). Inconsistent discipline, by which we mean punishment for doing a thing one day, and indifference, or even reward for doing the same thing at a later time, leaves a child unable to predict what will happen. (A boy once told us, in connection with a whipping his father had given him with a strap for calling a neighbor girl a foul name, "I don't really know what is bad until I do it." He had called his playmates names before without being punished, and then, for doing what he had done before, he was beaten severely without warning, and he might do the same thing again the next day in front of his father without being punished.)

Consistent discipline helps the child to learn that there is a moral orderliness in his world.

2. *To teach the child a reasonable degree of social conformity.* Discipline helps to teach a child the accepted toilet habits, to wear clothes, cover his genitals, control his aggressive feelings, keep his hands and face reasonably clean, eat in ways that are not disgusting to other people, be reasonably prompt in getting to school and keeping other engagements, sit reasonably quietly in church and the movies.

Certainly there is such a thing as too much conformity, and it may result from discipline; hence it is important to speak of a "reasonable degree" of social conformity, and to be cautious in employing discipline to teach conformity. Furthermore, there is some evidence, principally from simpler societies than our own, that social conformity will be learned to a considerable extent by imitation if adults are patient enough to wait until the child has formed the habit of imitating those who have prestige in his sight. Hence this function of discipline should be accepted with some reservations, lest it produce an unwholesome degree of conformity.

3. *To help the child develop self-control and self-direction.* Wholesome discipline consists in such treatment as will enable the child in due time to make wise decisions on his own responsibility. This is accomplished by the substitution of "inner" for "outer" control, or by the development of conscience in the child.

It appears from all that we know about child development that conscience, or the inner voice that guides, warns, and occasionally punishes the human individual, develops only in situations in early life that involve punishment by someone whom the child loves and looks up to. The child experiences the "teachable moment" for the development of conscience in the years from 3 to 6. He must be punished by someone he loves in order for him to take into himself the warning, punishing voice of the loved one.

A balance of consistent punishment combined with a great deal of affection on the part of parents seems to be the only formula for the development of self-control and self-direction.

☙ The Unwholesome Functions of Discipline

There are two unwholesome uses or results of discipline.

1. *To intimidate the child.* A veteran of World War II sat in a clinic talking with the psychiatrist about the nervous breakdown which made it impossible for him to carry on with his family and his work life. "When I was a boy," he said, "my father used to beat me every evening when he came home from work. If he was too drunk to do it, my mother would beat me. Sometimes I would be so frightened I would go away about the time my father was due to come home and stay away until I thought he would be asleep. Once I ran away for three days, afraid to come home." As a young man this person was so intimidated that he feared to face his employer and his associates when difficulties arose, and he found refuge in mental illness.

Discipline that is over-severe, whether it take the form of whipping and beating or the subtler forms of scolding and denial of love, can so intimidate a child that he will never become an independent adult. Even if discipline is not carried to the extremes illustrated above but is still severe and authoritative, it may turn a child into a dependent, submissive person who lacks self-direction.

2. *To release aggression by the disciplinarian.* Disciplining a child is sometimes a pure act of retaliation by a parent who has been frustrated by the child's misbehavior. This may not be altogether bad. Perhaps a reasonable amount of retaliation is the healthiest way for a parent to solve the minor frustrations of child-rearing. It is probably better for a child to receive a sharp slap on his buttocks for striking baby brother than to be locked in a room for an hour and to be told that mother does not love him. It is better partly because the punishment which comes more closely after the misdeed is apt to be more effective, and partly because the quick slap given in a moment of anger can be followed a few minutes later by caresses to assure the child that mother does love him. Denial of love by the mother is a much more dangerous punishment than spanking.

It has been said, "Never strike a child in anger," and there is some value in this aphorism, but there is more value in the opposite one of "Never strike a child except in anger." But the anger must be under control. The punishment must not be allowed to serve completely the cause of releasing aggression of a frustrated parent or teacher. Furthermore, there are cases, especially of emotionally disturbed children, in which punishment given in anger is the worst possible thing for the child.

If humans were like bears, it would be a simple and wholesome matter to discipline children by cuffing them as a mother bear does her cubs. Perhaps a family is fortunate in which something of this mother bear and cubs relationship exists, where punishment can be given and taken impersonally. But human emotions and human personality are too complicated to be dealt with on this level.

There are only two kinds of people who may safely allow the punishment of children to serve as a release for their aggression. Parents may do this safely within narrow limits, because they are so close to the child emotionally, and they give the child so much affection that the child can accept occasional aggression from them without doubting their love of him. Total strangers may also safely retaliate by punishing children for depredations on their property—for tearing up flower-beds, stealing fruit, breaking windows, stealing from a store counter, etc. This teaches the child that he will be punished for infringing on the rights of strangers, and unless the punishment is fearful or inhuman it does not intimidate him, but teaches him a proper respect for the rights of others.

People who have frequent relationships with children but are not very closely bound to them emotionally, such as teachers, club leaders, employers, and neighbors, should not retaliate when children do wrong. They may punish the children, but it should be done without aggression, and, on the whole, they will find reward more effective than punishment.

Action Research Improves an Aspect of Elementary School Guidance

IRA J. GORDON

In the elementary school, the relation between parents and teachers is an important aspect of the guidance program. Many attempts have been made to increase the amount and level of communication between parents and teachers as a method of aiding the total development of the child. Since most elementary schools have no professional guidance person, except on a district or area or county-wide basis, the task of fulfilling this function of the guidance program rests with the teachers themselves.

The following is a description of an action research project by four teachers[1] in Tampa, Florida, conducted as a part of their work in a classroom teachers work conference at the University of Florida, Gainesville. The project was conducted under the author's supervision and with consulting help from Dr. Victor Johnson, Director of Guidance in the Florida State Department of Education.

The group met four weekends, each about two months apart. The basic action research design presented in Corey and in Gordon, *i.e.*, defining a problem area, formulation of action hypotheses, data gathering, analysis of new hypotheses, further data gathering, analysis and tentative conclusions, was followed.

The initial problem developed was: If there were a complete understanding of the aims of parent-teacher conferences, more parents would seek conferences and there would be a better rapport between parents, teachers, and children at all times.

[1] The four teachers who were involved in this project are Ann Bock, Alice Cornelius, Bertha Hord, and Frances Hufford.

REPRINTED FROM *THE PERSONNEL AND GUIDANCE JOURNAL*, 37, 1 (SEPTEMBER 1958), 65-67, BY PERMISSION OF THE PUBLISHERS AND THE AUTHOR.

The group decided that parent-teacher conferences could be improved if parents, teachers, and children could see a "model" conference on TV which conveyed to them what guidance people believed to be basic principles of a good conference.

The first step in the plan to test this was to gather data from reading [see References] as to what was considered a "good" parent-teacher relationship.

The second step was to find out what parents, teachers, and pupils perceived a conference to be. A questionnaire, developed to tap these attitudes, was given in three schools.

Analysis of these two sources of data, readings and the answers of teachers, parents, and children, led these four teachers to develop a model conference emphasizing the following points:

1. More and more schools are making use of conferences for communication between parent, teacher, and children.
2. One of the most important points for parents and teachers to remember is that worth-while conferences must be planned.
3. The teacher must have concrete examples of the child's work, activity, and records available for observation.
4. It is helpful if the parent has a prepared list of pertinent questions and suggestions ready for the conference.
5. There should be at least two scheduled conferences a year.
6. Parents and teachers can get acquainted and additional information about the child is gained through conferences.
7. Scholastic, academic, and physical and social progress of the child is pointed up for parent and teacher.
8. Techniques of studying and learning can be emphasized in a conference.
9. Parent and teacher can become aware of progress of whole child.
10. Parents with children who have no "problems" can benefit from such conferences.
11. Children should be involved in the conference, although they need not be present the whole time.

These teachers then wrote a script and presented their "conference" on the commercial TV station in Tampa which gave them 15 minutes one morning a week before the schools' regular conference date. Notes were sent home with the children of the three schools involved, informing their parents of the date, time, and nature of the TV program.

Parents, Children, Teachers Report

After the next conference day, a survey was made to determine whether the program communicated and resulted in improved attitudes and better conferences. Data gathered from parents, teachers, and children led to the conclusion that the following changes took place in the thinking of interested persons viewing the television program. Parents felt more aware of the need for planned conferences involving the welfare of the whole child; follow-ups of suggestions made by parents and teachers in conference were thought to be the best procedures for helping a child to improve.

Children contacted liked being included in a parent-teacher conference; they wished that more information concerning their work could have been included, such as reading, reports on art, etc.; only one child indicated no more conferences were desired; the children liked having the parent know how they did their work at school.

Teachers expressed awareness of importance for cordiality as a means of freeing parent and child of any apprehension; teachers saw a need of positive approach, even when weaknesses were pointed out; teachers realized importance of using tact and diplomacy in terminating conference on schedule, yet making parent feel welcome to return. The teachers also reported:

1. Conferences helped teachers gain insight into children's backgrounds which was beneficial in understanding problems.
2. Teachers received valuable information which helped them understand child's behavior.
3. Teachers found parents very cooperative and interested in child's problems and scholastic progress.
4. Parents made an effort to be very punctual.
5. Parents with children who had no problems were as grateful for conferences as were the parents of those with problems.
6. Parents' friendliness and genuine interest in school gave the teachers a warm feeling.
7. It was notable that there were fewer "dropper-inners"—parents seemed to be more aware of the need for planned conferences.
8. Conferences provided opportunity for teachers to explain methods and techniques used in teaching subject-matter.

This project has implications beyond the improvement of these conferences. These teachers reported a great increase in their own feelings of professional adequacy; they felt that the task they had attempted, with intermittent help, was so challenging and the results so rewarding that in the process they had raised their own self-esteem and, therefore, felt more able to serve children and parents from a guidance point of view.

This change in their self-concepts is perhaps more significant for in-service education than the goals they accomplished.

In-service education of an action research type can serve to:

1. Aid in the solution of guidance problems facing the elementary school.
2. Provide teachers with professional research findings and suggestions in the guidance literature.
3. Enable teachers to increase their own feelings of adequacy as professionals, a feeling which will in turn be reflected in their total classroom behavior.

REFERENCES

1. Mauree Applegate, *Everybody's Business—Our Children* (Englewood Cliffs, N.J.: Prentice-Hall, 1950).

2. Stephen Corey, *Action Research to Improve Practices* (New York: Bureau of Publications, Teachers College, Columbia University, 1953).

3. W.K. Cummings, *This Is Educational TV* (Ann Arbor, Mich.: Edwards Bros., 1954).

4. James Lee Ellenwood, *Questions Parents Ask* (New York: E.P. Dutton, 1956).

5. Mary Frank and Lawrence K. Frank, *How to Keep Your Child in School* (New York: Viking Press, 1950).

6. *Fostering Mental Health in our Schools* (Washington, D.C.: Association for Supervision and Curriculum Development, 1950 Yearbook).

7. I.J. Gordon, *The Teacher as a Guidance Worker* (New York: Harper and Brothers, 1956).

8. James L. Hymes, Jr., *Effective Home-School Relationships* (Englewood Cliffs, N.J.: Prentice-Hall, 1953).

9. Grace Langdon and Irving W. Strout, *Parent-Teacher Interviews* (New York: John Day Company, 1953).

10. E. Leonard, D. VanDeman, and Z. Miles, *Counseling with Parents* (New York: Macmillan, 1954).

11. A. Levinson and B. Stasheff, *Teaching Through Radio and TV* (New York: Holt, Rinehart & Winston, 1956).

Some Criteria for Evaluating Elementary-School Guidance Services

WILLIAM COLEMAN

The modern teacher, according to widely held opinion, must understand and meet the needs of the children in his classroom if we are to have child-centered classrooms and guidance-centered schools. It is the purpose of this article to describe some criteria that a school might use to determine the extent to which it is providing adequate guidance services to implement this generally accepted goal.

Guidance services are frequently used to provide more complete information about the needs, abilities, and interests of individual pupils in order to facilitate instruction. With their background of training, guidance workers have more thorough knowledge concerning the tools and techniques for understanding the needs of individuals than most classroom teachers, and the counselor customarily works with individuals to relieve and reduce personal problems blocking learning. As teacher-pupil ratios are reduced and as classroom teachers acquire the special skills that counselors possess, the teacher will be in an advantageous position to expedite the total growth (social, psychological, and educational) of each individual in his care.

The criteria proposed below in the form of questions are recommended as a possible guide for a school's self-evaluation of its guidance program. The questions do not lend themselves to a quantitative score; rather, they are intended to provoke a self-criticism of existing practices. The questions may be answered by the principal, by an observer at the school, by a faculty committee, or by the whole faculty. Discussion of

REPRINTED FROM *THE ELEMENTARY SCHOOL JOURNAL*, 55, 5 (JANUARY 1955), 274-278, BY PERMISSION OF THE UNIVERSITY OF CHICAGO PRESS AND THE AUTHOR.

these questions should lead to better understanding of present guidance practices and a desire for improvement.

A list of bibliographic references for schools desiring to study further and to improve their present guidance program is provided at the end of this paper.

Criteria

1. Are the teachers sensitive to the feelings of individual pupils?
   (a) Are emotional feelings, such as gloom, discouragement, elation, and bitterness, recognized and dealt with?
   (b) Are pupils who are isolates or rejected by others helped to become members of groups?
   (c) Do teachers avoid sarcasm, criticism of individuals before the group, derisive remarks?
   (d) Are "free lunch" children accommodated without being embarrassed?
2. Are the teachers able to accept each child as he is in the classroom and to appreciate the individual differences that exist among children?
   (a) Are the admirable qualities in each child sought out and given expressed recognition?
   (b) Are the expectations held for each child reasonable?
   (c) Are provisions made in each classroom for a wide range of materials and learning situations?
   (d) Have reporting and promotional policies and grouping procedures been considered, adopted, and put into effect to meet fully the range of individual differences in abilities, interests, and backgrounds of pupils?
3. Are the teachers familiar with the growth and developmental patterns of children?
   (a) Do the methods of discipline indicate an understanding of normal behavior patterns? For example: Are six-year-olds expected to sit still for an hour or more at a stretch? Are twelve-year-old girls expected not to giggle in the presence of boys?
   (b) Are pupils encouraged to follow through their interests within limits, and are they given school time when it is needed to complete certain projects?
   (c) Do teachers realize that self-assertion, the desire for attention and

recognition, and a desire for independence may be behind the behavior of pupils?

4. Are the teachers familiar with, and do they utilize, the various methods of securing information on individual pupils?
   (a) Is there a cumulative record for each child? Is it kept up to date? Is the information pertinent and used?
   (b) Are visits made to pupils' homes and conferences arranged with parents in order to gain more information about pupils?
   (c) Are teachers trained in administering and interpreting tests of ability, achievement, interests, and values?
   (d) Have sociometric techniques and other methods been investigated for use in studying interpersonal relationships?
5. Are the teachers accessible to individual pupils for counseling?
   (a) Do individual pupils gain better understanding and self-insight concerning their skills and limitations as they progress in school?
   (b) Do the pupils receive help in meeting problems of emotional and social adjustment through conferences with their teachers and manipulation of school environment?
   (c) Do pupils become aware of the educational and vocational opportunities ahead of them, and are they assisted in making some general educational and vocational plans in collaboration with their parents?
   (d) Do all pupils feel that they have teachers to whom they can take a personal problem and receive help?
6. Is there an orientation program for beginning pupils?
   (a) Is there a handbook for parents of preschool children suggesting readiness activities in the home?
   (b) Is there a preschool clinic where parents are acquainted with the school and with things they can do to help beginning pupils?
   (c) Do teachers arrange to visit the homes of beginning pupils to learn about the children's backgrounds and needs?
   (d) Do teachers organize the first-grade room to accommodate the different levels of pupil maturity?
7. Is there an effective two-way communication system between the home and the school?
   (a) Do teachers and parents correspond or confer with one another regarding the problems of individual pupils?
   (b) Are there scheduled conferences with the parents of every child

in the school to discuss the child's development and possible problems?

(c) Do the report cards cover the things parents need to know about their children, including, for example, observations of personal characteristics?

(d) Do the parents make use of mediums at their disposal for indicating their reaction to the school's report on their child's growth?

8. Are all the teachers making use of appropriate community agencies to deal with some of the problems of pupils?

(a) Do teachers call upon the welfare agencies for assistance in providing food, clothing, housing, medical care, and other essentials?

(b) Do they call upon pastors and church groups to provide guidance pertaining to moral and spiritual matters for parents whose attitudes and patterns of behavior are detrimental to children?

(c) Do they ask community groups to help in programs for groups of children assisting individual pupils? For example, do they have 4-H Club leaders or civic clubs sponsor various projects, such as big-brother plans, visits, and programs?

9. Are all the teachers making certain that every child in need of it is securing remedial help in school?

(a) Is there a definite plan for identifying children needing remedial work?

(b) Is there an arrangement whereby children retarded in reading, arithmetic, or any other field can get special help, without neglecting or taking time from the other children?

(c) Is there a specially trained person available to help pupils with speech or hearing difficulties?

(d) Are the teachers willing to make the necessary arrangements for physically handicapped children, referring them to the "homebound" program only when it is necessary?

10. Is there a systematic plan for assisting pupils to make the transition from the elementary to the high school?

(a) Is information provided to the high school which will help get the entering pupils started properly?

(b) Is there an arrangement whereby the pupils visit the high school before they enter?

(c) Do you keep track of how your pupils make out in the high school?

(d) Do you meet with high-school people to examine the objectives and curriculums of your school and theirs, with the aim of making the transition of the pupils from elementary to high school as smooth as possible?

11. Have the necessary arrangements been made in your school to facilitate counseling individual pupils?
    (a) Has a guidance committee been organized that is representative of the faculty?
    (b) Do teachers have some time available for conferring with pupils individually or for talking with parents?
    (c) Do teachers have a room where they can talk privately with a pupil?
    (d) Are resource personnel available and used?
        (1) Are there available resource people, such as visiting teachers, school psychologists, and nurses, to whom children may be referred by teachers?
        (2) Are the teachers making use of such resource personnel when they are available?
12. Does the in-service training program include time for the discussion and consideration of guidance services?
    (a) Has the guidance committee assembled resource materials and information on such things as tests, reporting practices, and utilization of cumulative records?
    (b) Has the guidance committee stimulated thinking and growth in competencies in evaluation and guidance techniques among teachers?
    (c) Has the guidance committee assisted teachers with conferences on the problems of individual pupils?

Summary

Twelve general criteria have been suggested for elementary schools wishing to evaluate their guidance services. In the final analysis, however, guidance is a point of view, and the extent to which good guidance practices function will depend upon the point of view and attitudes of the individual teacher. Problems of learning, discipline, or pupil-teacher relations will be approached and handled in terms of the attitudes of teachers. No guidance program can be any stronger than the extent to which individual teachers accept each child, accord him respect as an individual, and reflect warmth of feeling for him.

REFERENCES

1. William Coleman, "Guidance in the Elementary School," *Tennessee Teacher*, **19**, 9 (May 1951).

2. ——— and E.B. Cobb, *Guidance Use of Test Results* (Knoxville, Tenn.: Tennessee State Testing and Guidance Program, University of Tennessee, 1951).

3. Walter W. Cook, Carroll H. Leeds, and Robert Callis, *Minnesota Teacher Attitude Inventory Manual* (New York: Psychological Corporation, 1951).

4. Ervin Winfred Detjen and Mary Ford Detjen, *Elementary School Guidance* (New York: McGraw-Hill, 1952).

5. Division of Research and Guidance, Los Angeles County Schools, *Guidance Handbook for Elementary Schools* (Los Angeles, Calif.: California Test Bureau, 1949).

6. Raymond N. Hatch, *Guidance Services in the Elementary School* (Dubuque, Ia.: William C. Brown Co., 1951).

7. Staff of the Division on Child Development and Teacher Personnel, *Helping Teachers Understand Children* (Washington, D.C.: American Council on Education, 1945).

8. Henry W. Magnuson, Carl A. Larson, and Thomas A. Shellhammer, *Evaluating Pupil Progress* (bulletin), **21**, 6 (Sacramento, Calif.: State Department of Education, 1952).

9. Willard C. Olson, *Child Development* (Boston: D.C. Heath & Co., 1949).

10. Louis Raths, *An Application to Education of the Needs Theory* (Bronxville, N.Y.: Modern Education Service, 1949).

11. Fritz Redl and William W. Wattenberg, *Mental Hygiene in Teaching* (New York: Harcourt, Brace & World, 1951).

12. Celia B. Stendler, "How Well Do Elementary-School Teachers Understand Child Behavior?" *Journal of Educational Psychology*, **40** (December 1949), 489-498.

13. Hilda Taba, Elizabeth Hall Brady, John T. Robinson, and William E. Vickery, *Diagnosing Human Relations Needs* (Washington, D.C.: American Council on Education, 1951).

14. Arthur E. Traxler, "Essentials of Guidance Services in Elementary Schools," *Elementary School Journal*, **53** (December 1952), 207-210.

Acceptance and Performance among Gifted Elementary-School Children

META F. WILLIAMS

It is generally conceded that wasteful numbers of intellectually gifted children in public elementary schools do not perform to capacity in academic and social areas. Over the years, corrective measures such as acceleration, enrichment, and segregation have been tried and found wanting. Nevertheless, evidence has been accumulating to the effect that curricular changes can render the gifted child more accepting of, and more acceptable to, his classmates. This article summarizes the results of the writer's research to determine whether acceptance, in turn, can significantly influence performance.

In the initial step, three elementary schools of suburban Connecticut furnished a sample of 117 children whose intelligence quotient was 130 or more as derived from the California Tests of Mental Maturity. These children, deemed "gifted" for purposes of the experiment, were then rated for academic performance by Stanford Achievement Tests, Metropolitan Achievement Tests, and Metropolitan Readiness Tests (administered to kindergarten groups) and for social performance by the California Test of Personality.

To establish extent of acceptance, sociometric data were gathered by application of the Classroom Social Distance Scale.[1] This instrument allows each child to register on a five-point scale his reaction to every other child in the classroom. By assigning numerical values to the scale items, one can arrive at two scores: (1) a "self social distance" score indicating degree of acceptance extended to the group by an individual,

REPRINTED FROM *EDUCATIONAL RESEARCH BULLETIN,* 37, 8 (NOVEMBER 1958), 216-220, 224, BY PERMISSION OF THE PUBLISHERS AND THE AUTHOR.

and (2) a "group social distance" score denoting degree of acceptance extended to the individual by the group.

The scale was chosen, in part, because it assays both types of acceptance at issue, and also because it relieved the writer of the task of defining or analyzing "acceptance" except in terms of test results; thus, on the strength of the investigations connected with creation of the scale, the writer could logically construe "friendliness" as a probable criterion of acceptance and, negatively, presume relative "rejection" to be a reasonable indication of relative lack of acceptance. The basis for these assumptions can be better comprehended upon examination of the scale items[1, p. 406]:

1. Would like to have him as one of my best friends.
2. Would like to have him in my group but not as a close friend.
3. Would like to be with him once in a while but not often or for long at a time.
4. Don't mind his being in our room but I don't want to have anything to do with him.
5. Wish he weren't in our room.

With certain adjustments devised by the writer to accommodate children in kindergarten and the earlier grades, the scale was administered to 888 children, a total comprising the 117 gifted children and a random sample of their classmates.

After the sociometric results were completed, intensive statistical study was undertaken. Academic- and social-performance scores were analyzed by correlation ratio (Eta), by chi square, and by numerical comparison. Eta revealed a possible relation between acceptance extended *by the group* to the individual and academic as well as social performance. Also apparent was a relationship between acceptance extended *to the group* by the individual and the two types of performance.

Thus, academic performance yielded an Eta of .22 (significant at less than the .05 confidence level) in relation to acceptance extended by the group and an Eta of .58 (significant at greater than the .01 confidence level) in relation to acceptance extended to the group. Social performance correlated with acceptance by the group gave an Eta of .37 (significant at just less than the .05 confidence level) and with acceptance extended to the group an Eta of .30 (significant at less than the .05 confidence level).

The most pronounced Eta correlation, then, was between academic performance and acceptance extended to the group. The corrected contingency coefficient (Cc) brought out by chi square analysis likewise showed marked relation in this category, but the relation between social performance and acceptance extended to the group was still more marked. In general, Cc indicated that acceptance extended to the group was more closely related to varieties of performance than was acceptance extended by the group. Relation between total performance and total acceptance—the combined data of acceptance extended by the group and to the group—was found the most emphatic of all.

TABLE 1 Statistical Relation between Performance and Acceptance

Kinds of Relationship (1)	*Chi-Square* (2)	*P* (3)	*Corrected Contingency* (Cc) (4)
Academic performance and acceptance extended by the group	5.78	$.07 < P < .08$	.31
Academic performance and acceptance extended to the group	16.09	$P < .01$	.50
Social performance and acceptance extended by the group	9.07	$P < .01$	.41
Social performance and acceptance extended to the group	20.00	$P < .01$	.57
Total performance and acceptance extended by the group	14.76	$.01 < P < .02$	.43
Total performance and acceptance extended to the group	22.98	$P < .01$	.51
Total performance and total acceptance	41.39	$P < .01$	.62

Table 1 shows the relation between two types of performance and two types of acceptance as indicated in statistical treatment by chi square. Corrected contingency coefficient (Cc) may be interpreted as signifying relative correlation between variables.[2, 3] Total performance (academic plus social) and total acceptance (extended by the group and to the group) show the most pronounced relationship.

Numerical analysis of the data revealed that more than four out of five children high in total acceptance were achieving within or beyond expectancy, whereas more than three out of five children low in acceptance were achieving below expectancy.

As a test of the findings, case studies were made of twelve children of the gifted sample, six of them highly accepted and six of them highly rejected. Techniques utilized, in addition to application of the scales previously mentioned, included the sociometric interview, the anecdotal record of classroom observations, the school-record digest, open-end questions, and the Van Pit Series-Wishes.

TABLE 2 Coincidence of Emotional Need Fulfillment and Acceptance Extended by the Group

Emotional Needs	*Number of High Acceptees in Whom Need Is*		*Number of Low Acceptees in Whom Need Is*	
	Met	Unmet	Met	Unmet
(1)	(2)	(3)	(4)	(5)
Belonging	4	2	1	3
Achievement	4	2	2	4
Economic security	2	4	5	1
Freedom from fear	5	1	1	5
Love and affection	5	1	....	6
Freedom from excessive guilt	2	4	1	5
Self-respect	2	4	1	5
Self-understanding	6	....	2	4

The Van Pit Series-Wishes data, summarized in Table 2, indicated need fulfillment among the intensively studied six gifted children highly accepted by classmates and the six gifted children rejected by classmates. The low acceptees showed greatest fulfillment in only one category, the need for *economic security*, which was met in five children of this group. The need for *love and affection* remained unfulfilled in all of the low acceptees; and in five cases each, the needs for *freedom from fear, freedom from excessive guilt,* and *self-respect* were not met. Among high acceptees, the need for *self-understanding* was fulfilled in every case. Of this group, five children had their needs for *freedom from fear* and *love and affection* met. The table indicates, then, a close relationship between acceptance and satisfaction of needs. If schools make a greater effort to fulfill the needs of gifted children by strengthening acceptance, the writer concludes that, in all probability, the performance of such children will thereby be improved.

The case-study findings paralleled and supported those of the general investigation and, in addition, indicated the effects of the school setting and curriculum on degree of acceptance, and therefore, on quality of performance.

In summary, there appeared to be: (1) no appreciable differences in intelligence between high and low acceptees; (2) an appreciable difference in both test-measured and school-evaluated social performance, favoring the high acceptees; (3) evidence of greater acceptance extended to the group by the high acceptees; (4) no difference between high and low acceptees with regard to the characteristics valued in friends; (5) greater permissiveness and wider variety of channels for learning in the experiences of the high acceptees; (6) more consistent satisfaction with interpersonal relationships among the high, and more consistent dissatisfaction among the low acceptees; (7) considerable differences between high and low acceptees in the fulfillment of their emotional needs, as indicated by the Van Pit Series-Wishes.

Significantly, none of the individually studied gifted children, accepted by classmates or not, appeared concerned with himself as a "big brain." None sought special attention on the grounds of unusual intellectual capacity. None was anxious for more school work or for special teachers or for a rarefied climate of any kind. The profuse data of the individual studies also indicated that all of the examined children, accepted by classmates or not, were willing, within emotional limitations, to attempt the work prescribed by the school.

Moreover, all were powerfully concerned with themselves as children, not as special children. They indicated the normal strong desire of children to use their bodies successfully, to build themselves physically into greater beauty and strength. They all wanted to love and be loved. And they wanted, above all, to consider themselves worthy members of a worthy peer group and to communicate this desire to their classmates. It seems reasonable to conclude, then, that those engaged in seeking better opportunities for our gifted children might with profit look to the child first, and only subsequently to his gifts.

If further investigation can demonstrate that the performance of gifted children is generally affected by considerations of group acceptance, as seemed true of the children in the study reported here, then the school must re-examine those practices which are inimical to acceptance and change them. Such change, aimed at cultivating the child rather than his particular gifts, might well prove less expensive and more effective than the practices now relied upon to help intellectually endowed children attain performance commensurate with their special capacities.

REFERENCES

1. Ruth Cunningham *et al., Understanding Group Behavior of Boys and Girls* (New York: Bureau of Publications, Teachers College, Columbia University, 1951), 401-406.

2. Charles C. Peters and Walter R. Van Voorhis, *Statistical Procedures and Their Mathematical Bases* (New York: McGraw-Hill, 1947).

3. J.P. Guilford, *Fundamental Statistics in Psychology and Education* (New York: McGraw-Hill, 1950).

Impact of First Grade Entrance Upon the Socialization of the Child: Changes After Eight Months of School

CELIA BURNS STENDLER
NORMAN YOUNG

In a previous paper we reported our attempt to get, by means of interviews with mothers, at certain changes in the socialization process as a result of first grade entrance.[7] From what mothers told us, we concluded that, contrary to the negative picture of sixness presented by Gesell, there is a decrease in behavior problems with most children at six, and a marked growth in general maturity, responsibility, independence, and self-control. Change in ego-development was noted, with the child reported as evidencing a marked increase in self-esteem. With first grade entrance comes a feeling of bigness, of importance, of participating in the kinds of activities older children and adults do, namely, reading, writing, and number.

These conclusions were reached from material presented to us by 212 mothers in an interview which took place after approximately three months of school. Our next interview was held after eight months of first grade life. Our purpose was to see (1) whether the improvement in adjustment noted by mothers persisted; (2) whether negative changes in adjustment noted by mothers occurred with change in attitude toward school and teacher; (3) whether parents differed according to social class in attitude toward the school.

REPRINTED FROM *CHILD DEVELOPMENT*, 22, 2 (JUNE 1951), 113-122, BY PERMISSION OF THE SOCIETY FOR RESEARCH IN CHILD DEVELOPMENT, INC., PURDUE UNIVERSITY, AND THE AUTHOR.

1. DOES IMPROVEMENT IN ADJUSTMENT PERSIST?

There are conflicting opinions in the literature concerning behavioral changes at six. With regard to kinds of change, we have the position of Gesell and others that the six-year-old is "out-of-focus"; that is, he is explosive, rebellious, rude, stubborn, brash, boisterous, and the like.[4, p. 89]

On the other side of the picture we have those who feel that the child is not highly emotional, explosive, expansive and undifferentiated—but is rather easier to get along with than ever, one who is controlled, less wilful, and gives less trouble generally than ever before. Bowley says, "There is less emotional intensity. The early violent feelings (before five years of age when control is weak) . . . are more controlled, repressed, or diffused. The child has learned to deal more adequately with internal tension and has normally made a fair adjustment to external conditions . . ." "In general, the period from 6 to 11 years is one of *comparative stability* and real intellectual advancement is achieved, unembarrassed by emotional difficulties."[1, p. 81]

It is obvious that this description gives us a different notion of what to expect from the six-year-old than the Gesell position. Bühler for the most part, is in harmony with Bowley on this specific point when she tells us, "The wilfulness and laxness of the 2-4 year-old is replaced to a certain extent by the serious attitude of the 5-8 year-old . . . It is, for instance, a matter of common knowledge that the child between the second and fourth year is especially difficult to handle" and "The 5-10 year-old presents relatively the fewest difficulties."[2, p. 142] The Bowley-Bühler picture of development is more in agreement with the kind of description of sixes which our parents gave us.[7]

While our interviews with mothers indicated improvement in behavior after three months of school, it was conceivable that the results might have been a function of the time factor. We hypothesized that there might have been a honeymoon period, and that after the glamor of entering first grade had worn off, the child might revert to the kind of six-year-old behavior Gesell describes. In this connection, Brooks reports, "The first reactions of children to school are not necessarily complete indications of the real personality of the children. A study of forty seven-year-old boys just entering school in Germany showed that 13 were confident, 16 indifferent, and 11 were shy. The early over-submissiveness to the teacher's authority tended to disappear during the first six weeks." [3] Our first purpose, then, in doing this particular study, was to see whether improvement in behavior persisted throughout the child's attendance in first grade.

2. WHERE NEGATIVE CHANGES OCCUR, IS THERE ALSO CHANGE IN ATTITUDE TOWARD SCHOOL AND TEACHER?

Not only are there conflicting opinions in the literature with regard to what kind of child the six-year-old is, but also with regard to the cause of changes in his behavior. On the one hand, we find the theory expressed that development is inevitable. The Freudian instinct-theories that attributed changes in development to biological causes might be mentioned in this connection. And although Gesell by no stretch of the imagination could be accused of being Freudian, we do find him stating with regard to the six-year-old, "New propensities are erupting; new impulses, new feelings, new actions are literally coming to the surface, because of *profound developments* in the underlying nervous system."[4, p. 89]

In our first report, we contended that any change in the child at six is not a function of the genes but is a result of the change from kindergarten and home to the elementary school. In discussing school entrance Skinner and Harriman state, ". . . there are bound to be factors . . . so potent in their influence upon the growing consciousness of the developing social being that the child has no pattern of behavior ready for the new set of social stimuli. One such set of circumstances occurs when the child leaves the kindergarten or the sheltered home environment for the regular elementary school group."[6, p. 229] Murphy and Newcomb take this very position when they say, "Entrance into the conventional first grade marks a sharp break in the actual structure of the child's experience. For the first time in the case of many children, they are expected to conform to a group pattern imposed by an adult who is in charge of too many children to be constantly aware that each child is an individual. Flash cards are flashed at the group all at once. Stories are told and everyone must listen whether he will or not. Drawing paper and crayons are handed out whether you happen to feel like drawing at that moment or not. One child who found this shift quite beyond endurance remarked after his first day in school, 'It's awful; all you do is mind all day long.' And another day he added, 'It is really awful. All you do is sit and sit and sit'."[5, p. 652] Conceivably such experiences could effect changes in behavior in the six-year-old. In order to see whether any negative changes in behavior reported by parents occurred with change in attitude toward school and teacher, we asked mothers to tell us when such changes, if any, occurred. We asked, also, about changes in attitude toward school, and about likes and dislikes for school activities.

3. DO PARENTS DIFFER ACCORDING TO SOCIAL CLASS IN ATTITUDE TOWARD SCHOOL?

Our third purpose, to see whether there were social class differences in parental attitude toward school that might conceivably affect adjustment, has received some attention in a previous paper.[8] Five different areas were examined in that paper: preschool attendance, parental educational aspirations for the child, preparation for school, parental criticism of the school, parental reception of report card. Significant social class differences in preschool attendance, parental expectations for the child's education and parental preparation of children for first grade skills were found. No social class differences were found in parental criticisms of the school. Parents were found to differ somewhat according to social class in the way in which they received the first report card.

In our third interview we wanted to see whether social class differences in two of these areas appeared toward the close of the school, namely, criticism of the school and reception of report card. As was noted in the previous paper, statements appear in the literature to the effect that lower classes are more hostile toward the school and more openly critical of it. While these did not appear during the first few months of school it was conceivable that they might appear later on. With regard to report card, it was reasoned that since the report card is an important indicator of how well the school thinks the child is doing, in those homes (upper-middles) where the values of the school are reinforced, the card would be seriously received. Good reports would be approved and poor reports frowned upon. Furthermore, upper classes might hold up higher standards of achievement and might so indicate in their rewards to the child. As has been indicated, some trend in this direction was noted in the second interview and a further check was desired at this time.

Procedure

An interview, the third in a series, was conducted with 202 mothers of first grade children in a Midwestern community approximately eight months after the start of first grade. Six experienced persons did the interviewing on the same sample of mothers as we had used in our two previous interviews.

TABLE 1 Distribution of 202 Families in a Midwestern Community According to Social Class

Social Class	*Number of Families*	*Per Cent*
Upper	8	4
Upper Middle	48	24
Lower Middle	59	29
Upper Lower	73	36
Lower Lower	14	7

Distribution of families according to social class is reported in Table 1. This distribution was obtained by using the technique worked out by Warner, Meeker and Eells.[9] Occupation, house type, dwelling area and source of income were used in class typing.

The interview form is included at the end of this report.

Results and Discussion

1. CHANGES IN BEHAVIOR NOTED BY MOTHERS

As can be seen in the interview form, each parent was asked to give her judgment as to whether her child showed more, less, or the same degree of a number of different traits. In the first of these, the term maturity or grown-upness was considered an over-all estimation of behavior; self-control, helpfulness, responsibility, patience, disposition, obedience, self-confidence, and getting along with playmates were subsumed as specific behavioral traits. Frequencies for each are reported in Table 2.

As can be seen from Table 2, an overwhelming majority of mothers reported children improved with regard to most of the behavioral traits in question. In only two instances do we find this not to be true. In respect to "patience" and "obedience" slightly more mothers reported the child was the same rather than improved. The reader will also note that a sizable minority of mothers reported change for the worse in regard to "patience," "disposition," and "obedience," more so than for any of the others. A *chi-square* analysis, however, showed that with regard to every trait except one there was a significant difference away from deterioration in behavior and in most cases toward improved behavior. The one exception was "patience" where no significant difference appeared.

TABLE 2 Frequencies of Change in Certain Behavioral Traits as Reported by 202 Mothers

	MOTHERS REPORTING			
	More	*Same*	*Less*	*Total*
Trait	*f*	*f*	*f*	*f*
Maturity	180	14	3	197
Self-control	104	72	21	197
Helpfulness	131	43	19	193
Responsibility	145	37	13	195
Patience	65	70	63	198
Disposition	95	58	47	200
Obedience	74	80	39	193
Self-confidence	157	26	9	192
Getting along with playmates	123	60	7	190
	1074	460	221	1755

The question of interpretation arises here. While the general picture of adjustment at six as reported by mothers is highly favorable when we total the positive responses to specific traits, it might very well be that the three traits of obedience, disposition and patience where we found many negative scores were highly important to mothers. Thus a mother might note that the child was more helpful and more responsible, but this might not be as important to her as to have a patient, obedient child with a pleasant disposition. Gesell reports, "Six is a trying age for many a parent. One of our parents reports that she dreaded to get up in the morning because it meant one continuous contest with her 6-year-old,—one long 'fight, fight, fight!' "[4, p. 117]

In order to see whether the negative scores for obedience, patience and disposition might outweigh the other traits in value to the point where mothers would find six a trying age, we posed that very question. We asked whether the year had been a more trying one, the same, or an easier one. Mothers responded thusly:

	f
The year has been more trying than the previous one	30
The year has been the same in this respect	60
The year has been an easier one	112

It would seem then, in so far as we can judge by what our parents told us, approximately 14 per cent of our mothers found the year more trying, 29 per cent reported it to be the same, and over 50 per cent of our sample said the year had been an easier one. In general, then, we can say that the improvement in behavior noted by parents during the first few months of school persists throughout the year and that our hypothesis regarding a honeymoon period was not substantiated.

2. NEGATIVE CHANGES IN BEHAVIOR AND ATTITUDE TOWARD SCHOOL AND TEACHER

Here we were interested in exploring possible causes for change in behavior. It was conceivable that improvement or deterioration in behavior might be tied up with a change in attitude toward school and teacher. In previous interviews parents had reported that children looked forward to school with great anticipation and that after three months in school children liked it and their teacher very much. Now we asked whether children seemed to like school and teacher more, less or the same as they did at first. The answers were:

	f		*f*
Liked school more	88	Liked teacher more	73
Liked school same	91	Liked teacher same	101
Liked school less	10	Liked teacher less	9

From what parents tell us, then, it would seem that first grade children like school, and that for many, liking increases with the school year. Where school was liked less or disliked, in seven cases teacher was also liked less. Where school was not liked, eight parents reported a more trying year. Because so few children disliked school or deteriorated in their attitude toward it during the year, no conclusion can be drawn as to whether attitude toward school has anything to do with changes in behavior.

Where liking for school increased, according to the mothers, the rationale for the change was mainly that the child was getting "acclimatized" to school. Explanations such as "He is getting used to the new situation," "increased and expanded interests," and "disappointed that she didn't learn to read right away, but when she started reading she was more interested" were comparatively prevalent. Some parents also reported, "She was worried about the big boys at first," "sense of achievement in going to school with the children," and "She used to be afraid of authority, but now she knows teacher better."

The things about school the child likes best were quite specific. Here we find reading far in the forefront with about 90 per cent of the responses in this direction. Next we find the answer "everything." A scattering of parents mentioned numbers, musical activity and art. But reading, according to parents, is almost synonymous with first grade in children's minds. This may represent wishful thinking on the part of mothers who want children to learn to read in Grade 1 or it may actually be the most popular activity, perhaps because of its prestige in the school and adult world.

We also asked what the child disliked most about school. The substitute teacher, the strictness of teachers, and the roughness of other children were most frequently mentioned. Here we see answers like "The substitute teacher jerked her around," "Teacher is mean," "too strict," and "Teacher wouldn't let child participate in activities." Some children complained about the little playground activity, others thought there was too much. Some said they didn't like working with clay or reading or writing, and "Teacher promises a surprise and then forgets." The reaction of the parents when children complained is generally to favor the school. Parents are apt to say, "Mind her (the teacher) and pay attention," "It's hard for a new teacher to walk into a strange class." "Help her by cooperating," "You have to get used to different teachers," and "Tell the teacher when the children are rough." A number of parents replied that they made no comment when the child complained and some even said, "I laughed!"

3. SOCIAL CLASS DIFFERENCES IN ATTITUDE TOWARD SCHOOL AT GRADE 1 LEVEL

As has been indicated in the introduction we were interested (1) in whether there were social class differences in parental attitude toward the school as indicated by criticism of the school, and (2) whether parents differed according to social class in reception of report card.

When we decided to analyze the data according to social class it was obvious that theoretical frequencies in the upper- and lower-lower class would be too small for valid testing. Hence, we chose to analyze the differences among the upper-middle, the lower-middle, and the upper-lower classes. We hypothesized that our data would fall in these social classes in the ratio 24:29:36, the same ratio as these classes fell in our total sample. Wherever there were three categories, one of which alone had a low frequency, causing significant *chi-square,* we decided to test for significant differences in the remaining categories. In this way we could get information as to the chief positive contributor to the significant *chi-square*. Answers to each question will be reported separately.

a. DO YOU THINK ANYTHING DIFFERENTLY SHOULD BE DONE BY SCHOOL OR TEACHER? *Chi-square* analysis revealed significant differences according to social class at the 5 per cent level in answers to this question. The main positive contributor was the upper-middle class. The difference between upper-middles and upper-lowers taken separately, however, did not yield a significant difference. Results are shown in Table 3.

TABLE 3 Responses by Social Class to the Question, "Do You Think Anything Differently Should be Done by School or Teacher?"

Social Class	*Yes* *f*	*No* *f*
Upper	6	2
Upper-middle	43	24
Lower-middle	16	16
Upper-lower	32	28
Lower-lower	3	9

Foremost among the criticisms of the school were "They should teach reading by phonetics," "The school is too overcrowded," and "inadequate playground facilities." There were varied complaints about the teachers. Among these were "too lax in discipline," "too much discipline," "teacher expects too much," and some implied that the teacher was "too nervous." Other complaints varied from "PTA should be improved" to "Emotional problems are teacher's fault, she lets children grow like weeds!"

b. DO YOU THINK YOUR CHILD IS GETTING A PROPER EDUCATION? As can be seen from Table 4, there was agreement that the child is getting a proper education and no social class differences appeared.

TABLE 4 Responses by Social Class to the Question, "Do You Think Your Child Is Getting a Proper Education?"

Social Class	*Yes* *f*	*No* *f*
Upper	6	2
Upper-middle	57	7
Lower-middle	41	6
Upper-lower	51	6
Lower-lower	10	1

c. WHAT DO YOU DO IF THE CHILD HAS A COMPLAINT ABOUT SCHOOL? The direction of responses for each class was obviously away from defending the child as Table 5 reveals. In the upper-middle class there was a significant difference in the direction of defending the school. In the "Other" category, 70 per cent of the replies said, "talk to the teacher and get the facts first" and most of the rest agreed that it would "depend on the problem."

TABLE 5 Responses by Social Class to the Question, "What Do You Do if the Child Has a Complaint About School?"

Social Class	*Defend School* *f*	*Defend Child* *f*	*Other* *f*
Upper	5	0	3
Upper-middle	43	2	21
Lower-middle	20	2	27
Upper-lower	23	0	32
Lower-lower	3	0	8

d. HOW DID YOU FEEL ABOUT YOUR CHILD'S LAST REPORT CARD? It should be noted here that the range in marks is not great in first grade, with the great majority of the students getting next to the best mark according to the marking system in the schools in this Midwest town. No significant social class differences were found. Results are shown in Table 6.

TABLE 6 Responses by Social Class to the Question, "How Did You Feel About Your Child's Last Report Card?"

Social Class	*Very Pleased* *f*	*Somewhat Pleased* *f*	*Displeased* *f*	*Very Displeased* *f*
Upper	5	2	1	0
Upper-middle	50	14	1	0
Lower-middle	33	12	3	1
Upper-lower	45	11	2	2
Lower-lower	8	2	0	1

e. DO YOU HAVE A SYSTEM OF REWARDS AND PUNISHMENTS . . . (WHERE REPORT CARDS ARE CONCERNED)? In categorizing the types of rewards and punishments 95 per cent were involved in increasing the child's "material wealth," i.e. gift or money. Money was mentioned explicitly in 58 per cent of the total affirmative responses. No significant social class differences were found. Results are shown in Table 7.

TABLE 7 Responses by Social Class to the Question, "Do You Have a System of Rewards and Punishments . . . (Where Report Cards Are Concerned)?"

Social Class	Yes *f*	No *f*
Upper	2	6
Upper-middle	15	52
Lower-middle	16	33
Upper-lower	16	45
Lower-lower	3	8

Summary

Follow-up interviews with 212 mothers of first grade children were conducted to see (1) whether improvement in behavior noted after school entrance persisted through the child's first grade year, (2) whether negative changes in adjustment noted by mothers occurred with change in attitude toward school and teacher, (3) whether parents differed according to social class in attitude toward the school.

Results indicated that the picture of improved behavior at six, described previously by mothers, persists according to what mothers tell us. With respect to every trait except one about which mothers were questioned, there was a significant difference away from deterioration in behavior.

Because so few children were reported as changing in attitude toward school and teacher after eight months of first grade life, no conclusion can be drawn as to whether change in attitude toward school has anything to do with changes in behavior.

With regard to attitude toward school, a significant difference at the 5 per cent level appeared in answer to the question as to whether anything different should be done by school or teacher, with upper-middle class parents most frequently responding affirmatively. Parents of all classes agree, however, that their child is getting the proper education. Upper-middle class parents are more apt to defend the school when their child complains. No social class differences were found with respect to reception of report card.

REFERENCES

1. Agatha H. Bowley, *Guiding the Normal Child* (New York: Philosophical Library, 1943), 81.

2. Charlotte Bühler, *From Birth to Maturity* (London: Kegan, Paul, Trench, Trubner, 1937), 142.

3. Fowler D. Brooks, *Child Psychology* (Boston: Houghton Mifflin, 1937).

4. Arnold Gesell and Frances L. Ilg, *The Child from Five to Ten* (New York: Harper and Brothers, 1946).

5. Gardner Murphy, Lois Barclay Murphy, and Theodore M. Newcomb, *Experimental Social Psychology* (New York: Harper and Brothers, 1937).

6. Charles E. Skinner, Philip L. Harriman *et al.*, *Child Psychology* (New York: Macmillan Company, 1941).

7. Celia Burns Stendler and Norman Young, "The Impact of Beginning First Grade upon Socialization as Reported by Mothers," *Child Development,* 4 (1950), 241-260.

8. Celia Burns Stendler, "Social Class Differences in Parental Attitudes Toward School at Grade I Level," *Child Development,* 22 (1951), 37-46.

9. William Lloyd Warner, Marcia Meeker, and Kenneth Eells, *Social Class in America* (Chicago: Science Research Associates, 1946).

Are Elementary Counselors Doing the Job?

ROBERT N. HART

Are elementary counselors doing the things that need to be done? Are they performing the duties that teachers feel are important? What can they do to improve their services to children and to teachers?

As elementary guidance gains momentum, such questions as these become increasingly significant.

Nearly everyone would agree that part of the elementary counselor's job is to help classroom teachers. Surprisingly, however, there is little evidence that elementary teachers have been consulted about the services they believe their counselors should offer.

In a study by L.M. Smith at Washington University in Saint Louis, a group of 42 elementary teachers enrolled in classes in the department of education were asked whether a need existed for specialized guidance workers in the elementary school.[2] Over 93 per cent of the respondents felt that there was a need for a guidance worker in the elementary school and that one of his duties might be to hold conferences with parents regarding pupil problems.

This minute evidence probably represents the only place in the professional literature where elementary teachers were asked what services their guidance counselors should offer.

Perhaps this lack of evidence exists because the guidance counselorship is a relatively new position in the elementary school. Few school districts employ such counselors as yet, but there is strong evidence that the position will become more common in future years. This is all the more

REPRINTED FROM *THE SCHOOL COUNSELOR*, 9, 3 (DECEMBER 1961), BY PERMISSION OF THE PUBLISHERS AND THE AUTHOR. DR. ROBERT N. HART IS CURRENTLY WITH LONG BEACH UNIFIED SCHOOL DISTRICT, LONG BEACH, CALIFORNIA.

reason for trying to determine what duties these counselors should perform.

Survey of Teachers

In a recent doctoral study[1] classroom teachers in 38 school districts throughout the United States where elementary counselors were employed were asked to indicate the most important duties for these counselors to perform.

Their answers were interesting because the duties they emphasized were sometimes not the duties that authorities in the field listed as important.

For example, these teachers felt that the most important duty for the elementary counselor to perform was counseling pupils with learning, physical, social and emotional problems.

Another part of this same study asked 20 authorities in the field of elementary school guidance to indicate the most important duties for elementary counselors to perform. The authorities felt that interpreting pupil data to staff members was the most important duty.

These authorities ranked holding conferences with parents regarding pupil problems as second in importance. Counseling pupils with learning, physical, social and emotional problems ranked third.

The teachers, on the other hand, felt that interpreting pupil data to parents was the second most important duty that elementary counselors should perform. Holding conferences with parents regarding pupil problems was ranked as third in importance by the teachers.

Other Duties

On other, less important duties that elementary counselors perform, a greater disparity of opinion between the authorities and the classroom teachers was noted. For example, the authorities ranked conducting inservice training in guidance for staff members as seventh in importance, while the teachers ranked it only twenty-sixth.

One conclusion that might be drawn from this comparison is that teachers felt themselves less in need of inservice training in guidance than the authorities considered them. Another possible conclusion is that the teachers felt the elementary counselor less well qualified to give this training than did the authorities.

TABLE 1 Rankings of the Relative Importance of Selected Duties for the Elementary Counselor to Perform

Item	Authorities' Rankings	Teachers' Rankings
Interpreting pupil data to staff members	1	4.5
Holding conferences with parents regarding any pupil problems	2	3
Counseling pupils with learning, physical, social and emotional problems	3	1
Interpreting pupil data to parents	4.5	2
Interpreting pupil data to authorized community agencies	4.5	10.5
Conducting in-service training in guidance for staff members	7	26
Acting as guidance consultant to all staff members on pupils' problems	7	9
Conducting case conferences	7	26
Selecting pupils who need special help (e.g., high ability pupils, those needing remedial work, emotionally disturbed, etc.)	9	6
Interpreting pupil data to pupils	10.5	16.5
Organizing and heading school guidance committee	10.5	24
Assisting in placement of pupils in proper classes (or special classes when needed)	13	4.5
Coordinating efforts of all specialists (psychologists, physicians, etc.) working on a case	13	8
Interpreting schools' guidance program to the community	13	14.5
Acting as liaison person between school and community agencies on pupil problems	15.5	7
Planning school testing program with principal	15.5	25
Fostering good mental hygiene among pupils and staff	17.5	20
Reporting to the principal annually on what has been accomplished in guidance for the year	17.5	10.5
Gathering information on pupils	19	14.5
Orientation of pupils to be promoted to next higher segment (junior high school or high school)	20.5	27
Maintaining adequate supply of guidance literature and materials for teachers and parents	20.5	23
Writing case histories	22.5	16.5
Conducting a follow-up program to check on pupils who have used guidance services	22.5	19
Conducting group guidance sessions for pupils	24	30.5
Supervising clerical workers assigned to counselor's office	25.5	30.5
Suggesting areas for curriculum improvement	25.5	35.5
Administering tests, inventories, etc.	27.5	12.5
Visiting pupils' homes	27.5	21.5
Orientation of pupils new to school	29.5	34
Planning future educational programs with pupils	29.5	29
Ordering tests and other guidance materials	31	21.5
Assisting in transferring procedures when pupils leave school	32	35.5
Encouraging and assisting teachers to carry on classroom research	33	32
Keeping adequate records on all pupils	34	18
Assisting in the enrollment of pupils new to school	35	37
Scoring tests	36	28
Counseling staff members on personal problems which may affect their work	37	33
Teaching remedial classes (reading, etc.)	38.5	39
Giving psychotherapy to emotionally disturbed pupils	38.5	38
Interviewing every pupil in school	40	40
Teaching regular classes (part time)	41	41

The teachers thought that one of the elementary counselor's main duties should be to assist in the placement of pupils in proper classes (or special classes when needed). The authorities saw this as a duty of counselors also, but ranked it as of only moderate importance.

On the other hand, the authorities thought that organizing and heading the school guidance committee was an important duty of the counselor, while the teachers felt that this duty was relatively unimportant.

Other relationships between the opinions of the authorities and the teachers on 41 duties that some elementary counselors perform can be seen in Table 1.

What is the conclusion to be drawn from these data for the practicing elementary counselor? If the premise is accepted that a large part of the counselor's job should be to help the classroom teacher, the obvious conclusion is for the counselor to ask the teachers in his school which duties he should perform to serve them best.

The performance of those duties recommended by the authorities in the field of elementary school guidance is not likely to result in as much teacher satisfaction with the services of the counselor as the performance of the duties that the teachers themselves recommend as most helpful.

The guidance needs vary from one school to the next, and while the recommendations of authorities may be followed as general guides, the wise counselor will consult his teachers on the specific duties he can perform which will be most helpful to them.

REFERENCES

1. R.N. Hart, "An Analysis of the Position of the Elementary School Guidance Counselor" (unpublished doctoral dissertation, University of Southern California, 1961).

2. L.M. Smith, "Informal Observations in Guidance: An Observation on Elementary School Guidance," *Personnel and Guidance Journal,* **35** (1956), 179-180.

Part Seven

INTERPERSONAL RELATIONSHIPS OF ELEMENTARY SCHOOL GUIDANCE PERSONNEL

Organizing for Guidance in the Elementary School

RAYMOND PATOUILLET

The printed word possesses a subtle authority for no other reason than that it *is* printed. Also, it is quoted equally to support prejudice and bias and to uphold honest inquiry. And when this printed word is in the third person it takes on the added authority of impartiality. The end result is rather frightening, especially in the field of guidance, where "common sense" so easily leads us to accept uninvestigated hypotheses. So that what I have to say will be clearly understood to be personal, subjective reactions to the subject at hand, I shall use the first person through parts of my presentation.

The problem of defining guidance as this term is used in the school setting has plagued all of us in the field for a long time. Some like to think of guidance as a program of services which may be clearly "defined, recognized, administered and evaluated. It then is possible to define a guidance program as a program of services which is specifically implemented to improve the adjustment of the individuals for whom it was organized."[1] I must confess that this term "adjustment" concerns me a bit and leads me to ask rather bluntly, "Adjustment to what?" Other writers define guidance similarly, as "services to assist the teacher in knowing the pupil and to meet his needs better, as well as to aid the pupil in understanding himself. . . ."[2]

Others of us shudder at the word services and prefer to think of guidance as enlightened teaching.[3, 4] A recent book defines guidance as a viewpoint which brings about services which in turn result in an experi-

REPRINTED FROM *TEACHERS COLLEGE RECORD*, 58, 8 (MAY 1957), 431-438, BY PERMISSION OF THE PUBLISHERS AND THE AUTHOR.

ential process with pupils.[5] This statement, in a sense, is an attempt to bring together two schools of thought.

As the reader probably suspects, I neither agree nor disagree with everything that has been said above. In my opinion the proponents of services and the proponents of enlightened teaching are not really as far apart as they would like others to believe. They have simply chosen to stress different dimensions of the same thing. I do believe, however, that the point of stress may well determine the nature of the guidance program. Let's examine these emphases more closely. Both camps agree, for example, that a guidance program involves services. They agree also that the teacher plays a major role in the guidance program. The basic issue is one of relationships and organization. How do people and services in the school setting relate to each other for the good of children? I should like to present some of my thoughts on guidance and on people who are involved in this area, and to suggest a plan of organization as I discuss this question.

Guidance

Guidance is a term that is often coupled with another multi-meaning word, adjustment. This is a potentially dangerous association. We must first define what we mean by adjustment. Adjustment to the status quo, for example, is not necessarily desirable. In a rapidly changing society like ours, marked by high mobility of the population, it is inadequate preparation for the future. In a democracy it can be fatal, for a democracy is strong to the extent that each individual contributes his greatest potential, his uniqueness developed to the fullest. The democratic answer to manpower shortages is human development rather than identification of talents for assignment to currently critical areas. Guidance can therefore be defined as the maximum development of an individual's potential for his own personal happiness and the welfare of society.

OLD AND NEW GUIDANCE

The idea of guidance is as old as the first teacher. A sound curriculum, adapted to the needs of youth and appropriate to their level of maturity, is sound guidance. A program of activities aimed at the development of social competence is likewise sound guidance. In these phases of the school program teachers have always played, and will continue to play, major roles.

More recently, guidance has developed specific techniques which are used by administrators and teachers as well as by school personnel specifically designated as guidance workers. Some of the better known instruments are cumulative records, psychological tests, counseling and group work techniques, and skills in human relations.

Originally, guidance was largely a remedial function, concerned with those in difficulty. The subtle assumption then was that pupils not measuring up to externally imposed standards (of achievement, behavior, and so forth) needed extra help or guidance. Schools soon realized the futility and waste involved in waiting for the casualties, and guidance began to assume a preventive function. The task then shifted to one of identifying potential casualties before they actually got to the disability lists. But even this has proved inadequate. In the face of the titanic struggle between communism and democracy, the optimum development of the individual has become more than the goal of a minority of progressive educators; it has become a necessity for national survival. Guidance is now being forced to assume a developmental approach. This means that it can no longer be solely or primarily concerned with the relatively few severely retarded or disturbed; guidance must be concerned with all pupils and must contribute to the maximum development of each.

Thus, while guidance will continue to serve remedial and preventive functions, its primary focus will be increasingly developmental. For example, rather than emphasizing testing to identify or predict strengths and weaknesses, it will emphasize enriching experiences to stimulate development so that tests will have more to measure. And there's something else here which I should like to make clear. The teacher's role is very definitely not that of junior psychologist, but of one who can translate subject matter into exciting experiences for children. That is the teacher's greatest contribution to education and to guidance.

. . . EVERYBODY'S BUSINESS

When guidance assumes a developmental approach, it inevitably involves all individuals and agencies which contribute to an individual's development. It is likewise concerned with the many facets of development—emotional, social, and intellectual, for example. The school can no longer arrogate the right to be *the* guidance institution of society. Often, it unknowingly assumes this responsibility, but wise parents have never permitted this. The school does, however, play a critical role. Because it deals with all the children of all the people, it is ideally suited to play the role of coordinator of guidance efforts.

Specifically, the school does not provide therapy, but it does provide a therapeutic climate. It also refers parents and children who need therapy to community agencies organized to offer such aid. Where no appropriate agencies exist, the school assumes a leadership role in establishing them. Similarly, the school does not assume the role of clergyman, den mother, or parent, but it does coordinate their efforts for the good of the child in the school setting.

THE CORE OF GUIDANCE

If guidance is everybody's business, then someone is needed to coordinate and integrate this emphasis in the educational program. The logical person is the guidance worker, and his task involves primarily skill in human relations. This is not to say, of course, that the guidance person need not have unique knowledges and skills in such areas as child development and diagnostic techniques, but rather, that these unique contributions may never be utilized if the guidance person is unable to relate positively to teachers, parents, administrators, community agencies, and groups of children as well as to the individual child within the counseling cubicle.

The guidance worker, therefore, is essentially a consultant in human relations who involves in a cooperative enterprise all those who affect the development of the child.

MENTAL HYGIENE AND HUMAN RELATIONS

Good human relations within a school contribute to a mentally hygienic atmosphere, and a mentally hygienic atmosphere allows people to be their own best selves, thereby encouraging sound human relations. The two are inseparable, and guidance cannot survive where they are not present. In order to insert a wedge into this circular relationship for purposes of study, I shall attempt to define a mentally hygienic atmosphere. I think it might be defined as an atmosphere which promotes physical health, a feeling of personal worth, and communication among members of the school community.

If pupils and teachers are enjoying good physical health, they are released from an area of worry that can in and of itself be disabling and inhibiting to good teaching and learning. Healthy pupils enjoy physical activity and seek to develop physical skills. Children in poor health are apt to look upon physical activity as a threat to their very being and to avoid it. They may react, as all human beings do to frustrating situations, by aggression or by withdrawal, both of which are roads to emotional disturbances.

A feeling of personal worth is a second factor in a mentally hygienic atmosphere. This factor is enhanced when one feels accepted as a person —not despite his differences or even because of them, but, more basically, because he is a human being and by that fact alone clothed in dignity. I do not believe that man gives dignity to man. If that were true, then man could take away dignity from man, a morally untenable position. For example, to fail a child because he is unable by nature to learn a certain task is just as immoral as ruling that no child shorter than four feet six inches shall be promoted to the fifth grade. It should be added that not all experience with failure is of a negative nature. A school program in which one experienced only success would be poor preparation for life. But failure that leads to a feeling of hopelessness, in turn leads to the possibility of serious emotional upset.

A third characteristic of a mentally hygienic situation is communication. This means multi-directional communication, rather than one-way-to-one-person communication. Figures 1 and 2 may prove helpful at this point.

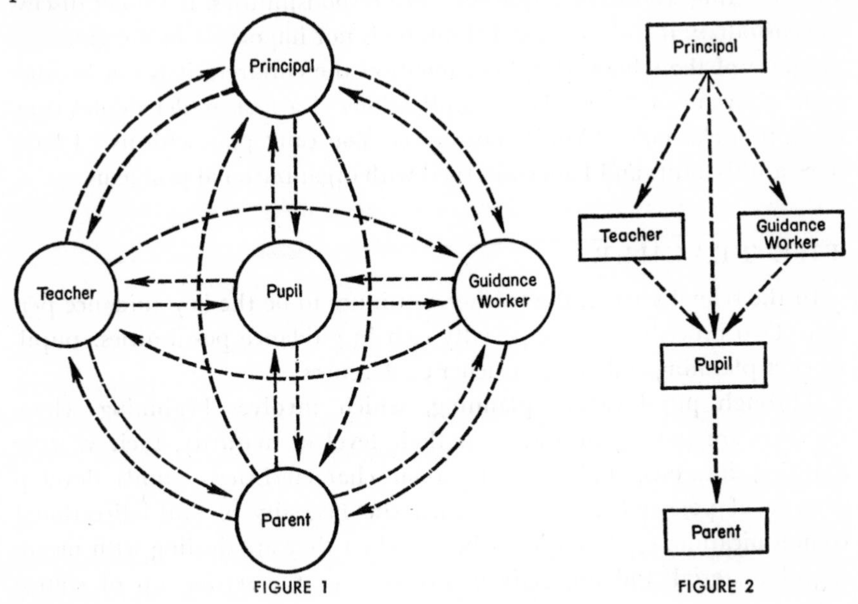

FIGURE 1

FIGURE 2

Represented in Figure 1 is an open society in which lines of communication are open. The lines in this figure should not be interpreted to be lines of responsibility or of authority, however, and the distinction should be kept clearly in mind. Unfortunately, most organizational charts usually clearly indicate lines of authority and little else. These tend to become lines of communication as well (as shown in Figure 2) and suggest a one-way communication process from "top" to "bottom," even though this may not be the intention.

In a situation where there is limited intercommunication, there is obviously limited opportunity to develop interpersonal relations, and potential resources for child development are isolated. Also, where there is a hierarchy of communication, creative energies of those beneath the top tend to be submerged in a feeling of hopelessness.

Thus, physical health, a feeling of personal worth, and multi-directional lines of communication are basic to sound mental hygiene. In turn, a mentally hygienic atmosphere is basic to human relations and to the guidance program of the school.

Guidance Personnel

In this discussion I shall direct my comments to those people in the school setting who have major guidance responsibilities. If I don't discuss the custodian, it isn't because I think he is not important in the guidance program of the school. If I don't mention the children, it is not because I am unaware of the guidance implications of a first grader's cruel comment to a classmate, "You're not pretty. You can't play with us." I have to establish limits and I am concerned with organizational problems.

THE TEACHER

In the school setting, the teacher continues to be the key guidance person. Two procedures are especially rich in guidance possibilities: pupil-teacher planning and parent-teacher conferences.

Through pupil-teacher planning, which involves beginning where children are (taking into account their level of maturity, their varying abilities, interests, and other personal characteristics), pupils develop a sense of personal worth and learn the necessity of multi-directional communication. Children learn better when they are dealing with meaningful material and are actively involved in the setting up of course goals, procedures, and evaluation, with the teacher serving as guide and resource person.

Through parent-teacher conferences the guidance responsibility of home and school is clarified and a cooperative, consistent approach is maintained.

THE PRINCIPAL

It is the principal who takes the lead in setting the guidance tone of the school. He involves his staff in policy making, thereby letting them know that they count as individuals. His position as democratic leader demands that he release the creative energies of his staff, rather than project his own needs upon them. He is skilled in human relations, in guiding his professional team through activities aimed at professional development. It has been said that "we do unto others as we have been done unto." This is especially appropriate in the field of teacher-administrator relationships. Teachers find it difficult to accept children as individuals if they themselves are not so accepted.

THE GUIDANCE WORKER

The school guidance worker (counselor, psychologist, visiting teacher) works primarily with and through teachers as well as with parents and the principal, serving as consultant and resource person to them. The guidance person works with children through the class setting, although individual conferences with parents and children are held if referral to an outside agency is indicated or if individual testing or interviewing is agreed upon by the teacher and guidance person.

I have grouped counselors, psychologists, and visiting teachers together under the general heading of guidance worker because I see an increasing number of similarities and a decreasing number of differences among their respective roles.

The term guidance counselor was probably first used in secondary schools with strong vocational emphases. The guidance counselor now finds himself involved in matters pertaining to educational planning and to personal and social development. He also finds that he is working with teachers, parents, community agencies, and groups of children, as well as with individual children. The term counselor therefore no longer adequately describes his function if we think of counseling as a one-to-one relationship. Thus, the guidance counselor has broadened his area of concern and is beginning to move into the elementary schools.

The role of the school psychologist too is assuming broader proportions. Initially, the psychologist was concerned primarily with the individual exceptional child.[6] He continues to be concerned with testing but has extended his concern to include the mental hygiene of the school. He works with teachers, parents, community agencies, and groups of children as well as with individual children. His area of operations is no longer restricted to the elementary school.

The school social worker or visiting teacher is moving in new directions too. Interest in prevention rather than remediation, wider use of referral rather than direct handling of cases, a realization of the need for visiting teachers in other than low-income areas, the growing use of visiting teachers in a consultative capacity, broadening the scope from trying to prevent truancy and delinquency to "helping all children with personal and adjustment problems,"[7] the extension of social work upward through high school—all of these trends seem to be drawing the visiting teacher closer to the guidance counselor and school psychologist.

It is clear that the teacher is the one who works with the guidance personnel and if she is to be helpful, guidance workers must understand her needs. The following list of functions prepared by a teacher attending the Thayer Conference of school psychologists is pertinent for all guidance workers.

What do I want of a school psychologist?

I want a person to help me with classroom problems on which I need help.

I want one to help me with a solution to my problem rather than give me a *diagnosis* of my problem.

I want one to *help me* solve my problems *within* my classroom setting (as much as possible) rather than to take my problem *from* my classroom.

I want one who may give me ideas on new techniques of teaching but not one who would do them for me.

I want one to give me advice on my relations with my fellow staff members if I need it.

I want one who would be a member of my staff, rather than an *assistant* in the administrative office.

I want one who would be a member of the *team*.

I want one whose personality traits are outstanding.

In teaching, we start with the child and get back to the child. *We are all in this together.*[6, p. 71]

From a study conducted by the National Association of Guidance Supervisors and Counselor Trainers[8] I was interested to learn that school systems were recommending the hiring of more guidance counselors, more psychologists, and more visiting teachers for our elementary schools. Frankly, I asked myself whether the schools responding to the questionnaire had comparable perceptions of these different guidance workers. In view of the discussion above, I think we can conclude that the teachers who responded were clearly indicating a need for assistance.

Guidance Organization

Let us assume for a moment that we are in an elementary school of 900 pupils; that we have a guidance counselor, a school psychologist, and a school social worker. Figure 3 represents these people. Theoretically,

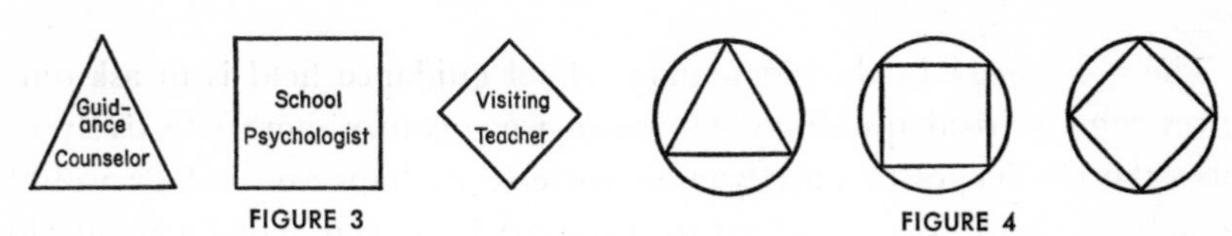

FIGURE 3 FIGURE 4

the triangle is taking care of the guidance counseling needs of 900 pupils, the square is responsible for the school psychology needs of 900, and the diamond is prepared to meet the visiting teaching needs of 900. In view of the preceding discussion we know that much overlapping of work will prevail and the teacher will not feel that she is getting any concerted assistance.

An alternative plan of organization would be to have three "helping teachers" or "child development consultants," each responsible for the developmental needs of 300 children. Both children and teachers would then stand a better chance of being served.

Of course the question that immediately arises is, What sort of training will these child development consultants need? My answer at this point would be a two-year program of graduate study including courses in guidance, developmental psychology, school psychology, social work, administration, and curriculum (including reading, an area in which teachers say they need help). Such a program is currently offered on an experimental basis at Teachers College, Columbia. The fully qualified school psychologist (a graduate of a four-year program) would still be needed of course, and would serve as consultant in our imaginary school to our three child development consultants. The proposed plan perhaps fills the need for more immediate assistance to teachers within reasonable financial limits.

An intermediate step which is probably necessary for the present is charted in Figure 4. While called child development consultants and performing similar tasks, each individual represented might have a different background and contribute unique strengths. The circle surrounding the triangle is the person who has had two years of graduate work in guidance; the one around the square is the two-year psychologist; and the one with the diamond in the center is the graduate of a two-year master's program from a school of social work. These three would work as a team, each serving as consultant to the other two.

Summary

The great need in the elementary school guidance field is to ask ourselves some critical questions. How can we organize more effectively to meet the challenges of our dynamic society? Perhaps an analogy would be helpful. If we use a rowboat to transport four men across a pond, do we use twenty-five rowboats to transport 100 men across an ocean or do we even build one huge rowboat? Perhaps we need to develop new means of transportation.

Whatever is done will have to be done with a thorough understanding of our children and our available resources. And it will challenge the efforts of *all* of us, working cooperatively, to establish the optimal relationship between the two.

REFERENCES

1. Raymond N. Hatch, *Guidance Services in the Elementary School* (Dubuque, Ia.: William C. Brown Co., 1951), p. 14.

2. Harold Wright Bernard, C. Evan James, and Franklin R. Zeran, *Guidance Services in Elementary Schools* (New York: Chartwell House, 1954), 5.

3. Janet A. Kelley, *Guidance and Curriculum* (Englewood Cliffs, N.J.: Prentice-Hall, 1955).

4. Esther Lloyd-Jones and Margaret Ruth Smith (eds.), *Student Personnel Work as Deeper Teaching* (New York: Harper and Brothers, 1954).

5. Harold F. Cottingham, *Guidance in Elementary Schools* (Bloomington, Ill.: McKnight and McKnight, 1956), p. 3.

6. Norma E. Cutts (ed.), *School Psychologists at Mid-Century* (Washington, D.C.: American Psychological Association, 1955), pp. 16-25.

7. Jean Pearman and Albert H. Burrows, *Social Services in the School* (Washington, D.C.: Public Affairs Press, 1955), p. 9.

8. National Association of Guidance Supervisors and Counselor Trainers, *A National Study of Existing and Recommended Practices for Assisting Youth Adjustment in Selected Elementary Schools in the United States* (Ann Arbor, Mich.: Ann Arbor Publishers, 1953).

Practical Guidance Services in the Elementary School

HELEN WHITE
MARY EDITH BANES

Every child is affected and guided by the influence of the individuals with whom he has contacts. For a number of years vocational guidance and counseling for those with specific problems have been used in the secondary schools. It is only very recently that organized guidance services have been recognized as a valuable and integral part of the individual's learning processes throughout life. These organized services are more successful when the constant alertness of the classroom teachers is incorporated with the incidental guidance and the personal interest shown to the individual.

Keeping abreast with the many problems of the times, Lafayette schools now use various services in their guidance program. The line of organization starts with a sympathetic, conscientious five-member school board. Next in line is a dynamic superintendent who stresses the four R's—readin', ritin', 'rithmetic, and human relations. Next, there are full-time principals in each building. The next link in this plan of service is the supervisory staff namely, general elementary, art, music, physical education, and speech and hearing therapy. Closely related to these is the school doctor, school health nurses, and the attendance officers. Special provisions have been made for teachers of the home-bound, physically handicapped, and emotionally disturbed individuals. In addition to regular classroom teachers in junior high school and senior high school there are orientation teachers and guidance counselors who compile handbooks for new students. To make the handbook more meaningful

REPRINTED WITH PERMISSION OF THE EDITOR, *TEACHERS COLLEGE JOURNAL*, 31, 3 (DECEMBER 1959), 58-62, INDIANA STATE COLLEGE, TERRE HAUTE, INDIANA.

a visitation day is planned for these groups. For example successful junior high students visit the sixth grade giving suggestions and answering questions concerning junior high school. The sixth grade is given a conducted tour of the junior high school building and welcomed by the guidance director.

Some special services in the school system are those of a testing director and as of September, 1959, a full-time teacher-counselor. Community resources include a Federal Child Achievement Center, State Clinical Services of Purdue University, and County Mental Health Center. Community organizations and United Fund agencies contribute support in this work.

The merit of these services is measured by the success of their use in meeting the needs of the classroom individuals. One case involved the boy, Joe, when he entered kindergarten. His foster parents were his own aunt and uncle. The paternal grandmother lived in the same home with them and required much care because of age and hearing disability. The first conference of the foster parent, teacher, and pupil was at the kindergarten round-up. It was recommended that he be enrolled in speech therapy at once. His behavior would be carefully observed during the six weeks of kindergarten orientation. The parents were assured that if his adjustment seemed difficult they would be called for special conferences during this time, and following that time they could visit the classroom. Three conferences were necessary on simple disciplinary problems stressing obedience for the child's own safety. Disobeying the parent's request not to ride his bike in the street nearly cost Joe his life; consequently, both he and his parents were convinced that discipline was necessary. From one of the conferences and from daily observation of Joe it was revealed that he was very upset and disturbed by the unorganized home situation during the morning routine. It seemed the hurrying and shouting contributed to his nervousness, poor speech pattern, and lack of social acceptance. Joe's constant annoyance in the classroom and his lack of muscular coordination prevented his progress as a normal pupil. Techniques found valuable in aiding him to overcome his difficulties were various forms of counseling with parent-teacher, parent-nurse, teacher-nurse, teacher-elementary supervisor, parent-elementary supervisor, teacher-physical education supervisor, teacher-pediatrician, teacher-speech therapist, and parent-speech therapist. In addition to these the readiness test and parent group-counseling aided in pin-pointing specific needs for Joe. He was referred to Purdue University Psychological Testing Clinic.

It recommended Joe's continuing in kindergarten until he could be enrolled in the Physically Handicapped School the following October. While there he continued speech therapy, and as he became more emotionally stable, he improved in his academic work. At the end of three years his progress warranted the recommendation that he return to the regular classroom.

When Bill, a quiet, polite, overgrown boy entered the fourth grade he was emotionally upset, below grade level in mastering academic work, and very despondent even to the point of threatening to take his own life.

In a conference with the mother the teacher learned that Bill's father and mother were separated, the father seeing the child once a week. The mother worked long hours leaving Bill alone before and after school. He ate lunch alone or at a drugstore.

Loneliness, insecurity, and lack of parental interest contributed to Bill's inability to stick with a job, either money-making or academic work. He was tested at Purdue University Psychological Clinic. This recommended him to the Physically Handicapped School because of an eye defect and a poor speech pattern. Before this took place his teacher showed a great deal of personal interest in him and took every opportunity to "spark" Bill's interest in academic work, in hobbies, and in friends. After much patient, incidental counseling the teacher noted an increased interest and "a sense of belonging" on Bill's part. This same teacher-interest continued in the Physically Handicapped School. After three years there Bill became sufficiently socially, emotionally, and academically adjusted to justify his return to the regular classroom.

Another type of guidance and one that has proved very worth-while is that of group-counseling with the parents following the orientation period in kindergarten. An evening session of kindergarten is held in which both of the child's parents are urged to participate and play the role of the child in a day's complete program. The purposes of this are to help the parents to understand the curriculum, to answer their questions, to suggest helpful home activities, to become acquainted with the teacher and other parents, and to give the teacher an opportunity to point out the value of parent visitations to the classroom, the time they should be made, and the proper behavior during the visits.

This basic plan gives the parents a feeling of belonging to and knowing the school. Consequently, they continue their interest through the elementary school and similar group meetings and visitations are held, in the upper classes, thus improving public relations.

In the kindergarten a second parent-group guidance conference is held in the spring upon the child's completion of two-thirds of the reading readiness booklet. Both parents have their child's booklet to follow as the teacher explains the object of each page. This enables the parents to decide for themselves if their child is mature enough to enter the first grade. It also points out problems for the needs of individual counseling, resulting in referrals to the various school and community services that are available. The Readiness Test program is explained to the parents to help them understand the total picture of maturation; emotionally, physically, mentally, and socially. The results of the test are recorded and used as a guide for first grade groupings.

A great deal of the success of the guidance services is contributed to the thorough continuous testing program administered from kindergarten through senior high school. These are carefully evaluated and the use of the results enables the teachers to be more effective in their teaching and counseling.

These elementary tests are selected by a nine-member testing committee composed of the elementary supervisor, principals, and teachers. The program is flexible and subject to change at any time. The tests are administered, scored, and recorded on cumulative records by the classroom teacher. The evaluation is made by a director of the testing program. Above is a chart showing the tests used.

The profile record of Susan's achievement at the 3.7 grade level indicated she was above average in comprehension (5.2), but very low in word meaning (2.5). At the beginning of the fourth grade the teacher increased the amount of word meaning drill, provided additional library reading, games, and an individual progress chart for her. At the 4.7 grade level she increased her word meaning score to 4.5. Similar use can be made of any test score. (Chart 1)

[Chart 2] is an evaluative table example of the total enrollment of a grade ranked in quartiles.

The effective use of this chart is to show the group strengths and weaknesses thus serving as a guide to the administrator and teacher. For example, when the third grade class ranked in the lower quartile in reading a remedial reading program was initiated in the fourth grade. Great progress was shown in the fourth grade tests.

ELEMENTARY TESTING PROGRAM

Grade Level	*Name of Test*	*Source*	*Time of Administering*
Kindergarten	Metropolitan Reading Readiness—Form R	Kindergarten Funds	6 weeks prior to the end of school year
I	Metropolitan Reading Readiness—Form S	School City Funds	Approximately 6 weeks after school starts in the fall, or prior to formal reading
	Scott, Foresman Reading Tests	School City Funds	After Pre-Primers, Primers, First Grade Readers
	SRA Primary Mental Abilities 5-7	Supervisory Funds	6 weeks prior to the end of school year
II	Scott, Foresman Reading Tests	School City Funds	After Readers 2-1 and 2-2
III	Otis Quick Scoring Mental Ability Tests	School City Funds	First week in November
	Scott, Foresman Reading Tests	School City Funds	After Readers 3-1 and 3-2
	Stanford Achievement Tests—Complete Battery—J	School City Funds	6 weeks prior to the end of school year
IV	Stanford Achievement Tests—Complete Battery—K	School City Funds	6 weeks prior to the end of school year
V	Pintner-Cunningham General Ability, Non-Verbal	School City Funds	First week in November
	Stanford Achievement Tests—Complete Battery—L	School City Funds	6 weeks prior to the end of school year
VI	Stanford Achievement Tests—Complete Battery—M	School City Funds	6 weeks prior to the end of school year
Any Level	Additional Individual and Small Group Tests	School City Funds	When requested as the need arises
Special Emotionally Disturbed Classroom Grades 3-4-5-6	Stanford Achievement Tests J. K. L. and M	School City Funds	4 tests during the year at 6-week intervals

CHART 1 Lafayette Public Schools—Stanford Achievement Test—Elementary Battery Form J—Group-Grade Equivalent

GRADE LEVEL 3.7			MAY, 1959					ENROLLMENT 613	
	Paragraph Meaning	*Word Meaning*	*Average Reading*	*Spelling*	*Language*	*Arithmetic Reasoning*	*Arithmetic Computation*	*Average Arithmetic*	*Battery Meaning*
Upper Quartile	5.2	5.2	5.2	5.3	6.0	4.7	4.4	4.6	4.9
Median	4.2	4.2	4.2	4.2	4.4	4.3	4.1	4.2	4.2
Lower Quartile	3.5	3.5	3.5	3.6	3.3	3.7	3.8	3.8	3.7
Span	1.7	1.0	1.5	1.6	0.0	3.9	2.0	1.9	1.8
	9.1	7.6	8.3	7.1	10.2	6.4	5.2	5.8	7.3

32 Pupils below 1.6 in Language

Prepared by S.R. McElwaine

Another factor contributing to the high ranking of Lafayette school children on these tests is the book rental system. Each child has a complete set of materials available on the first day of school. This book rental is provided at a nominal cost to all families and materials are furnished for those who cannot pay. The testing program director also administers the book rental.

CHART 2 Grade 4 Achievement Test, 1959

ENROLLMENT 625	GRADE LEVEL 4.7
44 pupils below 3.7	Battery Score
247 pupils above 6.0	Battery Score
106 pupils below 4.0	average reading
65 pupils below 3.7	average reading
210 pupils above 6.0	average reading

A child's progress is so dependent upon emotional and social stability that anecdotal records have proven beneficial to the classroom teacher. For example, the case of Denise was revealed in an anecdotal record. When she entered a new school apparently as a normal child she sat on the far side of the room away from the teacher's desk. When the teacher read the anecdotal record it was learned that Denise was an epileptic. She was immediately placed near the teacher's desk and the nurse gave instructions for her care. Many behavior traits can be better understood by the personal records such as fear and day-dreaming.

Just as anecdotal records are helpful to the teacher so are explanatory reports to the parents. The practice of using numbers or letters on report cards proved to be ineffective in conveying the complete story of the child's progress both individually and in relation to his peers. Through a long term co-operative study made by administrators, teachers, and parents a new system of reporting was devised to show the degree of achievement of the different facets of the subject matter. Although all of the needs have not been met by the revised system it does reveal pertinent information and the parents have been able to analyze a report more satisfactorily. It is also good for the teacher to have to evaluate the participation of each student. It is beneficial to the student to point out specific self-improvement needs and encourages continued progress.

In addition to the help of the complete reports to parents the sociograms have proved helpful to the teacher. In the fourth grade one was used to help discover group leaders for science projects. As a result of this grouping the pupils cooperated well and worked in a pleasant atmosphere with friends to obtain good results. The isolates were shown a special interest and this enabled them to adjust to a small group first, and later, to the entire class. Jane, one of the isolates, learned how to work with others well, and because of her capabilities, grew to be a popular leader in the sixth grade.

Children of any age love the art of role-playing. It proved helpful in solving the problem of teaching the pupils to be good losers in a ballgame. Dramas were written by the pupils and dramatized. Both good and bad characteristics were portrayed in the different roles. A game was played and pupils easily detected these characteristics. Improvement was definitely shown in later games and a change of attitudes was observed by both pupils and teacher.

Another facet of our guidance program which has indirectly created community interest or action in the schools is the cooperative administrator-teacher-parent coffee social on the opening day of school. The purposes of the social are to assist new patrons in becoming a part of the school community and to re-kindle the interest of former faithful parents. This similar plan is used during National Education Week to establish good public relations with administrative, community, and parent visitors. The informal manner creates good fellowship, a better understanding of the schools, and an increased sense of value of the educational program. A third example of school community relations is exhibited in welcoming parents during kindergarten round-up with a tour of the building terminating in the kindergarten room for a parent coffee social. The new enrollees also have a cookie social. These experiences result in both the parent and child feeling the sense of being an integral part of the school.

The guidance program is a continuous process. During the summer indirect guidance is given through recreation, crafts, drama, and reading for pleasure. This is a cooperative plan with the city park recreational program.

To summarize the successes of the practical guidance services in this school system we have considered the genuine personal interest of all those involved, the thorough and consistent testing program, and the wholesome attitude that no one is expendable. Contributing to other successes are the systematic organization of the services working in harmony with each other, and the individuals recognizing the need for and making use of the services. Imperfections of the system are recognized and remedial steps are taken by the appropriate personnel. Each one is constantly striving in a research manner to improve the guidance services. Verification of the worth of the services is in the amount of money spent each year for staff and materials. Beginning with very limited services Lafayette has increased the guidance budget to $133,000 in the present year. With the increased enrollment, the satellites orbiting into space, and the rapid pace of civilization, the demands on each classroom teachers are voluminous; therefore, the practical guidance services are a means of assisting the teacher in being more effective in the classroom role.

Roles of Guidance Workers in the Elementary Schools

SCIENCE RESEARCH ASSOCIATES, INC.

"I just can't do anything with Phil Marston," said his third-grade teacher. "His reading, arithmetic, and spelling levels are two grades below what they should be. I can't seem to reach him in class. Maybe he's shy, or maybe he just doesn't care. Anyway, with thirty other children in the class, I'm not able to give him the time he needs. I think he has some sort of emotional problem; it looks to me as though he needs special help."

Phil attends a large urban elementary school which is unusual in that its staff includes a guidance counselor, a school psychologist, and a visiting teacher. Before we look at what each of them can do to help Phil develop emotionally and intellectually, it may be helpful to review briefly the development and characteristics of guidance in our elementary schools.

Patouillet[1] sees guidance as originally serving a remedial function, designed to help children *after* they had become problems for the school; as progressing to a preventive function, designed to keep children from becoming problems, and at present as assuming a developmental function, concerned with the maximum growth of all students in all areas of human development. In its early stage, when guidance was primarily crisis-oriented, guidance personnel were considered responsible for helping students make occupational and educational choices, and for dealing with "behavior problems." In the elementary school, where students had no career or college choices to make, and where problem children could usually be cowed, coddled, or cajoled into submission by the teacher or principal, organized guidance programs were rare. Only in recent years, as a corollary to the developmental approach to guidance, have educators acted to establish elementary school guidance on a large scale.

All agree on the need for guidance in the early stages of a child's development, but there is little agreement on what constitutes a good guidance program in elementary schools. Because children's needs differ from place to place, there can be no hard and fast rules in this area. But guidance personnel seem to be in general agreement that programs and techniques that work in high schools cannot be carried over into the elementary schools without change. As one book puts it, "elementary school guidance must be defined in new terms, broader than the student- and services-oriented ones that customarily characterize other levels of guidance work."[2] Elementary school children are at a different stage of development than are those for whom secondary school guidance programs were devised; their needs are different, and different methods and techniques must be developed to help them.

Confusion of Roles

The roles of the different guidance workers in elementary schools must also vary considerably from the traditional roles of secondary school guidance personnel. There is considerable confusion among authorities and educational personnel as to precisely where, for example, the responsibility of the school psychologist ends and that of the counselor begins. In some school systems the psychologist will be concerned mainly with testing; in others he will be charged with promoting good human relations and mental hygiene throughout the school; in others he will function almost as a counselor.

Some factors that affect this variation of roles are the size of the school system, the attitude of the administrators toward guidance, the type of guidance program in effect, and the size and professional qualifications of the staff. Thus "the same title reflects increased specialization as the size of the staff and the system increases. Attempts by professional organizations to write uniform job descriptions to conform to job titles founder on this variation. . . ."[3]

Betty J. Bosdell, in her Ph.D. thesis at the University of Illinois, found that elementary school personnel themselves are not sure about just what guidance services they and their colleagues are supposed to furnish. Some of the duties she asked about were assigned as frequently to one person as to another. For instance, teachers and psychologists were with equal frequency assigned the responsibility for giving interest, intelligence, and sociometric tests. Bosdell also found that when her respondents were uncertain whom to assign a particular duty to, they tended to assign it to themselves. The majority of her sample were teachers.

The Co-operative Approach

Perhaps much of the confusion stems from an uncertainty about what guidance is and about how the various guidance workers are related to one another and to the program as a whole.

Patouillet's definition of guidance is appropriate in this regard. The goal of guidance, he feels, is "the maximum development of an individual's potential for his own personal happiness and the welfare of society." It follows that the goal of guidance is the same as the ultimate goal of education. The conceptual dichotomy of *teaching* (developing the child's intellectual potential) and *counseling* (developing his affective characteristics) then becomes largely a difference in emphasis: the ends are the same.

Now we are ready to look at the relationships between the roles of the various people who shape and implement the school's guidance program.

The importance of the teacher's role in elementary school guidance is too well recognized to need reiteration here. But in many instances the teacher may lack the time, skills, specialized knowledge, or attitudes necessary for effective guidance. In such cases she can help her students best by working closely with a guidance specialist.

The administrator is another key person in the guidance program, even though, as with the teacher, guidance as such is only part of his responsibility. The initiation and organization of the guidance program will depend largely on him; he will call the case conferences and faculty meetings that are essential to a co-ordinated program; his attitude can insure or impede the success of the program.

The guidance specialists have advanced training in either counseling, testing, or social work, and usually a background in psychology or guidance or both. Although, as we have seen, there may be considerable overlap between roles, each specialist has certain typical responsibilities. In almost all schools having a counselor, the position includes holding individual and group interviews and advising the teacher in matters pertaining to guidance. The psychologist is nearly always responsible for the testing program. The visiting teacher or social worker almost everywhere handles truancy problems, is concerned with home conditions that affect child development, and makes referrals to agencies outside the school.

An Ideal Example

As an ideal example of how the guidance specialists might work together to help a child, let's look at the case of Phil Marston that we mentioned earlier. After the teacher referred the case to the guidance counselor, he called Phil in for an interview. From the child's IQ score of 110 and from the alert and intelligent attitude he displayed in the conversation, the counselor concluded that Phil should have been doing better work. A few remarks Phil let slip about his home environment led the counselor to suspect that much of his trouble was centered on emotional problems at home. The counselor went to the principal, who called a meeting of the boy's teacher and all guidance personnel. After all available information about the child and his problems had been discussed and evaluated, it was decided to take three courses of action: (1) the counselor was to continue his interviews with the boy in an attempt to discover more about his problems; (2) the psychologist was to administer individual achievement, interest, and personality tests; (3) the visiting teacher was to interview the parents in the home. All three specialists were to inform the teacher of any findings that threw new light on the case.

Suggestions Toward Co-operative Guidance

What can those engaged in elementary education do to insure a co-operative effort for the improvement of the guidance program? One of the most effective methods was illustrated in the story of Phil Marston: the case conference, in which everyone concerned with a particular guidance problem has a chance to offer his observations and suggestions.

Another means of promoting co-operation is the faculty training session in guidance. Through such sessions the entire staff can share in the specialized knowledge of guidance experts.

Patouillet, in the article referred to earlier, suggests giving guidance personnel a common denominator. Under his plan, guidance specialists would be called *child development consultants* and each would be responsible for *all* the guidance needs of his share of the children in the school. Each specialist would have completed a two-year graduate program, with courses in guidance, psychology, social work, administration, and curriculum.

Some possible benefits of this change of labels: fewer jurisdictional squabbles, better co-operation among guidance workers, less overlap of roles, and better co-ordinated guidance programs. Every child, instead of having to go to a certain specialist whether he gets along with him or not, could be referred to the consultant to whom he relates most positively.

For reorganizing present staffs whose members have specialized degrees in guidance, psychology, or social work, Patrouillet proposes a modification of this plan. "While still called child development consultants and performing similar tasks, each one might bring a different background to the situation and contribute unique strengths. . . . These three would work as a team, each serving as consultant to the other two."

If what Patouillet and other exponents of the developmental approach are saying about guidance were reduced to capsule form, it would probably go something like this: Let's stop sawing the "whole child" into thirds, like the magician on the stage, with one segment set aside for the counselor to operate on, one reserved for the psychologist, and the other for the social worker. Let's realize that each of us is putting his unique knowledge and skills to work toward the same goal: the optimum intellectual, social, psychological, and physical development of the child. Each of us has something to offer; each of us has something to learn. One of the most promising ways to promote this team approach to guidance is to give teachers, administrators, counselors, psychologists, and visiting teachers a more comprehensive education in guidance, with emphasis on the relationships between the various roles rather than on the differences between them.

REFERENCES

1. Raymond A. Patouillet, "Organizing for Guidance in the Elementary School," *Teachers College Record* (May 1957).

2. Esther Lloyd-Jones (ed.), *Guidance in Elementary Education* (New York: Bureau of Publications, Teachers College, Columbia University, 1958).

3. Warren G. Findley, *Encyclopedia of Educational Research,* 3rd ed. (New York: Macmillan, 1960).

Self-Understanding in Childhood and Adolescence[1]

ARTHUR T. JERSILD

Historically the psychology of childhood and adolescence has been a science which some psychologists try to teach to other psychologists and to college students. My theme today is that we have held too restricted a conception of what child psychology is and what it might be. The proper study for all human beings from the earliest possible age is the human being himself.

Every child is actually or potentially a child psychologist. From an early age, without being deliberate about it, he acquires ideas and attitudes about himself and others. These are woven into the pattern of his life. They may be true or false, healthy or morbid. Their development is left largely to chance. This is not as it should be, in my judgment. I propose that the study of child psychology, designed to promote understanding and acceptance of self and understanding of others, should be a planned feature of the education children receive from nursery school onward.

Need for Understanding

There is one gloomy fact about children who now are growing up which underscores, as I see it, the need for such a program. A large proportion of children will move into adulthood troubled and unhappy about many things. Many will be afflicted by irrational fears which do not

[1] Adapted from a presidential address given before the Division on Childhood and Adolescence, American Psychological Association, State College, Pennsylvania, September 7, 1950.

REPRINTED FROM *THE AMERICAN PSYCHOLOGIST*, 6, 4 (APRIL 1951), 122-126, BY PERMISSION OF THE PUBLISHERS AND THE AUTHOR.

represent dangers in the external environment but unresolved problems within themselves. Many, as adults, will suffer from attitudes of hostility, vindictiveness, and defensiveness which are not a response to hostile forces in the outside world but represent attitudes carried over from unresolved childhood struggles. Many persons similarly will acquire persisting feelings of inferiority or other unhealthy attitudes regarding their personal worth which represent either an irrational estimate of themselves or a failure to accept themselves realistically as they are.

In numerous ways there is a vast carry-over of unhealthy attitudes regarding self and others from childhood and adolescence into adult life.

Is so much distress inevitable? I do not think we have to assume that it is. But I do not think the picture can be changed substantially if we simply try to extend the special services we now provide. These services are good, and need to be continued. But the answer cannot be found simply by offering more psychological counseling, psychoanalysis, or other forms of treatment of the kind now provided for severely disturbed people after they already are on the rocks. A bolder measure is needed for the benefit of the population at large. This measure, I maintain, must involve a vastly enhanced conception of the social functions of research in child psychology and of the role that child psychology might play in the education of children.

The Underlying Hypothesis

There is a general hypothesis underlying this proposal and it is this: human beings, from an early age, have more capacity for learning to face and to understand and to deal constructively with the realities of life than we have hitherto assumed in our psychological theories or in our educational practices.

Current Evasion and Neglect of Self-Understanding

It is a curious thing that the subject of self-understanding has been so neglected when we consider how eager we are to teach other things. Children learn to bound the states of the Union and they memorize the names and dates of bygone wars; they study the habits of beavers, learn about the distant stars, and the antics of Mother Goose. But the subject of human behavior, human motives, and the inner life of man has been pretty much ignored.

Much of what we do in education is an evasion rather than a way of facing problems that occur in the lives of children and adolescents. I have recently been involved in a study of children's interests in which several thousand youngsters in various parts of this country participated. [7] This study emphasizes, as some other studies have emphasized, that the interests children are induced to acquire often are superficial, stereotyped, and fail to lead the child on a road toward facing his real problems. However, we also found in this study that many of the older children expressed a desire to learn more about themselves and others, even though little was done in some of the schools they attended to encourage such a desire or to suggest that it might be fulfilled. What I propose is that we encourage this desire and try to fill it by developing a program to promote wholesome understanding of self and others as a basic feature of the general education of all children.

Implications of Self-Understanding

I have used expressions such as "self-understanding" and "self-acceptance" in describing my position. These particular words are not, in my judgment, as important as the intention and purpose which I am trying to express. But the concept of the self, especially as it has developed in recent literature in psychology[2] and in some of the newer theoretical formulations in psychiatry and psychoanalysis,[3] is a fruitful one in this connection. I believe this to be true even though in the present state of our knowledge the meaning of "the self" can be defined only in arbitrary and tentative terms.

When we speak of "the self" we mean, among other things, a system of ideas, attitudes, appraisals and commitments pertaining to one's own person. The person experiences these as distinctly belonging to him and all of them together constitute the person's awareness of his individual existence and his conception of who and what he is. These attitudes

[2] There is not space to properly acknowledge these contributions, but I would mention especially William James[5], and the later works of Mead[9], Murphy[10], Lecky[8], Rogers[11], and Snygg and Combs.[12]

[3] I refer especially to the works of Horney[3, 4], Harry Stack Sullivan[13], Allen[1], and Fromm.[2]

and ideas are, of course, influenced by learning. This is an obvious but very crucial fact.

The self has been defined as a perceiver and a thing perceived, a knower and a thing that is known. Probably the self can best be studied if viewed as a composite.

I shall not try to list all the features of the composite. But I will mention some of the things which children and adolescents themselves report when they describe themselves. Recently my colleagues and I have gathered compositions from several hundred children from the fourth grade through high school on "What I like about myself" and "What I don't like about myself" and other themes pertaining to self-description or self-evaluation.[6]

When evaluating and describing themselves, many children think, in part, of specific physical characteristics, including stature, facial features, posture, and bearing. (In passing I will mention that some of our preliminary data suggest that there is a great deal of irrational overrating, often in the form of self-disparagement, of physical characteristics during childhood.)

A very large proportion of children at all ages describe or appraise themselves favorably and unfavorably in terms of social criteria—their relations with people, their feelings about them, the attitudes others have toward them, and the attitudes they have toward others. Many children also assess their worth or worthlessness in terms of their relationship with their parents. Here again, as in connection with the development of other forms of self-appraisal, it appears that there are many possibilities for misinterpretation and irrational self-disparagement.

Also in the picture, according to our data, there may be attitudes which a person has concerning his inner resources, his talents, powers, and abilities, his weaknesses, his defects, shortcomings, past misdeeds, present impulses and temptations, his role or roles in life, and his responsibilities, and (mainly at older levels) his anticipation of the future. Some children emphasize awareness of religious affiliation and of moral obligations, and some mention commitment to values, goals, causes, which, as recognized by them, give content or direction to their individual ways of life.

Selfhood, in the literature, is often described by using "self" as part of a compound expression with modifiers which highlight one aspect or another of what the term denotes.

In the present context there are some modifiers that are particularly meaningful. We can distinguish, for example, between self-appraisal and appraisal by others and note that a person's self-estimation may be true or false or realistic or unrealistic when judged by group standards or by objective criteria. We can roughly distinguish between self-acceptance and self-rejection, as in the case of the person who lives comfortably with himself, or, by contrast, disparages himself or is ashamed of features in his past life or of his family background or is frightened by his present habits and impulses.

And to do a thorough job we would also have to try to distinguish between the "real self" and idealized or distorted versions of the self.

Needed Research

To carry out the program I am proposing we would need a vast amount of new research.

We especially need to study self-development from a genetic point of view, with attention to normal trends and the influence of various experiences on this development. We need to find out what is the nature of the growing child's perception of himself and of others. What concepts pertaining to understanding of self or others is he able to learn to use meaningfully and to apply? By what means is it possible to communicate with him? What are early symptoms and signs of false or morbid self-evaluation? These are only a few of the questions.

By way of an illustration or two: what is the approximate phase or level of development at which a child can appreciate the fact, say, that children who bully him are not simply unpleasant persons but troubled persons whose reproaches and adverse opinions should not lower his own self-esteem? At what juncture in his development might the child have the capacity for making allowances for others (or for himself) when they are peevish or irritable, or the ability to "see through" some of the arts and dodges, masquerades, concealments and camouflages of human motives, including his own?

Another research need is the need for finding out how children can be helped to use their capacity for self-discovery and for understanding others. In the literature there already are some promising leads.

Professional and Practical Ramifications

The subject I am dealing with raises questions that have a bearing on the definition of what our Division stands for and on our professional affiliations within the APA. There is a crisscrossing here of what we normally think of as matters belonging to several divisions.

Usually we think of something in the teaching field as belonging primarily to educational psychology. But the basic research here required is definitely in the field of genetic and developmental psychology—that is, in our Division.

Much of the information we now have concerning the kinds of problems children face and their capacity for coping with them has come from case work in the branches of psychology and psychiatry which deal with psychotherapy and psychological counseling. But the scope of what would be involved in my proposal goes far beyond the population now reached by these professional groups and involves research that goes beyond the conception which some mental hygienists have concerning the nature of their work, although we will still need to retain special psychotherapeutic services for deeply disturbed children.

The aim in clinical psychology and psychiatry has largely been to help individuals who have failed to make a comfortable adjustment to the conditions of life. The aim in the program I propose is to help the growing person while he is in the process of adjusting to these conditions, including conditions within himself. The aim in psychotherapy, according to one school of thought, is to bring conscious processes to bear upon hidden or unconscious sources of conflict. The aim in the program here proposed would be to try to discover and apply ways of reducing the hiatus between conscious or unconscious factors in the growing person's experience, by trying to help him to develop to the fullest whatever capacity he may have for understanding and interpreting the events of life as they befall, his ability to deal as forthrightly and knowingly as possible with his own feelings and impulses as these come into play, his capacity for discovering his potentialities, for acquiring a realistic appreciation of his assets and limitations, and his capacity for developing goals that might enable him to be true to himself rather than seeking to conform to standards that are out of harmony with what he is or ever could hope to be.

Unanswered Questions

I am sure all of you have thought of questions or misgivings regarding this proposal. Perhaps the greatest skepticism concerning the capacity of children to gain psychological understanding through everyday educational experience, as distinct from special professional treatment, will be found among psychologists themselves.

One misgiving may be phrased in the claim that the business of facing reality in a happy way is more an emotional by-product than a job that can be achieved by a studied approach. People don't make themselves happy by studying how to be happy. We might also phrase a misgiving as follows: If a child already is unhappy or anxious, would it not be impossible for him, while in such a mood, to gain in self-understanding by way of anything the school might offer? And if he is quite happy and free from anxiety, is there any reason why he should try to understand himself? Does it not follow then that the proposal in the first instance is hopeless and, in the second instance, needless? Again, someone might claim that the intellect can do little at the adult level to influence basic attitudes and it perhaps is even more powerless at the childhood level.

I agree that the learning of psychology on an academic level alone is not likely to make much difference, if any. A person can possess a vast knowledge of psychological facts and principles and still be an unhappy neurotic. Yet I do believe that a discovery about self that is first perceived on an intellectual level can sometimes initiate a chain of reactions that have profound emotional consequences in a person's life. And, besides, what I here propose is not just an intellectual or academic approach. In attempting this program we would have to recognize that the process of developing self-understanding involves all of the growing person's faculties for feeling and thinking.

The program would probably make much use of group projects as an aid to self-discovery and self-acceptance.

It would mean a greatly enhanced conception of the psychological possibilities inherent in a calculated use of present features of the school's program such as what is offered, for example, in physical education.

It would mean that each subject that is retained in the curriculum would be used, as far as feasible, as a vehicle for increased understanding of self or others. There is a rich psychological content, for example, in history and in the study of current events. If these subjects are properly scaled to the pupil's maturity level and if they are treated in realistic terms they give play to a wide range of human motives, hopes, conflicts and perplexities which the pupil can relate to some of the happenings in his own life.

While the program would definitely not be confined to academic learning, intellectual processes would certainly come into the picture. It is true that there are people in psychology who take a dim view of what the intellect can accomplish. Even those who have attached great importance to intelligence have sometimes underestimated the possibilities of intellectual growth. Actually, I don't believe we have begun to fathom what the human intellect can do.

In passing, I would add that, on the basis of limited observations, I have a hunch that the ability which enables a person to be wise to himself does not necessarily show a very high correlation with the kind of ability we measure by means of our common intelligence tests. From everyday observation it appears that a person can have a very high IQ and still thoroughly fool himself and that people with modest IQ's sometimes achieve a very canny and healthy picture of themselves.

One can overrate rational processes, it is true, but it is also absurd to belittle the role intellectual or cognitive processes may play in giving structure to experiences as they occur in life and in modifying or reconstructing the effects of experiences that have occurred. A crucial feature in many of the emotional experiences that might influence a child's self-evaluation is the child's perception of what is happening—a perception which leads him to react to an event as a form of success or failure, as a threat or an affront or a source of joy.

The question as to ways in which rational processes and emotional reactions interact in the course of self-development and in the process of self-discovery, and the question as to the interplay between a person's intellectual insights and the attitudes which govern his life, would constitute an important feature of the research demanded by the hypothesis I set forth early in this paper. Certainly at the present stage of our knowledge it would be ill-timed to settle this question by concluding in advance that understanding and insight occur only as incidental by-products.

Another question is, assuming that we could learn in theory how to do all this, where could we find parents or teachers who could put the theory into practice? That is not easily answered. But I believe that this question represents a problem of research and education rather than a theoretical obstruction that dooms the idea in advance.

To carry out the program it would, of course, be necessary to give careful attention to the selection and training of teachers. Moreover, child study would be a crucial feature of the teacher's job and a very important consideration in the school budget.

We might also ask, is it really possible for parents and teachers and children to establish the kind of relationship out of which mutual understanding and self-understanding might develop? The parent or teacher is a disciplinarian, we are told. He holds authority. He cannot permit conditions from which understanding such as here described might evolve. But this view may be questioned. This question should be raised as a problem for study, not as a problem regarded in advance as one that either can't be solved or is bound to yield a negative answer.

It might also be maintained that it is dangerous for teachers, or parents, to dabble with psychology. They might damage a child's mind just as an amateur surgeon might damage a child's body. This point certainly deserves attention. But let us be realistic. Every hour, every day, millions of parents and thousands of teachers practice psychology and, in effect, teach psychology in their dealings with children whether they know it or not. They are involved in situations in which children meet success or failure, acceptance or rejection, and countless other circumstances in which children are discovering themselves and developing attitudes regarding themselves for better or for worse.

This does not mean that we must try to get parents and teachers to take over the functions which psychiatrists and clinical psychologists are now responsible for. At best, there will always be a limit to what a parent and teacher, no matter how well-trained, can do in dealing with problems that arise in their relations with children who are in their immediate care from day to day. Actually, we need to learn more concerning the overlapping and the distinctive and exclusive roles of the parent and teacher, on the one hand, and the specialist in psychology or psychiatry, on the other. Among other matters, we also need more light on the question as to how, in the *education* of children, we might achieve some of the things which the psychological specialist tries to achieve in the *re-education* of his patients.

So I say, let us as far as possible bring the forces which now operate in darkness out into the light. Let us recognize that the most important psychological facts in a child's life are his relationships with others and his relationship to himself. These relationships are constantly in the process of development and are constantly involved in the learning that goes with the business of living. Learning which pertains to anything so crucial should properly be part of the child's planned education and indeed should, in my judgment, be regarded as the most important part of the educational program.

Each child is a student of human nature within the limits of his maturity level and what he has had an opportunity to learn. The home, the classroom, the playground, and other situations are psychological laboratories in which he is now a subject and now an observer. Child psychology will fully come into its own when it discovers the capacities children have for learning from these laboratories and explores the conditions under which these capacities can best be developed.

REFERENCES

1. Frederick Allen, *Psychotherapy with Children* (New York: W.W. Norton, 1942).

2. Eric Fromm, *Man for Himself* (New York: Holt, Rinehart & Winston, 1947).

3. Karen Horney, *The Neurotic Personality of Our Time* (New York: W.W. Norton & Company, Inc., 1937).

4. ———, *Our Inner Conflicts* (New York: W.W. Norton, 1945).*

5. William James, *Principles of Psychology* (New York: Holt, Rinehart & Winston, 1890).

6. Arthur T. Jersild, "Self-Evaluation During Childhood and Adolescence: A Preliminary Study" (unpublished).

7. Arthur T. Jersild and Ruth Tasch, *Children's Interests* (New York: Bureau of Publications, Teachers College, Columbia University, 1949).

8. Prescott Lecky, *Self-Consistency* (New York: Island Press Co-operative, 1945).

9. George Mead, *Mind, Self and Society* (Chicago: University of Chicago Press, 1934).

10. Gardner Murphy, *Personality* (New York: Harper and Brothers, 1947).

11. Carl Rogers, *Counseling and Psychotherapy* (Boston: Houghton Mifflin, 1942).

12. Donald Snygg and Arthur Combs, *Individual Behavior* (New York: Harper and Brothers, 1949).

13. Harry Stack Sullivan, *Conceptions of Modern Psychiatry* (Washington, D.C.: The William Alanson White Psychiatric Foundation, 1947).

* A more comprehensive statement of Karen Horney's position was published after this address was written. See K. Horney, *Neurosis and Human Growth* (New York: W.W. Norton, 1950).

The Consultant in Elementary School Guidance

DON C. DINKMEYER

There is a real need for a clear-cut definition of the role of the guidance specialist in the elementary school. At present, we find members of various professions working with varying levels of effectiveness in the elementary school guidance program.

Many schools service their entire guidance program through the school psychologist and his perception of the task. This program frequently is diagnostically strong but lacks the scope of a guidance program. Other schools use a Social Worker as their source of guidance. Here, greater emphasis is placed on individual counseling and home-school contacts. Some school systems use personnel who would be more closely aligned by their education with the members of the American Personnel and Guidance Association. For these people there has not been a definite philosophy for their program, and as a result, they frequently function in a manner similar to the high school counselor.

We would like to present another view on the role of the guidance specialist in the elementary school. This will be called the Role of the Consultant in Elementary School Guidance. It will attempt to include the psychiatric, psychological, social work, and guidance viewpoints. It will recognize that this service goes on in a school, and as a result, must function in relationship to school administration, teachers and children. This program seeks to keep in mind the need for services to all children. It is based on the belief that in practice the teacher must serve in the role of doing the original diagnostic work, and that the teacher must carry on certain counseling services in the elementary school. This does

REPRINTED FROM *GUIDANCE*, 1, 4 (SPRING 1962), 95-101, BY PERMISSION OF THE PUBLISHERS AND THE AUTHOR.

not make the teacher either a school psychologist or a psychotherapist, but it does place her as a key person both in detecting difficulties and in assisting in the successful management of behavior difficulties.

This role of the guidance consultant arose from a need on the part of administration, the teaching staff, and the guidance specialist to build a program with real payoff. Careful inspection of the literature related to elementary guidance soon convinced us that there was a need for a new look at elementary school guidance; and that there was a body of knowledge available which could serve as a solid foundation for this new approach.

The major purpose of this program is to maximize the development of each child. It was felt that there was a real need for earlier identification and effective handling of the adjustment problems of pupils. It was felt that the elementary school program should not be just a repetition of high school guidance; but that it needed to consider the specific characteristics of the children, and to recognize the role and the relationships of the elementary teacher to her class.

Counseling, then, should be an added service which results in improved guidance by teachers, not in less guidance by teachers. This program, then, only works through establishing an effective relationship with the teachers. This can be done by in-service education and through close contact with their actual classroom situations. Obviously, it is most effective when it produces a change in a child or situation.

The program attempts to assist teachers in dealing with guidance problems at their level of demonstrated competency. It strives continuously to raise the competency of the teacher. It does not seek to build a large "private case load" but to help the teacher solve the problems in her classroom. It recognizes that many problems are directly related to the relationship between the teacher and the child, and until this relationship is improved, frequently, outside contact cannot be efficacious. The consultant is concerned with establishing a continuous flow of information between each classroom and his services.

The teacher serves as a screening device and as the person who carries out the daily relationship with the child. She selects the type of child she feels needs special assistance. Once a contact has been established with the consultant, she also carries out recommendations. Recommendations must always be formulated after observation of the child in the classroom setting, study of the cumulative record, and some personal contact with the child. Suggestions to the teacher are always tentative in the sense that she knows her situation and her capacities, and hence recommendations must be realistic for this child, teacher, and setting.

The guidance consultant performs a number of functions in relationship to the testing program, the coordination of services, referral, individual pupil counseling, group counseling, preventive mental hygiene, the promotion of research, and parent education. For the purposes of this paper, we shall attempt to stress the function of a consultant on learning and behavior problems.

The guidance specialist begins each school year by explaining the purposes of the program to the total staff. This should be done verbally at a total staff meeting, and in writing to all concerned. The consultant should be available for any questions related to his specific relationship to the classroom teacher. Once the original clarification of role has been presented, observation in all classrooms is a primary task. This observation must be with a purpose. It is to look for: behavior problems, learning difficulties, and difficult group relationships. However, the consultant must do more than merely observe as a motion picture camera, he must also act to establish purpose and causation as related to the behavior he is observing. The child is seen in the classroom setting in order to come up with a realistic diagnosis and plan for treatment. The teacher's handling of the child and the child's response soon makes clear the "psychological movement" that is going on in the social setting. This enables the specialist to develop practical recommendations that fit a specific situation in contrast to the classical generalizations that frequently arise from individual testing. Thus, the child is seen in relationship to the teacher, the group, the learning atmosphere, and the specific learning task.

Teachers are requested to provide a list of children with whom they especially desire help. They are also requested to list suggested times when they might meet to discuss the situation with the specialist.

The list of children requests the name of the child and a specific description of the learning or behavioral difficulty. At this point they should indicate what they have attempted to do about the problem, how the child has responded, and any background information that is pertinent. Insofar as possible, anecdotal records related to this child's specific problem are requested. Access to the pupil's cumulative record should be available at the time of referral.

Regularly scheduled appointments should be set up with all the teachers to discuss their problems. While it is important that each teacher feel free either to use or not use the service, it is also important that the consultant have some opportunity to develop a relationship with the teachers so that they are able to choose whether they can benefit from the service or not. This can only be done if the consultant is aware of the time each teacher is available for consultation.

It is apparent that a major part of the consultant's work is to fill in the gaps in the teacher's education. Typical teacher education programs do not provide the teacher in training with skills in handling guidance problems. Textbooks do not address themselves to this problem, frequently, and college instructors often are unable to stimulate interest in problems that college students do not have; or the college instructors are not qualified by their experiences to answer the questions of the rare student who has raised a guidance problem. The elementary guidance specialist must come up with real answers to meet the concerns of the teacher on the job. It is obvious that his batting average on recommendations must be fairly high or the teacher will not continue to come to him with her problem. The consultant can only be successful when recommendations are mutually developed, tested, and revised when the situation warrants such action. This provides an exciting challenge to the specialist in child development and guidance, for here he is able to see certain principles work with a variety of children and teachers. There is continual opportunity for him to check his theories in relationship to the laboratory of the classroom.

Aside from regularly scheduled appointments with the teachers, there should be provision for other in-service contacts. These contacts can be facilitated through pre-school workshops, institute days, staff bulletins, and released time for professional meetings. A variety of topics can be handled in such meetings and through written materials. Obviously, they should be topics of concern to the staff, preferably selected by the staff.

Some topics which are effective include: Individual Differences, Diagnostic Cues, Influencing the Child, Understanding the Child's Life Style, Changing Goals and Behavior, Learning as an Emotional Disability, Discipline, Cumulative Records, Recording and Using Anecdotes. It is also productive to schedule opportunities for groups of teachers to discuss mutual problems, related to guidance. If the consultant is able to develop a good working relationship with a high percentage of the teachers, he will also find them contacting him regularly through notes in his mailbox or on an informal basis.

The diagnostic skills of the teacher can be developed in many ways. Careful inspection and analysis of achievement test results can be most productive. Interest inventories, check lists, problem inventories, all help give a view of the life's space of the child. The typical paper and pencil personality test can be of value not only as a screen, but when used to see the specific response of the child to certain questions. Creative writing and the development of autobiographies provide other insights. The teacher can be trained to be more effective, in observing, as she comes to recognize certain principles. The consultant assists her to see that each child must be understood in terms of the child's subjective view, that all behavior is purposive, and that there is a unity and pattern in the style of life of each child. Each child tells us much about himself if we will only develop and use both the "third eye" and "third ear."

The treatment procedure is more difficult to discuss in general. It must be based on a thorough understanding of a specific child, a specific situation, and the teacher's capacity for managing the total situation. This necessitates adequate diagnosis and the recognition that many children are best understood when a tentative diagnosis is formulated. This tentative diagnosis is sometimes stated to the child in terms of "Would you like to know why you are acting the way you are?" or "Could it be?" or "Is it possible that?" This tentative testing of the diagnosis of the child helps to formulate the recommendations. The recommendations are tested in the classroom and are always subject to revision when experience with this specific child indicates they are inappropriate. This obviously places a great emphasis on regular communication between the consultant and the teacher.

This guidance approach implies that each child should be following an educational program tailored to his specific developmental rate and his specific needs. This can only be accomplished when adequate developmental information is available, and functional cumulative records are developed. Bi-weekly staff meetings to discuss the meaning of a child's behavior in the light of his cumulative record are held. These meetings are not only used as a typical case conference, but to illustrate general developmental and guidance principles.

This program places its emphasis on sharpening the guidance skills of all the teachers. Some individual pupil counseling is accomplished but only after thorough screening, and indication that this problem cannot be managed on a consultant basis with the teacher. Most counseling contacts are designed to be short-term, and to produce specific recommendations for the classroom teacher. At present, children who need intensive, long-term counseling, are not handled in the school setting.

The consultant assists in making arrangements for them with other facilities.

Group counseling is another method used to spread the services. Some group counseling is being done by teachers who have been specially trained and who work under the supervision of the guidance specialist. This is usually worked with groups of fifteen set up on the basis of grade levels. The guidance consultant also does some group counseling with the children who have specific problems which are similar and appear to be servicing effectively through a group approach. These children are selected in consultation with all of the teachers concerned.

This program, in action, has been a rewarding one, for both the consultant and the teachers. It has provided the opportunity to test a specific role in guidance and to see many teachers develop skills in understanding and guiding individual children more effectively. It appears that a wider scope of diagnostic services are possible when all teachers are concerned in contrast to the individual psychological examination by the specialist. This implies that all teachers must be made aware of the kinds of behavior which indicate the need for service, and that they must have available certain tools which enable them to locate children with problems.

An Administrator's Thoughts About Counseling

W. FREDERICK STAUB

Most specialists who work in the field of education are likely to experience, at one time or another, a lack of acceptance, a feeling, on the emotional level, that they are sociological strangers. It was a feeling I knew first as a counselor and later on as an administrator. Putting the experiences in perspective, I can see with greater clarity than I was able to at the time, that rejection has its values, that it sharpens the sensitivities of the specialist and enables him to develop a more operational type of empathy, and thus effectiveness, toward those with whom he works.

An example is perhaps in order. A number of years ago I had just completed administering an individual intelligence test to an elementary school youngster. I accompanied him to his room, knocked at the door, and paused in the hall where I hoped to chat for a few minutes with his teacher. She stood there, peering at me through the door which was left purposely ajar. Her eyes, her general demeanor told me long—or it seemed eternally so—before her words did, that, "If you had taught, young man, you would know that all the boy needs is. . . ." Dawn broke, and I'm afraid I wasn't able to suppress a trace of glee in my tone when I replied, "You're right, I believe, I had a similar youngster in one of my classes seven years ago." Open sesame, rapport was established, for "I, too, had passed that way," and we could then begin to work productively.

This phenomenon, the rejection of the specialist by the classroom teacher, is often a very understandable one, and one which perhaps finds its explanation in the log-teacher-student syndrome. Organizationally, education is a rather unique enterprise, without much of a tradition in

REPRINTED FROM AN UNPUBLISHED PAPER PRESENTED AT THE OHIO STATE UNIVERSITY (MARCH 1962), BY PERMISSION OF THE AUTHOR.

hierarchical structure, and at the core is the teacher and pupil in the learning environment. Between teachers and those professionals in education not engaged in classroom teaching in the classical sense, the interrelationship is often poorly defined and imperfectly understood. Communication, articulation, and coordination present special kinds of problems, in this venture, where youngsters and their learning are central.

Through the years, as perceptive teachers have studied the learner, and as specialists from other disciplines, such as psychology, anthropology, and sociology, have contributed to our understanding of the complexity of the learning processes, we have broadened our grasp of how intricate the teaching-learning act really is. Thus, we in education have arrived at the very realistic position that it is a rare teacher who knows enough about the psychology of learning, the vicissitudes of behavior, the physical, mental, and emotional abnormalities of the learner, to do the job unassisted. Specialties, as a result, have developed, and practitioners have entered the field of education to ply their unique competencies in the better solution of learning problems presented by youngsters with hearing and visual losses, by those with orthopedic impairments, mental retardation and acceleration, and a host of other deviations. Rather grossly to overstate the case, these specialists, who may or may not start with a base of classroom teaching experience, implicitly say to the regular classroom teacher, "I exist because you don't know enough about the specialized ramifications of the teaching-learning process." This, obviously, is rarely ever said, but it does not have to be. Adverse working relationships can often result from a diversity of causes. The specialist in education often comes to his position with more preparation than many classroom teachers. For this reason, and often because his services are in part subsidized by state foundation allocations, his salary is higher than would be expected, if the often traditional preparation-experience factors were determining his position on the schedule. His pupil ratios may be less, his facilities may be better, all giving an external "trappings" picture to the regular classroom teacher that the specialist, indeed, is in a privileged position.

Every discipline which is yet young, and imperfectly understood both from within and without, has the problem of creating an optimum environment within which to work. Knowing the acceptance factor inheres in "newness," its practitioners need to work as sensitively as possible in confronting this problem. Educational administrators, for example, are still fighting this battle inherited from board examiners and their representatives who punctiliously pried into the manners and morals of those who taught.

Counseling, as a formal discipline, is even younger than administration, and may, too, in some quarters, be regarded as an interloper in the educational enterprise. This may be especially so because it has "thrust upon the scene" as the result of some fortuitous circumstances. Man power studies which revealed some critical national shortages, Dr. Conant's trenchant look at education and its many problems, pupil population explosions and our insufficient resources to cope with sheer numbers, dramatic developments in our technology, and cold-war insecurities have created a climate which has nurtured counseling as a vitally needed vehicle, if not panacea, for that which appears to be upon us in education. As an administrator, I raise a note of caution and suggest that counselors, because of skirmishes perhaps too easily won at the outset, may need to work with considerable diligence and insight if the campaign of acceptance ultimately is to be won. I should like to suggest some ways in which the counselor might do this, by capitalizing on what I regard to be his stock in trade skills.

First, it is my observation that counselors are—within the discipline—concerned with a delineation of their appropriate professional roles. May I urge that this not be a totally parochial process? Anyone who works within education needs to have a role concept to function with purpose and integrity. Roles in education, however, because of some of its rather unique characteristics, are of necessity interrelated. There are perceptions of roles, which can have marked effect on how the role is played, which exist in the minds, and become manifest in behavior, of teachers, administrators, pupils, boardmen, parents, and members of the public-at-large. A counselor, then, working at times with all these groups, may need an attitude of role flexibility to maximize his operational effectiveness. Let there be time, I suggest, for the counselor to become familiar with his own working environment, and the unique needs and problems presented by it, and thus have an opportunity to parlay his own strengths in the winning of personal and professional acceptance. In my judgment the counselor must parlay the following factors:

1. Focusing on the counselor, I state, somewhat categorically, that he is, by training, the best understander of the youngster. He knows him, specifically, as well as in the generic sense, as an individual, with needs, drives, and a personality in foment. The counselor understands his mani-

festations of behavior, the compulsion to conform, the almost uncontrollable urges to rebel, his amazingly mercurial mood swings. Understanding these things and being relatively in a nonthreatening relationship as he works with the pupil, the counselor is in a uniquely favorable position to give invaluable assistance to those who often threaten and are threatened by the youngster—namely teachers, parents, and administrators in particular.

2. Next, the counselor is a specialist in the problem-solving process. So adept must he be in this, that he can help a pupil, often touched in a raw nerve end by some buffeting circumstance, to see beyond the irritation to the problem, and from the problem to some rational steps for its solution, or at least better control. As the counselor works in this situation, be his role catalytic or otherwise, his skill as a motivator often is put to the test, for he knows that the problem will only be solved if the youngster actively engages in the process. Adroitly, he may need to work with him to confront reality, to assess those areas of the problem over which he can develop some control, and those to which he may need to effect a temporary or permanent adjustment. It is in this process that a counselor becomes very knowledgeable about a youngster, and that knowledge which he gains can be the very type of information which the classroom teacher is seeking.

3. Since problems rarely are solved, it seems to me, in the microcosm of counselor and counselee, vis-à-vis, the counselor develops considerable competence in the area of coordination. He builds on his academic knowledge of the importance of peer groups, church, family, school, and community forces as they seem to bear on a problem-at-hand, by becoming familiar with these forces as identities and as processes. He learns how these can be marshalled as resources, coped with as people, confronted as problems' sources. In a sense, the skilled counselor helps to develop a curriculum from which each counselee can learn that which he needs to know to effect a solution to that problem which confronts him. This, too, I believe, is a skill of considerable value upon which the counselor can draw to enhance his relationships with his classroom teaching colleagues.

Now I should like to turn to some very specific things which an administrator might logically expect from a counselor.

These expectations are seen in a context of organizational productivity, for this, of necessity, is a dimension of particular concern to the administrator. A brief consideration of organizational productivity, as it relates to an educational enterprise, is perhaps needed as a backdrop to this discussion. Broadly, of course, it is the amount and kind of learning which the pupil attains in the school setting. It's the complex of skills, attitudes, understandings, and appreciations which are often mandated or often developed as guidelines by such agencies as the state, by accrediting agencies, by professional associations or by a professional staff, and by the community in each school district through its elected policy making body, the board of education. In a specific sense, organizational productivity gets extraordinarily complex and becomes mixed in ways that are difficult to unscramble. Productivity is often extremely hard to measure, although it is sometimes said to be "sensed." A community, for example, may feel that its schools are excellent and that morale and effectiveness of both pupils and teachers are high. At the same time, all concerned, professional educators as well as laymen, may be hard pressed to present supportive data.

In order to make meaningful inroads into organizational productivity, it is necessary to make explicit some specific objectives, see these in terms of observable, measurable behavior, and agree on what constitutes admissible evidence that can be used in assessing the degree to which these objectives have been accomplished. Let us consider a couple of these for illustrative purposes. One commonly held by many school districts is the objective of teaching pupils critical thinking. Another often refers to character training and self discipline. As stated, it becomes readily apparent that these objectives need to become manifest in behavior, that is spelled out grade level by grade level, and at times pupil by pupil.

It is at this point that the counselor can perform yeoman's service, by bringing his skill to bear on the task of spelling out objectives in recognizable, behavioral terms. Perspective is his, because he knows the individual and the group, both normatively and by expected range of behavior.

Secondly, an administrator has the right to expect that the counselor be a sensitive communicator about his own operation and about the function of a counseling program. Flexibility is a key dimension in the communication process, for a counselor often needs to be a skilled adapter to the situation which confronts him. If his own role concept is too rigid, and that which he wishes to do conflicts with the perceived needs of those with whom he works, there can be problems which could jeopardize his effectiveness. Communication, too, implies that the counselor find ways—and here is where his experience as a teacher can combat his sociological stranger proneness—to assist the teaching staff in understanding that there is a definite relationship between his work and that which is done in the classroom.

A third expectation is that the counselor have a policy-consciousness. An administrator has the right to assume, I believe, that the counselor is able to recommend policy which can be the guidelines for achieving the objectives of the counseling program and for lending order to the operation. The work of the counselor, by its very nature, has broad implications for staff and pupil morale, and in a wider sense for public relations as well. Consciously to act with a sensitivity to these things, is an attribute which certainly will be appreciated by administrators.

In the fourth place, there is an expectation that the counselor be a collector, clarifier, digester, of problems in the school setting, which are behavioral in nature. Sharply must he see them as problems, while at the same time must he appreciate that many will need his help to approach them by first getting off the dead-center of symptoms. The inventiveness which the counselor displays in seeing the research possibilities of these problems, will be a prized commodity, particularly if that research can markedly effect a reduction of the problem and bring about more purposeful behavior.

May I conclude my suggestions with what sounds like a crass note? The counselor, a student of human behavior, becomes increasingly knowledgeable about the more esoteric forces, and their subtle interplay, which govern the actions of men. As his skill grows in this complex arena, let him be mindful of the factors which best will facilitate his work in the school setting. Space needs to be allocated, time must be made available, schedules have to be constructed, materials require ordering. Concomitant with the development of requisite skills in his admittedly complex discipline, let the counselor also become a good budgeter who can speak clearly, and with sufficient detail, about that which he needs to do his job. Administrators admire those who can do this and do it well, giving evidence as they express their needs that those needs are seen in clear focus and in perspective.

If the counselor can do these things with skill and understanding, he will be an exemplification of his profession, a well-adjusted person who can confront problems intelligently, and who can exhibit the mature, adaptable behavior which he seeks to nurture in others.

❧ Part Eight

ISSUES IN ELEMENTARY SCHOOL GUIDANCE

Developmental Issues in Child Guidance: Plasticity, Direction and Conformity

DAVID P. AUSUBEL

Every person professionally engaged in child guidance work either implicitly or explicitly takes a stand on three important developmental issues that in large measure determines his philosophy and objectives in this field of endeavor. First, how plastic are children? To what extent can their behavior be molded or modified by guidance procedures to more desirable ends? Second, assuming that some degree of modification is possible, from what direction is it ordinarily effected? Does the impetus for change arise from within or without? Does the guidance specialist initiate change or merely facilitate its emergence from existing potentialities within children? Lastly, are we primarily concerned with helping children realize their individuality to the fullest extent or with helping them conform to the expectations of society and of their peers? What light if any can the field of child development throw on these three issues?

Plasticity

For those who are professionally concerned with influencing the behavior and development of children, no theoretical issue is more central than that of plasticity. Once conspicuous change has occurred in the organization of a child's personality, it is important that the possibilities of reorganization be assessed realistically and with a reasonable degree of accuracy. Exaggeration of these possibilities raises false hopes for every-

REPRINTED FROM *JOURNAL OF NATIONAL ASSOCIATION OF WOMEN DEANS AND COUNSELORS,* 22, 3 (APRIL 1959), 106-112, BY PERMISSION OF THE PUBLISHERS AND THE AUTHOR.

one concerned, whereas undue pessimism leads to defeatist attitudes and therapeutic nihilism.

Unfortunately, however, "the plasticity of the human personality and its responsiveness to reorganization are not issues that can be resolved by doctrinal assertion but are matters for explicit empirical determination. . . . Furthermore it is extremely unlikely that one blanket generalization could ever suffice to cover all [important] aspects of development." [1] In the absence of sufficient particularized research data bearing on this issue, I will merely attempt to consider some of the major factors limiting plasticity as well as the kinds of variables that must be taken into account in estimating behavioral modifiability.

Why is it that children exhibit a sizable nucleus of stubborn individuality that remains relatively stable in the face of various environmental influences? Three kinds of factors seem to be involved: those originating from (a) within the child himself, (b) his family environment, and (c) various integrative and self-perpetuating factors involved in the organization of personality. The child contributes to the longitudinal consistency of his personality development by furnishing a core of genically determined temperamental predispositions that in many cases are strong enough to resist considerable training and cultural pressure in the opposite direction. Recent research has shown that these genic influences are largely mediated through the neurohumoral system.

Parents, on the other hand, contribute to the continuity of the child's individuality by providing a relatively constant interpersonal environment in which their influence is maximized by the fact that it is typically recurrent, pervasive and affectively toned. The prepotency of their influence also reflects the significant advantage of *primacy.* In the unstructured and necessarily restricted attitudinal field of children from which most competing influences are excluded, the specific values of parents naturally tend to become pre-emptive in their patterning effects. These effects also tend to perpetuate themselves by making the individual selectively sensitive to the conditions that bring them about and by creating needs for similar kinds of experience. Thus, the very fact that development proceeds in a given direction makes the child progressively less plastic. Once such commitment occurs, susceptibility to other kinds of stimulation as well as other ways of responding to the environment and of differentiating a general potentiality necessarily become limited.

Further enhancing the effect of primacy is the fact that childhood embraces many critical periods of development in which maximum susceptibility to environmental influences prevails. Also, since children lack an adequate experiential background with which to interpret and respond to environmental trauma, the young child tends to be more vulnerable to the damaging effects of such experience than the older individual, provided, of course, that he is sufficiently mature to be susceptible in the first place.

Finally, personality resists reorganization because it is organized in relation to certain integrative factors that give it cohesiveness, and because, like any complexly regulated biological or behavioral equilibrium, it obeys the principle of inertia. As a result of characteristic ways of interacting with significant persons in his environment, the child acquires more or less permanent constellations of ego needs and habitual modes of self-evaluation. Once these are consolidated they tend to remain relatively intact in the absence of substantial cause for change. The child tends to react to the environment in ways that maintain the same orientations, habits, adjustive mechanisms, and techniques of striving and reacting to others that he used before. Even if the objective properties of the environment undergo marked change he may attempt to force the altered stimulus content into familiar perceptual molds so as to avoid the need for personality reorganization. Thus, for example, in dealing with peers and other adults outside the home, under-dominated children continue to reflect the influence of their parents' attitudes and expectancies even though this leads to obviously maladaptive behavior.

These considerations by no means point to the life-long freezing of childhood personality structure. Many of the more desirable personality outcomes of favorable early upbringing can be vitiated in part by severe deprivation, serious interpersonal conflict or crippling disease in adolescence or adult life. Similarly, balancing forces—from siblings, peers, relatives, teachers and other adults—are usually available to counteract extreme parent attitudes in the home. Nevertheless, even under the best of circumstances it must be appreciated that complete plasticity never exists and that the possibilities of reorganizing personality on a more wholesome basis are always limited by the child's developmental history.

In estimating the chances of reversing the effects of early significant experience one must obviously consider the direction and severity of the trauma, the degree of damage sustained and the type of trait involved. Immaturity of personality structure in children (dependence, hedonism, passivity, low frustration tolerance, etc.), for example, when conditioned by extreme parental overprotection, overdomination or underdomination (rather than by genic factors), ordinarily tends to be much more reversible than catastrophic impairment of self-esteem attributable to severe rejection by parents. In the first instance, the damage can be counteracted in large measure by re-educating the parents and by bringing maturing influences to bear on the child outside the home and within the counseling relationship.

In the second instance, however, self-esteem is so irreparably damaged that the individual can never completely recover from his feelings of inadequacy to cope successfully with his environment. At best, his tendency to over-react with fear (i.e., neurotic anxiety) to any anticipated threat to his self-esteem can be made more tolerable and kept from becoming acute and disabling. In either case, however, the nature and timing of counteractive measures must be taken into account. Much depends on whether re-educative experience is introduced early or late; whether it is consistent or sporadic, intensive or superficial; and whether the child still retains a reasonable measure of plasticity in responding to new environmental influences.

Direction

Historically, the issues of plasticity and direction are closely related. Theorists (e.g., Rousseau, G.S. Hall, Gesell) who allowed for little plasticity and believed that the course of development was more or less predetermined because of the child's phylogenetic inheritance, tended to advocate a highly permissive and non-directive environment that would not interfere with the prearranged sequences of spontaneous maturation. *Tabula rasa* theorists (humanists, behaviorists, cultural relativists and situational determinists), on the other hand, conceived of the child as infinitely malleable, and hence perceived the directional control of development to lie essentially in the environment. The school of client-centered therapy, however, departed from this traditional relationship of ideas and combined an extremely optimistic clinical estimate of human plasticity with an emphasis upon a permissive and non-directive environment. The principal purpose of self-direction in its view was not to allow for the simple unfolding of a predetermined personality structure but for the active *self-creation* of a personality with almost limitless possibilities for reorganization.

In any case, insofar as the regulation of development was concerned, the source of directional control tended to be dichotomized between internal and external determinants. Ranged in one camp were the environmentalists, believing in unlimited plasticity, and stressing the importance of external controls and sources of change and of externally derived needs and insights. Ranged in the other camp were those who highlighted the significance of internal controls and sources of change and of endogenously derived needs and insights. The latter group encompassed both hereditarian predeterminists who discounted the notion of plasticity, and client-centered therapists who viewed an active self as the principal directional force in development and emphasized the extent of human plasticity.

The major difficulty with these points of view, in my opinion, is that they posit a false dichotomy that is not consonant with the actual regulation of human development. Human beings are neither wholly plastic and helpless creatures of their environment nor wholly governed from within by endogenous factors and predispositions. At every stage of development, internal and external factors interact to pattern and limit the ensuing direction of growth. Those who inveigh against external standards and controls and assign a sacrosanct status to endogenous needs seem to forget that most needs and standards originate within the culture, and can only be internalized if they exist externally to begin with and are initially enforced by external sanctions.

Transitional periods of human development (e.g., infancy to childhood), which are marked by radical changes in biosocial status, are especially dependent upon external pressures and are never solely a product of spontaneous maturation. They are induced in large measure by altered cultural expectations and demands regarding appropriate behavior, responsibilities and prerogatives as children move from one age level to another. Thus, a common cause of maturational failure is insufficient environmental pressure to overcome inertia and resistance to change. The inertia stems from the various regulatory devices discussed above that tend to perpetuate the sameness of personality structure, whereas resistance stems from ambivalence about exchanging an established and familiar status for one that is more advanced but also more insecure and uncertain.

Thus, since normal personality reorganization in children ordinarily takes place under the impact of mature social demands and expectations (which also includes relevant moral considerations) why should similar external stimulation be excluded from the counseling relationship? Why shouldn't the counselor initiate as well as facilitate the emergence of new perceptions and motivations? In either case it is the individual himself who must take final responsibility for the reorganization of his personality since no real change is effected without internalization. No matter how unthreatening or benevolent his approach, the counselor still represents to the client

> the expectations of the social reality to which he has not yet succeeded in adjusting adequately. Much of the stimulus for change in motivation, attitude and adjustive behavior during the period of [guidance] . . . comes from the expectations of the [counselor] in his role of social reality surrogate. If the latter, however, take the position that it is the [client's] prerogative to structure the framework of expectancy and set the limits in the relationship, the [client] not only feels under no pressure to abandon his unrealistic, autistic or immature frame of reference, but also feels justifiably encouraged to seek adjustment within such a framework with the tacit approval, support and sanction of the [counselor] . . . Similarly, if the [counselor] articulates no moral expectations and fails to express ethical judgments, the [client] is justified in assuming that the former either approves of his immoral behavior or else considers that *any* type of ethical solution he [the client] is satisfied with is also satisfactory to the [counselor]. In the latter case [guidance] takes place in an amoral setting . . . Proper timing, good rapport, and tact on the part of the [counselor] are necessary, as well as a constructive approach rather than an attitude of condemnation. If, however, in spite of skillful handling the [client] discontinues treatment because of the [counselor's] expression of moral judgment, it is doubtful whether he could have benefited from it in the first place.[2]

It is undoubtedly preferable for the client to discover for himself his underlying attitudes and motivations rather than for these to be communicated to him by the counselor. Such insights are not only more readily acceptable to him but also represent the fruits of a more active, meaningful and profitable process of self-inquiry. Nevertheless there is no good reason why the client cannot "avail himself of the insights . . . of the counselor in modifying his perceptual and motivational patterns and his adjustive techniques. Not only is self-discovery not an indispensable condition for the acceptance of insight or the initiation of change, but it is frequently an impossible and unrealistic goal."[3] Many clients, anxiety neurotics for example, are not free independently to discover or utilize beneficial insights because of their chronically maladaptive ways of learning, perceiving and setting goals or because of their fixed and rigid defensive mechanisms.

Conformity

The problem of striking a desirable balance between conformity and individuality is currently a matter of urgent professional concern to the child guidance specialist. In America today, tolerance for heterodoxy has declined to an unprecedently low level and the cult of the extroverted, outgoing personality is at an all-time high. The most highly valued person in our society is the skilled manipulator of people, the smooth talker, the good mixer, the man who knows how to sell himself effectively. In this type of cultural climate it is extremely important to have safe, unoriginal, dependable ideas, never to rock the boat, never to take an unequivocal position. Thus, it is hardly surprising that modern youth overvalues conformity and expediency and shies away from independent thinking and ideological commitment. Taking their cue from their elders, adolescents seem more concerned with being accepted by their fellows and "getting ahead" on the basis of social poise and likability than with expressing their individuality through striving and achievement.

For this shift in the relative social value of conformity and individuality as personality traits, guidance experts bear some of the responsibility. Over the past twenty-five years they have consistently exaggerated the importance of being an outgoing, socially facile, conforming person, and have overemphasized the dire mental hygiene consequences of introversion, non-conformity and social unpopularity. Formerly a pupil would be referred to the school psychologist if he were boisterous, aggressive and refractory to discipline. Now it is the child who is reserved, contemplative and unconcerned about the opinion of his peers who is viewed with alarm. The tendency for psychologists to sanctify "adjustment" as an end in itself, irrespective of its ethical implications, has also contributed to the growing unconcern for moral and human values and a corresponding overvaluation of success at any price. When a man's worth is measured in terms of his market value, then opportunism, expediency and conformity obviously become more important traits than personal integrity, moral courage, and intellectual honesty.

These considerations, of course, do not in any sense detract from the importance of conformity as a legitimate goal of development. The very existence of a culture depends upon a certain degree of communality in the values of its members. Before they could ever hope successfully to adjust to the culture in which they live and to share in its perpetuation, developing individuals must also assimilate for the most part prevailing patterns of behavior in their social milieu. Even during childhood, the crucial role of the peer group as a socializing agency and source of security and status counsels an optimal degree of conformity to its standards.

The peer group is the only cultural institution in which the child's position is not marginal, in which he is offered status and a social identity among a group of equals and in which his own activities reign supreme. By achieving acceptance within the group he also gains a measure of intrinsic self-esteem that is independent of his performance ability. Finally, it is only in the peer group that children have sufficient opportunity to acquire approved techniques of sociability, self-assertion, competition and cooperation, and to learn how to enact their appropriate age and sex roles. Hence, children who are *completely* rejected by their peers not only forfeit all of these important developmental advantages but are also placed in some jeopardy of withdrawing into themselves or into a compensatory world of fantasy.

Nevertheless, those who counsel children would be remiss in their responsibility if they failed to appreciate the importance of non-conformity for the optimal differentiation of personality structure, and for the development of moral courage, inner-directedness and the ability to stand alone without group support. The mental hygiene dangers of nonconformity have been vastly over-rated. It is possible in most instances for children to maintain their membership in the peer group without conforming abjectly to its standards, without surrendering their individuality or special interests, and without sacrificing their moral scruples. Children and adolescents tend to exaggerate the degree of conformity required for peer group acceptance. In the first place, acceptance or rejection is seldom completely unanimous in any sizable group or as unequivocal as appears at first glance. Second, sociometric studies show that children consistently overestimate the status of popular individuals and correspondingly underestimate the extent to which deviant or low prestige persons are accepted by the group. Some evidence also points to the conclusion that apparent disregard for the group's approval tends to enhance the individual's sociometric status by making him appear above the need for currying favor with others. Hence, many "safe" opportunities for the expression of individuality are lost.

Popularity is by no means coextensive with adequate social adjustment. An ostensibly popular individual may be little more than "a stranger in his group" in terms of the depths of his attachments, or may be popular simply because he is docile, conforming, and willing to be "used" by others. Contrariwise, the child who is unpopular because of temperamental shyness or strong personal interests is not necessarily socially maladjusted or inevitably fated to become so. A follow-up study of 54 children referred to a child guidance clinic because of shy, withdrawn behavior, showed that 16 to 27 years later two-thirds of them were satisfactorily adjusted and only two were mentally ill. Introversion would stand a much better chance of becoming socially acceptable again if professional workers in guidance placed a less ominous prognostic label on it.

REFERENCES

1. David P. Ausubel, *Theory and Problems of Child Development* (New York: Grune & Stratton, 1958).

2. ———, *Ego Development and the Personality Disorders* (New York: Grune & Stratton, 1952).

3. ———, *Theory and Problems of Adolescent Development* (New York: Grune & Stratton, 1954).

Guidance Foci in Elementary Schools

CLAUDE W. GRANT

In order to present a discussion of guidance in the elementary school it will be necessary to review rather briefly some aspects of the historical background of guidance. Only from the historical perspective will we be able to understand some of the difficulties involved in developing a concept of guidance at the elementary school level.

Historical Development of the Guidance Concept

Frank Parsons, a lawyer, is credited with fathering the "Guidance" movement. Parsons noted that because of increased technocracy and the centralization of industry, the process of choosing an occupation was becoming more and more difficult. It could no longer be assumed that a son would follow the craft of his father, or become absorbed into his neighbor's small business. Appalled by what seemed to be inefficient methods of selecting a vocation, Parsons directed his energies towards providing some sort of vocational choice assistance. Growing out of Parsons' efforts the vocational bureau was established at the Civic Service House in Boston in 1908.

Parsons' philosophy was based upon principles such as the following:

1. It is better to choose a vocation than merely hunt a job.
2. No one should choose a vocation without careful self analysis under guidance.
3. Youth should have a large survey of the vocational field.

REPRINTED FROM *FRONTIERS OF ELEMENTARY EDUCATION,* 1 (1954), BY PERMISSION OF THE PUBLISHERS AND THE AUTHOR.

4. Expert advice must be better and safer for the young man than the absence of such advice.

Parsons felt that to choose a vocation a person should have three things.

1. A clear understanding of himself.
2. A knowledge of the requirements and conditions of success.
3. True reasoning on the relation of these two sets of facts. (That is, a fitting of one's self into job specifications.)

As we consider the historical development of Guidance there are three things we should keep in mind.

1. The Guidance movement is of relatively recent origin, less than 50 years old.
2. The original emphasis was centered on vocational choice.
3. Because of its recent origin early leaders and their students holding to the vocational emphasis still play an influential role in the field of guidance.

From the vocational choice point of view guidance in the elementary school is absurd since a vocational choice is not a problem with this age group.

In looking at the beginning of the guidance movement we should be aware that there were no existing psychological tools for the appraisal of the individual. The first published tests appeared in the achievement testing area. In 1908 and 1909 two different tests were published to measure achievement in elementary arithmetic. Tests of value in appraising vocational fitness were an aftermath of World War I. It was not until the 1930's that there existed sufficient measures of abilities, aptitudes and interests for clinical use in vocational decision making.

Of considerable importance in shaping the concept of guidance presented here are two other forces, each beginning about the same time as the vocational guidance movement. The mental hygiene association which has grown out of the National Committee for Mental Hygiene was started by Clifford W. Beers in 1909. The early history of clinical psychology seems to be centered around treating the deviate child, and with the advent of the Binet Intelligence test became for all practical purposes synonymous with mental testing. As the emphasis moved from mental testing to psychotherapy, clinical psychologists developed many concepts about individuals and the counseling process that were adopted by counselors in the field of "Guidance."

While the National Committee for Mental Hygiene as an agency was organized to correct conditions in hospitals for psychotics, by the early 1920's, due to the work of Freud and others, it was recognized that efforts at the prevention of behavior must begin with children. For this reason between 1925 and 1929 this committee organized and operated several experimental child guidance clinics. It is important to note that these clinics were operated outside of schools and were staffed by a psychiatrist, a psychologist, and a social worker. The child guidance movement thus got its start and continues to operate under essentially psychiatric auspices, concerned primarily with children whose behavior proves sufficiently deviate to gain them admission to the clinic.

This child guidance movement should not be confused with guidance in the elementary schools, nor should the emphasis on treating deviate youngsters be considered to be the emphasis of guidance in the elementary schools. "Guidance" is seeping down into the elementary schools from the high school and junior high school rather than from agencies outside the school.

The concern with behavior on the part of disciplines engaged in understanding human relations led to the accumulation of a wealth of information on the psychodynamics of adjustment. By the 1930's psychologists felt that they could rather accurately analyze an individual's behavior and determine the underlying causation of this behavior. Most counselors of the 1930's seemed to hold the point of view that if you could interpret a subject's behavior to him and point out the causation for this behavior the subject could on the basis of will to change his behavior change it. Thus the primary role of the counselor was that of diagnosing his subject through psychological tests and factfinding interviews, pulling this information together, interpreting to the client, and setting forth a plan of action. It is observable that this practice was in keeping with one of Frank Parsons' original principles, e.g., expert advice must be better and safer for the young man than the lack of such advice. The basic premise upon which such an approach is based is that the individual concerned is able to profit from such analysis, interpretation and advice—that the "Will" controls behavior. This is almost an inherent concept in our culture and seems to be rooted in religious philosophy.

In contrast to this approach to adjustment and choice problems there were some, notably Jesse Taft and Otto Rank who emphasized the importance of developing a non-threatening relationship with the client. Carl Rogers refined and expanded this point of view. His book published in 1942 was a fresh though controversial approach in human relations activities. The following points are some which seem apparent from Rogers' writings.

1. An individual possesses all of the necessary resources to the solution of his own problem.
2. The role of advice and/or interpretation in human relations seems to have negative value.
3. Each individual has a drive toward maintaining himself at the highest level of adjustment possible.
4. The important thing in changing behavior is providing a permissive accepting situation governed by certain limits, in which the individual does not feel the necessity of defending himself against various forms of threat, but can direct his energies toward growth in self understanding and self decision.
5. The individual must be responsible for his own decisions.

Rogers called his approach non-directive, or client-centered. He referred to the existing approach to the solution of choice and behavior problems as directive, thus leading to the rather highly emotionally conducted "directive vs. non-directive" controversy. While the majority of us in the field of guidance and counseling cannot go along with Rogers *in toto,* we must give him credit for calling attention to the over-emphasis on advice and interpretation in counseling and guidance activities. It is extremely important when drawing from Rogers' contributions to remember that his approach to the solution of adjustment problems was developed in a clinic to which came clients seeking help with emotional conflicts and not in a typical clinic established for working on general educational-vocational problems, and again, not in the classroom.

Contributions from mental hygiene, clinical psychology, and others have focused our attention on the importance of the adjustment process. We are now aware that decisions made by an individual, such as choosing a vocation, involve the total adjustment of that individual. The trend in the guidance movement is to be concerned with the whole individual and not just his vocational choice. Many consider a vocational choice to be a vehicle by which one person tells other persons who he is.

Historically then, guidance was centered on vocational choice. The process was one of analysis and advice. With the development of interest, aptitude, and ability tests, and a reservoir of knowledge about the psychodynamics of adjustment, counselors felt they were in a position to give accurate advisement.

Research on the importance of emotions in decision making pointed up the limitations of interpretation and advisement, and introduced more democracy into human relations. It is clear that "will to do" is not sufficient to change behavior. We are discovering that working in the field of human relations requires training far beyond that possessed by the typical guidance counselor of a few years ago.

We have now moved far enough in the development of principles of learning, the psychology of adjustment, tests and measurements, and skills in human relations to establish an effective guidance program in schools. There are however, in this writer's opinion three specific blocks or hurdles which must be overcome. Each is rooted in the historical development of Guidance.

1. The five services concept which has become synonymous with the Guidance program in the secondary school is too limiting and possibly misleading. In order to define "Guidance" as something apart from teaching, five guidance services were outlined by a committee headed by Jones in 1941 and later sponsored by the U.S. office of Education through Harry Jager, then chief of the division of Guidance. These services are: (1) individual inventory, (2) information giving, (3) counseling, (4) placement, (5) research.

It will be noted immediately that with the exception of the individual inventory service the other services do not in their original form fit into the elementary school, even though some current writers in the field of elementary school guidance attempt to make them. If the guidance concept is limited or defined by these five services, then Guidance at the elementary school level is not possible. There are many who take this point of view. We must break free of the five services concept in order to develop Guidance concepts at the elementary school level and to do justice to Guidance at other school levels.

2. The second hurdle is the result of the emphasis on vocational choice and the feeling that this choice was basically a matter of appropriate information and sound advice.

3. Building status for the school's counselor based upon his competence in human relations activities. Up until 1951 it was possible in New York state to receive certification in Guidance with a minimum of 6 appropriate hours. I am sure that this 6 hour Guidance counselor was very limited in competence in the area of human relations and felt very insecure in his job. This insecurity led into the trap of becoming a junior grade administrator and frequently an academic handy man around the school. The academic handy man role seems to prevail (in many places)

as the characteristic role of the Guidance Counselor. It is going to take completely trained school counselors a long time to effect a reorientation in school administrators, teachers and community as to their most effective role.

Based upon this background I feel that we are now ready to move ahead with the discussion of guidance in the elementary school. The setting of Guidance is of course in the school. No one would disagree that the primary responsibility and reason for existence of the school is to educate youngsters. If we did not believe that youngsters need the type of education that schools provide, we would not provide schools.

Formal education seems to be centered in the classroom, and is based upon teachers being able to provide appropriate learning experiences for pupils. There are a number of conditions which must be met as a basis for providing appropriate learning experiences, some of them are as follows:

1. A healthy relationship between teacher and students.
2. A healthy relationship among the various pupils in the class.
3. Motivation on the part of the student to learn.
4. An adequate understanding on the part of the teacher of individual pupils in terms of their
   (a) Social and emotional development
   (b) Level of growth in each of several scholastic aptitudes
   (c) Rate of growth in these same scholastic aptitudes
   (d) Remedial needs (personal, social, academic, physical, etc.)
   (e) Interests.

It is apparent from these points that while the learning process is placed in an educational setting, the determinants of learning are rooted in psychological processes and understanding.

Guidance personnel in schools, while primarily educators, must be well grounded in psychological understandings and techniques. The primary role of a guidance counselor in a school is that of (1) working with teachers and students for the purpose of reducing unfavorable conditions which impede student learning, and (2) working with teachers and students in the process of assisting students to operate at higher levels of efficiency. It must be remembered always that the teacher-pupil relationship is the important thing in the school since it is during the teacher-pupil interaction that learning takes place and/or is guided. Thus the guidance program must be set up for the purpose of facilitating this relationship, and guidance personnel should be selected on the basis of their competence to carry out those activities necessary to support the teacher in her role.

The basic purposes of guidance at the elementary school level and the secondary school level are the same. The basic competencies of Guidance personnel should be similar at each level. However because of differences characteristic of elementary school youngsters as contrasted with secondary school youngsters, and in the organization of the schools, there are basic differences in foci.

Let us look briefly at the elementary school. There are some factors in the structure of the elementary school that need to be carefully noted.

1. One teacher has the same pupils during the entire school day for one or more years.
2. The emphasis at the elementary school is not as centered on subject matter as is true at the secondary school level.
3. There is a possibility for a more informal atmosphere in the elementary school grades.
4. Teachers are not concerned about Regents examinations.
5. Parents seem to be more sensitive to the development of their children during their early years.
6. No one is worried about vocational opportunities or pressed with the immediate decisions connected with post-school plans.
7. In brief, in the elementary school teachers are in a position to know individual youngsters well and at the same time are sufficiently removed from the pressures of Regents, post-school realities, etc., to be able to modify class procedures somewhat to give individual youngsters more attention.

I would now like to consider what I believe to be the main emphasis of guidance in the elementary school:

1. RECORDING AN ACCURATE DEVELOPMENTAL HISTORY OF EACH INDIVIDUAL PUPIL. In contrast to a fast growing trend, or fad, to do away with comparative evaluations of pupils in elementary schools a focus of Guidance is that of very carefully evaluating each pupil. The underlying purpose is the creation of a developmental history of a youngster to be used not only by the current teacher, but by subsequent teachers and counselors and the youngster's parents. The elementary school teacher, having each pupil for periods of at least a year at a time, is in a position to make careful observations of youngster's behavior. There are several areas in which descriptions of pupils are necessary. A pupil needs to be described in terms of: (1) mental ability, (2) differential achievement, (3) apti-

tudes, (4) interests, (5) personality development. He needs to be redescribed in each of these areas yearly. Adequate tests do not exist for measurement in all of these areas. The fact that teachers can observe their pupils over a period of a school year offsets in part the lack of appropriate tests. For example, a teacher can describe a youngster in terms of his typical behavior characteristics. She can also describe him in terms of his strengths and his weaknesses. She can compare him with his classmates from the standpoint of artistic ability, music ability, social maturity, mechanical knowhow, verbal ability, numerical ability, and the like. These group comparisons along with recommendations should be an important part of the school's developmental history of every youngster. There are some who argue that objective information should not be passed along from one teacher to the next on the grounds that the new teacher may be biased by this information. From my point of view, if a teacher cannot handle information professionally she shouldn't be teaching. A first responsibility of a principal in a school is that of getting his teachers to treat data about pupils professionally.

2. Adult-child relationships. The second focus of Guidance in elementary schools is adult-child relationships. I am referring specifically to parent-child relationships in particular and in general to all adult relationships a given child may have. I would like to list two or three points which are basic to considering the importance of healthy adult-child relationships.

(a) The importance of a youngster being able to identify with adults in the development of characteristics, attitudes and values appropriate to our culture.

(b) The importance of a healthy relationship existing in any situation where learning is to take place. The most important characteristic of healthy human relations is *acceptance*.

(c) Parents have expectations for their children which are too often reflections of their own desires rather than in keeping with their children's abilities, interests and personality characteristics.

It is clear that a child's relationship with his parents shows up in school in many ways, such as in his work habits, his attitudes, his social behavior, and his way of regarding his teacher. The child's relationship with his parents must become a concern of the school. The school's concern is that the pupil's parents understand and accept him in terms of his level of maturity (physically, socially and emotionally) and in terms of his various abilities, interests and potentialities.

Starting with the kindergarten and continuing each year, parents should have the benefit of what information the school can impart about Johnnie's total development. The school has the responsibility of not only imparting information about Johnnie to his parents, but doing it in a manner such that Johnnie's parents understand and accept Johnnie and make realistic demands on him as he is developing, and realistic plans with him for the future.

3. A THIRD FOCUS—THE EXPLORATION AND DEVELOPMENT OF INTERESTS. The measurement of vocational interests in elementary school youngsters has no meaning. Expressed vocational interests during this period typically have meaning only in terms of immediate need satisfaction; that is, the expression of an interest in flying an airplane cannot be construed to mean the youngster will become a pilot, but that in his world of fantasy flying an airplane would allow him to satisfy a need which exists at the moment, but which may in all likelihood not exist in a few weeks. The concept of vocational interests involves the concept of time. To a youngster the future typically means no more than not today.

Vocational and avocational interests seem to be reflections of a combination of four things, (1) inherent characteristics which make it easier for a person to do something with a higher degree of skill than other things, (2) a society with a highly developed system of values attached to various types of behavior, (3) the satisfaction of receiving approval for one's activities with an increased like for those activities one can do well enough to win approval, and (4) the concept one has of himself as an individual. The elementary school period is one in which the individual should be exploring himself in relation to his environment.

The lack of rigidity of the elementary school makes this exploration possible. While current interests at this age should not be thought of as having vocational implications, they do serve as motivations to learning and can be capitalized on by teachers as stimuli to motivate exploration into new and different areas of the pupil's environment. Such exploration allows the individual to place himself in various roles, test various aptitudes and form a broad base upon which to draw in the development of stable satisfying interests.

4. THE FOURTH EMPHASIS OF GUIDANCE IN THE ELEMENTARY SCHOOL IS THE DEVELOPMENT OF SOCIAL AND EMOTIONAL MATURITY. Basic to all adjustment, to good work habits, to representative achievements, to evidences of feelings of self worth, to the selection of an appropriate occupation, to taking one's place as a contributing member of society and

ad infinitum, is social and emotional maturity. At a time when best estimates indicate that one out of every sixteen children in elementary schools will spend some time of his life in an institution for the mentally ill, the problem of social and emotional maturity is indeed an important one.

There are no adequate tests to determine emotional and social immaturity for use by the elementary school teacher. This does not, however, mean that symptoms of poor adjustment cannot be discerned in youngsters. The fact that teachers in elementary schools have youngsters 6 hours a day, 5 days a week for the school year in a relatively flexible program makes it possible for them to become acquainted with various adjustment problems of pupils. It would seem as important to keep a development history of a pupil's social and emotional growth as it is to keep a record of his growth in academic skills, aptitudes and interests. Each student should be described in terms of emotional and social behavior by his teacher at each grade level. This short description should be a part of his cumulative record. There must be a conscious effort to improve social and emotional adjustment as part of the school program. This, of course, means that (1) teachers must have sufficient training in this area to understand the nature of adjustment processes, and (2) sufficient training in techniques and methods to be able to work competently within the classroom on adjustment problems.

It should be pointed out that providing teachers with a set of techniques will never change the situation. Techniques in human relations are of value only as they grow out of, or are reflections of a philosophy about human behavior. Basically the first step in improving the mental health of youngsters is developing in teachers an understanding of behavior. These are, of course, certain skills which when they truly reflect acceptance and understanding on the part of the teacher can be used to alleviate stresses faced by a child in a classroom. Teachers should be acquainted with the broad area of creative arts, creative drama, creative dancing and other means of self-expression.

Teachers should be acquainted with psycho-drama techniques used to help an individual youngster find meaning in his own problems, and with the value of socio-drama to effect changes in group attitudes toward a given youngster, race problems or school issues, and as a means of developing positive plans of action in project work.

Kindergarten and primary teachers could profitably use some techniques developed in play therapy for use in their informal class activity groups. The teacher can determine phases of adjustment which prove uncomfortable to student through such approaches as sociometric devices, careful observation of individual behavior within the class group, noting previous teachers' comments and careful examination of cumulative records for discrepancies between measured ability and achievement, or an inconsistent achievement pattern. To facilitate the learning process adjustment problems need consideration.

The child guidance movement early emphasized the importance of working on adjustment problems during childhood. The elementary schools have been slow in following this lead. In the last analysis what has been gained if we succeed in imparting certain pieces of subject matter to students if their stability will not allow representative and profitable self-expression.

Summing up, Guidance Foci in the Elementary School are as follows:

1. Recording an accurate developmental history of the youngster's growth in areas of mental ability, achievement, aptitudes, interests and social and emotional adjustment.
2. Building healthy adult-child relationships.
3. The exploration and development of interests.
4. Social and emotional maturity.

It is observable from this discussion that the teacher is the central figure in these Guidance emphases. The place of the Guidance specialist consists of working with teachers and pupils in the following ways.

1. He works with teachers (a) in the process of assisting students to operate at higher levels of efficiency, and (b) in reducing unfavorable conditions which impede student learning.
2. His work with students would be typically limited to (a) obtaining information which the teacher could profitably use in her work with the youngster, and (b) in obtaining understandings which would help him give some direction to the teacher in meeting the students' needs in the classroom.

Guidance Functions of Elementary School Personnel

BETTY J. BOSDELL

In recent years increasing attention has been focused upon the provision of counseling and guidance services at the elementary school level. The concern of pupil personnel workers for the developmental and preventive aspects of guidance has contributed to a fuller realization of the possibilities inherent in the elementary school setting for counseling and guidance.

Elementary school guidance is seen as an organized systematic approach to helping every child realize and utilize his unique potential. It is an integral part of the total elementary school program and is consistent with the curriculum and characteristics of the elementary school.

The following assumptions will serve as a basis for this consideration of elementary school guidance and the functions of the various elementary school personnel. First, the elementary school guidance program emphasizes prevention and healthy personality development. Remediation and treatment are included in the program, but are not the primary functions of the program. Second, guidance and counseling is provided by many elementary school personnel working in a team approach and is available to and utilized by all pupils in the elementary school. Third, the teacher is a key person in the program due to his day-to-day contacts with his pupils and the unique opportunities that exist in the self-contained classroom for guidance experiences. However, the teacher is limited by virtue of time, his skills, and his training in what he can do. Fourth, specialized personnel in elementary school counseling and guidance are essential to the success of a program.

REPRINTED FROM *GUIDANCE JOURNAL*, 1, 3 (WINTER 1961), 47-54, BY PERMISSION OF THE PUBLISHERS AND THE AUTHOR.

This article will examine (1) how teachers, counselors, principals, and school psychologists allocated responsibility for various specific guidance services; (2) what trends are becoming evident in role functions; and (3) some of the implications these findings might have to the elementary school guidance program and to the training of elementary school personnel.

In a recent study, the author sought to delineate the unique responsibilities of each person as perceived by himself and by his colleagues. The respondents were teachers, counselors, principals, and school psychologists. Each completed a questionnaire listing 60 specific guidance services by specifying which person in the elementary team he felt was responsible for providing each of the services. Although the questionnaire did not assume to be all inclusive, prior use demonstrated that it did include services typically found or recommended as desirable for elementary school guidance programs. A replication of the first study and other data obtained during the past three years confirm most of the major findings of the first study. However, it has become apparent that some new trends are developing and some modifications have been made in the earlier trends. These may give some insight into the directions that elementary school guidance seems to be taking. The existing assignment of duties for each of the various personnel is given, followed by the current trends and modifications.

The majority of the elementary school personnel felt that teachers were primarily responsible for providing the following services.

- Recording observations of pupil behavior
- Administering group achievement tests
- Interpreting achievement test results to pupils
- Helping pupils develop positive attitudes toward school
- Helping pupils discover their own strengths and weaknesses
- Helping pupils understand and recognize their attitudes and feelings in everyday life
- Providing additional help in subject matter areas where the pupil is weak, excels, or shows special interest
- Giving pupils an opportunity to talk over their problems in a group setting with other pupils
- Interpreting achievement and mental test scores to parents
- Providing remedial instruction for the average child
- Helping gifted pupils with special projects
- Orienting pupils to the next grade or school

Recent trends have delegated the last four responsibilities to other personnel. The counselor is seen as assuming responsibility for the interpretation of achievement and mental test scores to parents and for helping in the orientation of pupils to their next school experience. The trend also seems to be for special teachers to be responsible for providing remedial instruction to the average pupil and for helping the gifted pupils. If such persons are not available, then the school psychologist is delegated this responsibility. These trends toward the utilization of specialized personnel may be due to a greater awareness of the availability of special personnel or a felt need for such programs. Present trends indicate that the teacher is viewed as appropriately helping pupils examine their educational and vocational plans. Also teachers are increasingly seen as responsible for providing pupils with occupational information appropriate to their maturity.

Some of the teacher responsibilities mentioned earlier are duties for which teachers are usually inadequately prepared. The question of whether the teacher can also serve effectively as a counselor has long prevailed. Perhaps in the past some of these things had to be done by the teacher if they were to be done at all, hence, teachers assume it is just accepted practice. This hypothesis is substantiated in part by teachers expressing a need for additional in-service work in guidance and for more elementary school guidance and counseling personnel to help them in their classrooms as well as with individual pupils. The use of elementary school pupil personnel workers as consultants to teachers is one of the most evident trends in elementary school guidance.

The elementary principal is designated as responsible for the administrative and public relations aspects of guidance:

- Interpreting school services to parents
- Disciplining pupils who are habitual offenders
- Providing teachers with an opportunity to discuss the problems they face at school

The only trend away from these duties has been toward the school psychologist or counselor also providing teachers an opportunity to discuss school problems. Most school personnel feel some problems can best be handled by the principal while others are more appropriate for the psychologist or counselor.

The elementary school supervisor was delegated the responsibility for providing in-service education in the area of child study and for providing group guidance materials to the teacher for his use in the classroom. However, recent trends see the supervisor's role differently. Currently the elementary school supervisor is seen as assuming responsibility for helping teachers to adapt the curriculum to pupil needs and to provide for follow-up studies of elementary school pupils. The provision of group guidance materials and in-service education tends to be shared with the elementary school counselor or is seen as his responsibility.

The visiting teacher is seen as responsible for working with pupils who are habitual absentees and for working with the parents of these pupils. The visiting teacher is increasingly seen as responsible for the work that is done with the home environment in aiding parents. In many respects the visiting teacher's role most closely approximates that of the school social worker.

Health personnel are held responsible for the health of pupils, for the recognition of physical difficulties, and for working with pupils who have health problems. They are also seen as a referral resource for teachers for recommending pupils with health disabilities or parents whose health practices or standards may need improvement or help.

Special teachers are seen as responsible for working with children who are on a homebound program and for providing remedial instruction for slow learners. Educable and trainable mentally handicapped students are seen as the responsibility of special teachers. As mentioned earlier the trend is also to assign special teachers responsibility for working with all remedial problems and for working with gifted pupils.

The school clerk or secretary is seen as responsible for recording test results in school records, for keeping cumulative folder information up-to-date and for scoring tests. All personnel felt that most of the necessary clerical work with records and testing should be done by a clerical staff, thus releasing other personnel for more professional duties.

In those instances in which none of the above special personnel are available, elementary teachers and principals see as their role the assumption of these duties. The school principal usually assumes the responsibilities attributed to the elementary supervisor and the visiting teacher, with the classroom teacher providing the remainder. However, as most school personnel commented, when there is a lack of trained specialists these things are either not done or at best occur on a hit-and-miss basis. When such conditions exist what is accomplished in any school is dependent upon its teachers and the principal.

Generally, in discussing elementary school guidance the two major professional specialists mentioned as sharing direct counseling and guidance responsibilities are the school psychologist and the school counselor. Perceived functions for both are in a state of definition and clarification.

Initially the school psychologist was assigned the following duties:

- Administering individual tests (achievement, intelligence, aptitude, etc.)
- Administering special tests to groups (all tests other than achievement)
- Selecting pupils for special classes
- Diagnosis of atypical children

The role of the school psychologist as described initially is what most often is perceived as the role of the psychometrician. Whether this in part reflected reality situations, a felt need for better evaluation programs, or a lack of vision as to the wider functions of the school psychologist was not determinable. Recent trends indicate an expansion of the above role. Previously mentioned was the tendency to assign to the school psychologist the responsibility of providing teachers an opportunity to discuss problems they face in schools, helping the average child with remedial problems and working with the gifted. Where previously it was felt that the school was not responsible for providing mental health assistance for teachers, this is now seen as the function of the school psychologist. Although the counselor and school psychologist are still seen as sharing responsibility for helping teachers understand themselves better in relation to their pupils and for completing case studies of atypical children, these are more frequently seen as the psychologist's function. Although the counselor was formerly seen as responsible for making referrals to agencies outside the school, this function is increasingly seen as the school psychologist's responsibility.

Counselors and school psychologists are still sharing responsibility for providing play therapy experiences for pupils in need of this service. Present trends also indicate they should share responsibility for providing in-service training in guidance and for working with parents to improve parent-child relationships. In those instances in which continued contact is necessary, the school psychologist is seen as the more appropriate person.

What then is the role of the counselor? The elementary school counselor is seen as being primarily responsible for the following services:

- Counseling with pupils with emotional problems
- Counseling with pupils about family problems
- Working with parents of children who have problems
- Arranging referrals
- Working with parents to improve parent-child relationships
- Helping teachers with mental health aspects in their classrooms

This tendency of the initial respondents to see the counselor as primarily a trouble-shooter rather than as a preventive agent might be related to the actual manner in which elementary school counselors were functioning, or to the feeling that teachers are generally in the best position to serve as preventive agents; hence, this is their responsibility. Counselors are increasingly seen as responsible for helping teachers learn better ways of working with pupils, particulary with those with social and emotional problems. Counselors are also seen as responsible for providing group guidance materials for classroom use, for in-service education in child study, and for aiding in the orientation of pupils to their next school or grade. There is some tendency to feel that counselors are more responsible for organizing group activities for those with similar problems than any of the other school personnel.

Where there is either a counselor or a school psychologist in a system, but not both, then the one who is there tends to be perceived as responsible for providing the services of the other. The only limitation in this trend is in terms of lack of training of the psychologist or the counselor to assume some highly specialized responsibilities.

In summary, then, it can be seen that although delineation of job responsibilities is beginning to differentiate clearly between roles, there are still many areas of overlap and some areas for which no one is perceived as responsible.

In the past, necessity has required the teacher to do many of the things for which he is not trained. Where counselors have functioned in schools, their roles have been largely trouble-shooting and not preventive. Trends presented indicate that current thinking is moving toward the developmental and preventive role of counselors, with the majority of their time spent in working with teachers and pupils. The challenge that faces elementary educators and pupil personnel specialists is to discover and implement the best methods of fulfilling the aims of elementary guidance services.

❧ Let's *Not Tell* Parents Their Children's I.Q.'s

JOHN A.R. WILSON

So you are going to tell parents the I.Q. of their children!

In principle, I heartily agree with the idea that parents should know the capabilities of their children. It would make it so much easier to plan for their future. After all, there is not much point in spending years of heartbreaking struggle trying to prepare for college if a young person is not capable of doing college work.

For the slower students—shall we say those in the lower quarter of the population?—it is best that they get on with the job of finding a comfortable niche that will not be too taxing and that can be the basis of a pleasant and worthwhile life. Pushing these young people into aspirations to be college presidents, lawyers, and school teachers can only lead to frustrations and eventual mental ill health. It is better to be a good ditchdigger than it is to be a poor doctor; better for the person and better for society.

Conversely, is it not desirable that the bright be identified early so that they can be encouraged to work a little harder to enable them to fulfill their promise? We need all the good minds that we can locate and develop. Why, then, is there any question about telling parents the I.Q.'s of their children?

I think there are two good reasons. The first one is that we do not know the I.Q., and the other is that, if we did know the I.Q. of an individual child, there is no way of communicating this information to the average parent.

I shall elaborate. I have before me the I.Q. scores for a small class, se-

REPRINTED FROM *PHI DELTA KAPPAN,* 40, 9 (JUNE 1959), 343-345, BY PERMISSION OF THE PUBLISHERS AND THE AUTHOR.

lected because the students in it were well above average in ability. These scores were obtained at different times from kindergarten through grade 8. Let us look at them [see Table 1].

TABLE 1 Intelligence Tests and Grades in Which Administered

	CTMM*								SRA†	WISC‡
Individual	*K*	*1*	*2*	*3*	*4*	*5*	*6*	*7*	8	8
Student 1					140		136		130	139
Student 2	129	129	112		122		130		119	131
Student 3			116	134	115		130		105	133
Student 4					94		131		98	133
Student 5		125	127		126				123	143
Student 6	119		136		123				116	133
Student 7	124		107		131				107	117
Student 8						117	128		129	134
Student 9	122		130		128		130		118	118
Student 10	125		126		120	109	135		127	112
Student 11									117	122
Student 12	147				135		134		123	125
Student 13	136		127		131		133		119	131
Student 14					118		129		102	130

* California Test of Mental Maturity
† Science Research Associates Primary Mental Abilities Test
‡ Wechsler Intelligence Scale for Children

Portrayed in this array of figures is the first major dilemma of the conscientious administrator who wants to inform a parent about the ability of his son or daughter. It makes quite a difference to the parent of Student Number 14 whether he is informed that his child has an I.Q. of 102 or of 130. Both of these scores were obtained within a very few months of each other. Looking over the array, it seems as though the WISC test yields scores consistently, and sometimes substantially, higher than the SRA test. About the time that this fact begins to dawn, Student Number 10 shows up with a score of 127 on the SRA test, the second highest score in this particular list. However, this student obtained a score of only 112 on the WISC test, lowest in the group by a good five points. Over the years, the record for Student Number 10 would seem to indicate that the 127 score is the more accurate of the last two. In his case, analysis of his WISC results indicates that he had a high verbal score but quite low performance on four of the five tests. Is this information important in the interpretation of this youngster's intelligence? (It may be a clue to the fact that he was in a gifted but non-motivated group of students.)

Which Test Will You Use?

When you decide that you are going to inform parents of the scores their children earn on intelligence tests, which test are you going to use? Are you going to explain to the parents that these scores might have been either higher or lower if different tests had been used? Are you going to base your results on one test only? (To use only one test obviates many difficult decisions, of course.)

From this problem of choosing which I.Q. you tell the parent about, let us turn to the problem of communicating with the parent.

You have been trained over many years to understand the meaning of the I.Q. It is only natural that you assume that everyone is almost as conversant with the concept as you are, at least with the vocabulary. But everyone is not. If you wish to test this statement, ask a number of your teachers—not counselors or test experts—to explain to you the meaning of the standard error of measurement as it relates to an I.Q. test. Unless you intend to report the test scores in bands such as those that the SCAT test uses, you are almost certainly going to have to explain to the parents the concept of the standard error of measurement. The I.Q. score is not sufficiently stable to permit you to avoid this concept, even though you might avoid the name. If your teachers cannot tell you what this means, even though they have recently had to pass an examination which presumed such knowledge, how do you expect the parents to understand you?

The parent who wishes to push his youngster will interpret your explanation as meaning that there is a real chance that his child is actually two standard deviations above where his score places him. On the other hand, the punitive parent will interpret your report as meaning that his child really did well on the test, but that the test results were probably a fluke and that his child is probably not as intelligent as the score given would indicate.

Some Horrible Examples

I have seen the harm that I.Q. information has done to individuals who have been informed of their scores. I am sure that you have also. The following example will illustrate the point I am trying to emphasize: A friend of mine, while in the junior high school grades, was told that he had an I.Q. in the 90's. This bit of information haunted him through the years, although he must have been aware that the information was erroneous, for in a university noted for the quality of its graduates, he earned a degree with distinction, completing a joint major in mathematics and physics. He went on to graduate school and earned a master's degree with straight A's. He is currently the superintendent of a large school district and handles the job very capably.

Another example will describe a different danger to which people supposedly intelligent enough to know better are subject. There were three partners in a business, all university graduates who had taught school. One of them had been a school principal. By one means or another, they had all learned their I.Q. scores, which were 135, 133, and 132. The man with a score of 135 quite seriously pointed out that he was smarter than the other two partners and that the partner with the I.Q. of 133 was smarter than the one with the score of 132. It was bad enough to have this conversation take place, but it was worse to find that none of the men would accept the fact that the scores were so close that there was absolutely no basis for feeling that one partner was more capable than the others. These people were gifted, yet unable to understand the significance of the scores.

How Well Do *Teachers* Understand?

My students would be quick to point out the danger that is inherent in using isolated cases to prove a point. They would be entirely correct. Therefore, before authorizing your teachers to give I.Q. scores to parents, try a little experiment to learn just how well the teachers understand the meaning of the scores. If this test is passed, test the same subjects to see how well they can pass on their information to a *thoroughly biased* individual.

Having said all I have about the danger of giving I.Q. scores to parents, some of you will probably come to the conclusion that the scores are so unstable that they are meaningless. This is not so. They are just a bit more difficult to interpret than it at first seems.

If you are willing to make the necessary effort to verify the accuracy of scores by checking them against other tests and against performance, and if you have the patience and the skill to work carefully with the parent of a youngster who needs the kind of a push that this kind of information might supply, by all means go ahead. Most of you have been working on this basis with parents of the mentally retarded already. You have used individual scores to confirm teachers' judgments and group scores. You have conferred with the parents and have explained the nature of the program for the slow learner and the advantages of his being in this special class. It does not always mean that the parent accepts your evaluation of the situation, but usually he does.

Similarly, if you are willing to go to the same lengths with the bright and the average pupil, if you are aware of a real need for a course of action that is dependent upon the parent understanding the level of intelligence of his child, and if you are willing to verify the teacher's judgment and the results of the group test with an individual test properly administered, then by all means go ahead. Tell the parent what he should know, but tell him in such a way that he can understand and follow up the information with action.

If you are going to give out scores of a routine group test to parents so that they can play with them at the bridge table, using the information to maim each other in subtle ways, then it would seem to be inadvisable. Remember that I.Q. scores are one of the most dynamic status implements obtainable. This is particularly true in certain socio-economic groups, usually the ones that would like to have the information made available. It is an implement that can damage as well as aid. Please make sure that these scores, if you make them available, are used to benefit and not to harm.

Let's *Tell* Parents Their Children's I.Q.'s

ROBERT TOPP

Every once in a while professional people discover to their surprise that the clientele they serve is much more capable of understanding "professional" matters than they had thought possible.

Physicians are learning they can explain a cardiograph to patients and by doing so secure cooperation in therapy otherwise unobtainable. Dentists find that insight into theory underlying decay will result in improved dental hygiene for the people they serve.

So it is with respect to education: parents are being informed about many matters formerly considered either beyond their comprehension or not within their ability to accept with reasonable objectivity.

Information about their children's I.Q. is one of these matters.

Up to now we have played a hush-hush game with the I.Q. because we wanted to protect parents from what might be bad news to them or from what they might view as good news which in itself is not. They might assume, we believed, that a low I.Q. means that their child is destined to failure in whatever he tries; or, conversely, that a high I.Q. promises success for the asking. They would be wrong, of course, in either case.[1]

Time and again we heard ourselves saying, "Parents of bright children will become overbearing and parents of dull children ashamed." Or, "Parents who tell their children their I.Q.'s will cause those who are high to loaf and those who are low to become discouraged and quit."

But even these frightening thoughts are not justification for keeping the I.Q. secret from parents. The anticipated consequences come about, if

[1] Cronbach writes, "Some persons of I.Q. 110 make significant contributions and some of I.Q. 160 lead undistinguished adult lives."[1, p. 123]

REPRINTED FROM *PHI DELTA KAPPAN*, 40, 9 (JUNE 1959), 342, 346, BY PERMISSION OF THE PUBLISHERS AND THE AUTHOR.

they do at all, not from knowledge of the I.Q. level of children but from *attitudes* of the parents toward this information. Some parents boast about their child's ability to climb to the top of the jungle-gym and others are embarrassed by their adolescent boy's squeaky voice. Keeping parents in ignorance of facts which concern their children because their attitudes might be wrong seems indefensible.

Our reluctance to discuss the I.Q. has had much to do with the present unhealthy state of affairs. As in sex education, the more secretive we were the more intriguing the subject became. And as with sex, everyone talked about it but most of what was said was exaggerated. Paradoxically, while we refrained from telling parents we continued to use I.Q. information for the very same reasons that would make it useful to parents.

Which brings us to the most important argument for telling parents the I.Q.'s of their children. It constitutes one additional, significant measure of a set of qualities possessed in varying degree by all people. Parents ought to have information if they are to plan the future with their children. They guide children through the "long haul" while we teachers of necessity are concerned only for a year or so in the lives of the young people we guide. Yet teachers feel that this is essential information to have about each child. And so should parents know about the potential of their children in order to plan intelligently for further education and make hundreds of other decisions that affect their children's future.

If there is a cardinal principle of mental health, it is "know thyself." Know your own (in this case your children's) weaknesses and strengths and accept them, governing yourself accordingly. I.Q. information seems to be this kind of essential knowledge, especially during the elementary and secondary school years.

We have been correct, however, in assuming that if parents were told the I.Q.'s of their children without qualification and explanation some misinterpretations would be made. Consequently, explanation and instruction to parents (and to many teachers) is in order.[2]

They can well be told, individually and in workshop groups, that the I.Q. is a measure established by two or more paper-and-pencil group tests. They can be told that, in spite of the general constancy of the I.Q., there can be some fluctuation over the developmental years, and great fluctuation in rare instances. Usually, appreciable change in I.Q. comes

[2] Smith writes, "Ideally, parents and teachers should work as a team in sharing information for the welfare of the child. But parents as well as teachers must thoroughly understand the meaning of intelligence test scores before they can use them to the child's advantage."[2]

about only through rather extensive "interference" with intellectual functioning such as emotional illness, physical illness or handicap, or an impoverished environment such as might prevail at a poorly-operated orphanage. In other words, for most children the I.Q. is relatively constant.[3]

Another aspect that can be pointed out is that I.Q. does not represent *general* ability, but specific abilities related to the manipulation of verbal-abstract symbols. For example, the I.Q. one possesses does not assure scholastic achievement but contributes to it. Other abilities and attitudes that contribute to school success are at least equally significant: seriousness of purpose, social insight, mechanical aptitude, to mention a few. McDaniel writes, "The student with highest test scores is not always the achiever, nor is the student with a low score inevitably doomed to failure. Many factors other than intelligence enter into scholastic success; and, at best, a test represents only a sampling of the individual's abilities."[4] Ruch supports this point of view when he notes that ". . . a person can be intelligent in one field and not in another, indicating there is not a 'general' intelligence which includes all abilities." [5]

Don't Undervalue I.Q. Significance

Just as we should avoid attaching too much importance to the I.Q., so we should not depreciate its significance. We could very well point out that the median I.Q. of college freshmen in American colleges is about 109, but to graduate from a high grade college with average marks and normal effort an I.Q. of 120 may be necessary. We could tell parents that the mean *minimum* I.Q. of students doing average work in the high-school academic curriculum is approximately 104.[1] We should tell them that the theoretical average I.Q. in an unselected population is 100, but that this average increases the higher the group on the educational ladder.

When we inform parents about the I.Q. of their children there is no reason why we should not engage in some "directive" group and individual counseling. Just as we suggest to parents that it is unwise to compare school marks of children in the same family (or of any children, for that matter) in the presence of the children, or as we admonish them not to

3 Ausubel states, "Generally speaking, once the I.Q. approaches stability it tends to remain relatively constant. . . . At the age of nine, for example, the probable error of an I.Q. is about five points. This means that one-half the tested persons do not deviate more than five points on retesting."[3, p. 593]

overprotect, so we should urge them to consider the desirability of using I.Q. information in an appropriate way.

Parents may be told at this time that there is nothing to be gained by using I.Q. data as a "threat" or a "promise" to get a child to work harder or feel prouder. They may be informed that it is probably unwise to tell the child his I.Q. until he is old enough to understand its significance, and that this perhaps should be left to the high-school counselor to do, if he feels it wise. If we handle it delicately enough, we might even suggest to parents that none of this information, whether it consists of scores on standardized achievement tests, school marks, results of aptitude tests, or I.Q., need be shared with other adults but should be used only as valuable background as they guide their children.

Much of the present unhappy misunderstanding between the public and educators has come about simply because many of us in education have failed to recognize that parents must be informed about what is going on in school.[4] Education that moved ahead with changing needs and improved methods was labeled "progressive" and earned a poor reputation, almost certainly because the public (and not a few teachers) failed to understand what it was all about.

Times have changed. Parents are more interested in the problems of education and are more capable of understanding the many complexities involved. They want to know the facts, deserve to know the facts, and should be given the facts. I.Q. information may well be included.

[4] If we do not supply the information, the public may demand it. By legislative action, schools in California will be required to show parents the permanent records of their children beginning with the school year of 1960, if the parents request it.

REFERENCES

1. Lee J. Cronbach, *Essentials of Psychological Testing* (New York: Harper and Brothers, 1949).

2. Henry P. Smith, *Psychology in Teaching* (Englewood Cliffs, N.J.: Prentice-Hall, 1954).

3. David P. Ausubel, *Theory and Problems of Child Development* (New York: Grune & Stratton, 1958).

4. Henry B. McDaniel, *Guidance in the Modern School* (New York: Dryden Press, 1956).

5. Floyd L. Ruch, *Psychology and Life,* 3rd ed. (New York: Scott, Foresman, 1948).